D0918687

This

. . . is an authorized facsimile made from the master copy of the original book. Further unauthorized copying is prohibited.

Books on Demand is a publishing service of UMI. The program offers xerographic reprints of more than 136,000 books that are no longer in print.

The primary focus of Books on Demand is academic and professional resource materials originally published by university presses, academic societies, and trade book publishers worldwide.

UMI
BOOKS ON DEMAND™

UMI
A Bell & Howell Company
300 North Zeeb Road ❧ PO Box 1346
Ann Arbor, Michigan 48106-1346
800-521-0600 ❧ 313-761-4700

Printed in 1997 by xerographic process on acid-free paper

SOCIAL CONTROL

SAGE FOCUS EDITIONS

SOCIAL CONTROL
Views from the Social Sciences

edited by
Jack P. Gibbs

SAGE PUBLICATIONS
Beverly Hills / London / New Delhi

For information address:

SAGE Publications, Inc.
275 South Beverly Drive
Beverly Hills, California 90212

SAGE Publications India Pvt. Ltd.
C-236 Defence Colony
New Delhi 110 024, India

SAGE Publications Ltd
28 Banner Street
London EC1Y 8QE, England

Printed in the United States of America

Library of Congress Cataloging in Publication Data

HM
73
.S626
1982

Main entry under title:

The Future of social control.

(Sage focus editions ; 51)
Based on a symposium held Dec. 8-9, 1980 near
Omaha, Neb.
Bibliography: p.
Includes index.
Contents: The notion of control in sociological
theory / Lewis A. Coser — The notion of control
in psychological theory / Eugene Burnstein — The
politics of control and the control of politics /
Samuel Krislov — [etc.]
1. Social control—Addresses, essays, lectures.
I. Gibbs, Jack P.
HM73.F87   303.3'3   82-5774
ISBN 0-8039-0615-3   AACR2
ISBN 0-8039-0616-1 (pkb.)

FIRST PRINTING

Contents

Preface

This book stems from a symposium on social control funded by the Research Division of the Boys Town Center for the Study of Youth Development. The symposium was held over December 8-9, 1980, in the Center's facilities near Omaha, Nebraska; and the participants express their appreciation for the support and efforts of three persons affiliated with the Center: Dr. Luther Otto, Director of the Research Division; Ms. Sandra Wendel, Secretary for the Research Division; and Dr. Morton Weir, Director of the Center (now Professor of Psychology, University of Illinois, Champaign-Urbana).

The symposium was organized in the conviction that the notion of control has potentialities that are far from realized, one of which is furthering the integration of the social and behavior sciences, including jurisprudence. Interest in promoting that integration has waned in recent dacades; but the boundaries of the various disciplines have not become less arbitrary, nor is there any more basis now for regarding those boundaries as conducive to scientific or scholarly progress.

As suggested in the Introduction to Part I, a major issue haunts the conceptualization of social control. For various reasons, there is a reluctance in the social and behavioral sciences (sociology in particular) to emphasize the conscious and deliberate character of control, with some definitions of *social control* going so far as to suggest that intention is irrelevant. That reluctance borders on a grossly unrealistic denial or belittlement of the purposive quality of human behavior. Since that quality is not limited to any social, cultural, political, economic, or purely psychological sphere of life, control is surely an interdisciplinary notion.

Still another argument pertains to the evolutionary trend toward greater sociocultural complexity. That trend does not result in attempts to manipulate human behavior *and* nonhuman objects on an ever increasing scale; rather, complexity *requires* it. Hence, whatever the rationale for the past slighting of the notion of control in the social and behavioral sciences, that rationale will become increasingly indefensible.

7

In recognition that the foregoing arguments are disputable, no attempt was made to support them in recruiting symposium participants. Indeed, some of the symposium participants and contributors perhaps do not share my convictions about the importance of control or my preference as to conceptualization. Similarly, while the contributors were encouraged to speculate about the future of control, "futurology" is a dubious enterprise; and some of the contributors proved to be reluctant prophets. But all of those considerations are secondary to the main point. The contributors represent a great deal of talent in various disciplines, and for that reason alone they neither wanted nor needed very much editorial *control.*

—Jack P. Gibbs

PART I

The Notion of Control

The term "control" could become central for the social and behavioral sciences because it can be used to describe virtually any type of human behavior, be it the modification of inanimate things, the domestication of plants and animals, or social interaction. For that matter, the term control can be used at any level—macro, micro, or intermediate.

At the macro level, numerous social phenomena (e.g., law, government, war, advertising, propaganda) cannot be described without at least implicit reference to control. To be sure, at least in most countries various phenomena at the macro level, such as the degree of urbanization or the division of labor, appear uncontrolled. But even those phenomena give rise to an important question: Why are such phenomena uncontrolled and how could they be controlled?

Then consider human behavior at the intermediate level, meaning in the context of particular organizations or associations (e.g., corporations, churches). If only because of the commonly hierarchical character of organizations or associations—superordinate and subordinate positions in particular—much of human behavior in those contexts is subject to control in the purely conscious and deliberate sense.

Control in the conscious and deliberate sense may appear to be rare at the micro level; but everyday interaction is a study in attempts at control. If requesting an item in a store, hailing a cab, asking a friend over for dinner, or simply dialing information is not attempted control, then we should abandon the English language. Surely it would be astonishing to argue that such acts are not attempts at control because they are benign.

It is not claimed that the term "control" has been used extensively in all of the social and behavioral sciences, and it may well be that the utility of the notion of control depends appreciably on the kind of behavior and the level of analysis. As a case in point, the term *"social* control" has been used more extensively in sociology than in other disciplines, perhaps

9

because sociologists study diverse kinds of human behavior at different levels. The subject matter of psychology is hardly less diverse, but by conventional standards most psychological studies are at the micro level. Accordingly, since space limitations precluded chapters on the notion of control in all disciplines, sociology and psychology have been taken as strategic fields.

In Chapter 1 Lewis Coser succinctly describes the history of the notion of social control in sociological theory. As the description rightly suggests, the notion has been important but not central. The major reason is that most sociologists have treated social control only in connection with norms and social order; hence, social control has been a secondary concept. More specifically, throughout the history of the concept and in keeping with a tradition established by E. A. Ross (*Social Control,* 1901), sociologists have been prone to think of social control as any sociocultural phenomenon that maintains or contributes to social order. One correlative belief is that social order is largely based on normative consensus, and by that tacit line of reasoning social control is virtually equated with the influence of norms on human behavior. Such reasoning ignores or belittles not only social conflict but also the conscious and deliberate manipulation of human behavior. When sociologists speak of norms, they rarely suggest that norms are created to manipulate behavior; rather, norms are commonly described as unplanned or beyond human control. Sociologists do recognize that some norms are *created* (as in the case of laws), but they often express doubts as to whether such norms effectively control behavior. Even the "internalization of norms" is presumed to be somehow automatic, meaning that it need not be promoted consciously and deliberately.

So it is not surprising that Coser does not identify one major sociological theorist who has emphasized the conscious and deliberate quality of social control. However, Coser does recognize that most prophecies of "future worlds" (e.g., Orwell's *1984*) depict social control as manipulative in the extreme. Hence, it may appear that from the perspective of traditional sociological theory the prophecies are grossly unrealistic, but Coser stops short of dismissing those prophecies.

Eugene Burnstein's observations in Chaper 2 suggest both contrasts and similarities between psychology and sociology as regards the notion of control. Sociologists use the term social control extensively; but the term scarcely enters into major sociological theories, and those theories offer little to anyone who seeks an answer to this question: How can human behavior be controlled? Unlike sociologists, psychologists rarely use the word control, except in studies of the "locus of control"; but there is a similarity in that no major theorist in either field has been preoccupied with control. Nonetheless, Burnstein's survey indicates that psychology offers more than sociology to those who seek an answer to the question about controlling human behavior.

It is true that much of the literature examined by Burnstein appears to bear at most only on the notion of self-control, a notion commonly ignored in speculation about social control, especially at the societal level. Yet truly effective totalarian social control may require the shaping of self-control throughout society. Accordingly, insofar as psychoanalytic theory and theories of the moral development of individuals can be stated so as to emphasize the importance of socialization practices, they are relevant in devising means of control at any level. Learning theory and such notions as operant conditioning are more immediately relevant only because they point to means of control independent of personality or character development.

1

The Notion of Control in Sociological Theory

LEWIS A. COSER

The notion of social control emerged in American sociology around the turn of the century. The term was first used by one of the founders of American sociology, Edward A. Ross, in a series of papers that he later incorporated in a volume entitled *Social Control,* and published in 1901. Ross assumed that human nature existed prior to social interaction and was constituted by an already existing complex of drives and impulses. Hence social control to Ross (1896) referred to "the moulding of the individual's feelings and desires to suit the needs of the group." He used the term in an imprecise manner, but one gathers that he was mainly concerned with those regulative institutions that insure that individual behavior is in accord with group demands. He refers not only to policemen or agents of the judiciary system, but also to beliefs in the supernatural, ceremonies, public opinion, morals, art, education, and related phenomena that, so he argued, maintain the normative structure of society, and constitute the mechanisms by which society exercises its dominion over component individuals and enforces conformity to its norms and values.

Ross's contemporary, William Graham Sumner, another of the founders of American sociology, attempted a somewhat similar task in his famous *Folkways* (1906). As the subtitle of the book, *A Study of the Sociological Importance of Usages, Manners, Customs, and Morals,* indicates, Sumner was primarily concerned with the ways standardized group norms serve to insure individual conformity. "Folkways," in Sumner's terminology, are "habits . . . and customs . . . that become regulative for succeeding genera- tions, . . . they very largely control individual and social undertakings" (1906: iii-iv). Sumner attempted to account for the centrality or the peripheral character of various norms in terms of a typology of negative sanctions that were customarily applied in case of their breach. Relatively peripheral customs, which he called folkways, encounter only mild and informal sanctions in case of nonobservance. Norms surrounding activities considered more central for the functioning and well-being of the community, which he called mores, are enforced by more stringent sanctions in case of infringement. Finally, the central core of the group's norms, values, and beliefs calls forth stringent legal sanctions in case of nonconformity.

These early analysts highlighted the ways in which social control affected individuals, but their major focus of attention was on the mechanisms by which society manages to curb given and preconstituted individual passions and desires and makes individuals fit for social cooperation. As James Dealy put it in 1920, "The process of socialization is difficult and contrary to crude human nature. Society must build through social control and education a type of mind that will become individualistic through social service" (Dealy 1920: 385-386).

Early sociological investigators significantly enlarged understanding of social control by pointing out that there exists a wide variety of control mechanisms, and that law, which had earlier been seen largely as the only important mechanism, was one of many, and possibly not even the most important one. Yet these analysts, proceeding on a dualistic model according to which previously constituted human nature was shaped by external controls in the quest for societal stability and order, never satisfactorily explained the manner in which external control comes to be incorporated into the personality of the individual. When faced by this problem, they typically tended to use a series of *ad hoc* concepts, such as suggestion or imitation. Such concepts, however, not only failed to help analyze the concrete mechanisms involved; they also proved to be not much more than convenient labels for as yet unexplained phenomena.

Matters took a different turn when several social scientists as varied as George Herbert Mead and Charles Horton Cooley in America, and Emile Durkheim, Sigmund Freud, and Jean Piaget in Europe, argued in their otherwise often divergent manner that human nature, the human self, far from being simply given, was in fact developed through social interaction. As Cooley once said, "Man and society are twin-born." I shall be able to highlight here only a few of the formulations of these authors.

Emile Durkheim, after having initially attempted, especially in his *The Division of Labor* (1933), to explain social control largely in terms of external constraints by "social facts," was led in his subsequent work to argue that social norms, far from simply being imposed on the individual by the surrounding society, came to be internalized in the personality of social actors. They are, so he argued, "society living in us," and become part of the individual's psyche through both formal and informal processes of socialization. Durkheim maintained in his mature work that the essence of social control lay in the individual's sense of moral obligation to obey a rule, the voluntary acceptance of social duties, rather than in simple external conformity to outside pressures. The moral demands of society, as Durkheim sees the matter in his mature work, are constitutive elements of the individual personality.

While Durkheim stressed internalization of societal demands as the most important element in social control, the American social philosopher George Herbert Mead, and the Austrian psychiatrist Sigmund Freud, made, unbeknownst to each other and working in different intellectual traditions, further significant contributions to the understanding of the internalization of social norms. Mead argued that a person's self-image, the "me," develops through social experience as the person becomes aware of and susceptible to the expectations and appraisals of others in his or her significant environment. The attitude of "significant others" becomes internalized and broadens out to constitute the "generalized other," the foundation of the moral conscience of the person. In this reflexive manner, the expectations of others in society form the character of the individual. Conscience is a societal creation.

Sigmund Freud's construct, the superego, is too well known to require discussion here. It is arrived at from a different point of view than Durkheim's or Mead's conceptualizations, and Freud uses a different terminology, yet it dovetails with Mead's or Durkheim's formulation, as Hans Gerth and Charles Wright Mills argued a quarter of a century ago in their much neglected *Character and Social Structure* (1953). Freud, who held that in the process of attaining maturity, the "external policeman" is largely replaced by an "internal policeman," sees, just like Durkheim and Mead, that the internalization of societal norms through the incorporation of the expectations of others is built into the psychic structure, so that significant social control operates from within rather than from without.

The brilliant Swiss psychologist Jean Piaget, while taking a different approach than the other social scientists discussed here, nevertheless also stresses the centrality of internalization for the process of social control. Especially in his early work, *The Moral Judgment of the Child* (Piaget 1948), he develops the thesis that mature autonomous moral judgments develop and become internalized on the basis of cooperative social relations with peers, whereas heteronomous moral judgements that characterize early stages in the development of the child emanate from conformity with the authoritarian pronouncements of parents and other superordinate figures. Types of individual morality are thus seen as deriving from the types of social structures in which persons, and especially maturing children, are variously involved.

All these trends of thought focusing attention on internalization as the central mechanisms for social control culminate in the work of Talcott Parsons. Attempting to synthesize the pertinent work of Durkheim, Freud, and the American school of social psychology, especially Cooley, Mead, and W. I. Thomas, and focusing in particular on the convergence of the views of Durkheim and Freud, Parsons writes as follows:

> In Durkheim's work there are only suggestions relative to the psychological mechanisms of internalization and the place internalized moral values in the structure of personality itself. But this does not distract from the massive phenomenon of the convergence of the fundamental insights of Freud and Durkheim, insights not only as to the fundamental importance of moral values in human behavior, but of the internalization of these values. This convergence, from two quite distinct and independent starting points, deserves to be ranked as one of the truly fundamental landmarks of the development of modern science. It may be likened to the convergence between the results of the experimental study of plant breeding by Mendel and of the microscopic study of cell division—a convergence which resulted in the discovery of the chromosomes as bearers of the genes [1964: 19].

Parson's formulations, despite his repeated disclaimers, seem to lend themselves to what Dennis Wrong (1961) has called an "oversocialized conception of man." Especially when combined with the uses Parsons made of the notion of cybernetic control in his latest writings, they seem to suggest that human beings are in the last analysis passive executors of the structural and symbolic agencies of social control. There is, to be sure, a contrary strain, that of voluntarism, which can be found in all of Parson's work, but he has not been overly successful in reconciling the twin notions of voluntary action and societal control.

Such a successful reconcilation is accomplished, however, in the work of another master of functional analysis, Robert K. Merton. To Merton, the notions of structural control and individual choices are complementary rather than contradictory. As Arthur Stinchcombe puts it in his brilliant reconstruction of Merton's analytical scheme, "The core process that Merton conceives as central to social structure is *the choice between socially structured alternatives*" (Stinchombe 1975: 12). To Merton, institutionalized social control patterns define and shape alternatives of choice for social actors. Such patterns provide motives as well as possible sanctions, be they positive or negative, that have bearing on the alternatives presented to the actor. Structural controls limit the alternatives open to given actors, but in turn, institutional consequences of action act back to shape the nature of the alternatives that people will subsequently encounter. There is no one-way street from control to action, but the choices that people make under the constraints of socially structured alternatives lead in their turn to a reshaping or persistence, as the case may be, of the system of social control. This view of the matter is, I would submit, the most sophisticated conceptualization of the notion of social control hitherto attained.

The Limits of Internalization

In the rest of this chapter, I shall attempt to show that the notion of internalization has indeed constituted a significant advance in the understanding of social control, but that it has also tended to focus attention too narrowly on only one particular, though admittedly crucial, aspect. Central features of modern social control, from Nazi concentration camps and Stalin's Gulags, to thought control during the Chinese Cultural Revolution, and to .the totalitarian controls that the rulers of South Africa exercise over the black population of that country, or most of the total institutions studied by Erving Goffman to just give some especially drastic examples, can hardly be understood in terms of internalization. As these few examples should make plain, any notion of social control that omits a consideration of power is bound to be seriously deficient in accounting for many social phenomena that are in the forefront of modern consciousness. Moreover, exclusive focus on internalization obliterates the crucial distinction that Robert K. Merton and Rose Laub Coser have made between behavioral and attitudinal conformity, that is the distinction between conformity that is not accompanied by a sense of internal conviction and conformity that is indeed based on an inner sense of commitment (Merton 1959; Rose Laub Coser 1961).

We can approach the matter by way of a suggestive typology developed by Amitai Etzioni (1961). He argues that there are at least three different types of social control mechanisms, and hence modes of compliance that come into play in different types of organizational settings.

Etzioni argues that organizations can be classified according to their predominant compliance patterns as coercive, utilitarian, or normative. Coercive organizations are those where the major means of control over lower participants rely on the threat of the use of force and where high alienation characterizes the orientation of most lower participants. Typical cases are concentration camps, prisoner-of-war camps, correctional institutions, and mental hospitals. Coercion in these organizations is the major means of control, and their main purpose is to keep inmates in. Whatever conformity can be exacted from them is behavioral conformity backed by the power of negative sanctions. No, or hardly any, internalization of norms takes place, and inmates would run away were the restraints on their movements lifted.

In utilitarian organizations, in contrast, remuneration is the major means of control over lower participants. Calculative involvement characterizes the orientation of the large majority. These, blue-collar, white-collar, or professional workers, typically exhibit mainly behavioral conformity, even though a measure of attitudinal conformity may also be present, especially among "old timers." In any case, should the expected remuneration not be forthcoming, lower participants would typically leave the organization. They accept social control on the part of superordinates only as long as they are being compensated by appropriate remuneration.

Finally, only in normative organizations does one find high degrees of attitudinal conformity. Here, normative power is the major source of control over most lower participants, whose orientation to the organization is characterized by high commitment. In this case, compliance rests principally on internalization of directives accepted as legitimate. Religious organizations, some types of voluntary organizations, some political organizations such as ideologically oriented political parties, and some labor unions rest, at least in considerable part, on normative and internalized types of control. It should be kept in mind, however, that Etzioni describes ideal types. He is well aware that, for example, normative organizations may also harbor many participants who join them for utilitarian motives.

I am not concerned to defend the details of Etzioni's classifactory scheme. It is meant only to illustrate the point that social control through internalization turns out upon inspection to characterize only some, surely not all, organizational settings. Moreover, recognizing the ability of those high in the hierarchy to influence the behavior of those lower down even against their wishes highlights the central part that power plays in social control. Yet power is totally left out of the picture in most writings on internalization.

An adequate understanding of power relations, that is of relations in which some can determine the behavior of others even against their will, involves a knowledge of the grounds on which a power holder claims obedience, and in terms of which the obedient feels compelled to obey. In any given social order we may expect to find both willing, conscientious consent and coercion, even though in many settings the one may predominate over the other (Gerth and Mills 1953). A good deal of analytical confusion arises when, as in most of Talcott Parsons's work, the general notion of power is collapsed into the notion of authority, that is, when general capacity to determine the behavior of others is largely dealt with in terms of the much narrower realm of legitimate authority, i.e., the situation where the commands of the superior are indeed followed through voluntary and willing compliance of the subordinate.

The Dark Side of Social Control

The liberal era of the nineteenth century could indulge in a Panglossian vision of the present, and even more of the future, in which force and coercion were successfully minimized, and benign social guidance on utilitarian principals came to prevail over the barbarous coercive regimes of the past. But this rosy version found it hard to survive the impact on laymen and scholars alike of two world wars, the Holocaust, Gulag, and Nazi concentration camps.

What is more, we have become sensitized in the latter part of the twentieth century to forms of social control that, while eschewing the use of force and coercion, seem to pursue malevolent rather than benevolent goals. Power holders use force when they inflict bodily harm upon subordinated individuals or when they threaten such harm. But there is another form of social control, manipulation, which is exercised not when the bodies of subordinate individuals are harmed or threatened to be harmed, but when their minds and wills are violated by symbolic means. Propaganda and many aspects of modern advertising are cases in point. In these cases, those manipulated are typically unaware of the fact that control over them is covert rather than overt, and they are not able to mobilize their defenses.

The dystopias of twentieth-century writers, from Zamiatin's *We* to Huxley's *Brave New World,* and Orwell's *1984,* typically are shown to rest on forms of total control and domination that are based on a mixture of coercion, induced consent, and the manipulation of symbols. Pessimistic projection of the future by such authors as Max Weber and Harold Lasswell rest likewise on a combination of coercive and manipulative-persuasive means of social control. In Weber's iron cage of mechanized petrification or in Lasswell's garrison state, the powerful herd it over the powerless by means of a combination of force and manipulation.

One major resource that power holders have always used when exercising social control has been a monopoly or near-monopoly of knowledge. When, as in medieval society, knowledge was the privilege of a small stratum of churchmen and lay experts, the underlying population being deprived of access to knowledge was powerless to resist the demands of their churchly or secular masters. This monopoly was largely broken when the Bible and other sacred books were translated into the vernacular and when literacy, largely through the invention of the printing press, spread into ever wider strata of that population.

Yet universal literacy is surely not enough. Our age has witnessed access to significant portions of knowledge being monopolized by relatively small circles, and such knowledge withheld from even highly literate portions of the public at large. Weber pointed out a long time ago that bureaucracies zealously attempt to keep much of their knowledge secret because monopoly on knowledge helps reinforce their power of discretion against both political leaders and the population at large. Such is the case in contemporary America, even after the passage of the Freedom of Information Act. As long as officials are free to classify documents as secret or supersecret, withholding them from dissemination, the knowledge of the population at large and even of the scholarly community must remain restricted, and the chances for manipulation increased.

What is more, sociologists such as James Rule (1974) have shown the inherent threat to individual and social freedom that is posed by the increasing accumulation of knowledge about individuals' behavior, both licit and illicit, that computerized knowledge, public and private, can now provide. Credit bureaus, credit card organizations, banks, draft authorities, the Bureau of the Census, motor vehicle registration offices, the Internal Revenue Service, social security administrations—all now have created pools of information that may well be used to restrict and restrain recalcitrant or potentially recalcitrant individuals. Police files keeping track of deviant individuals have been used for a long time. But the art of keeping track of average individuals has been enormously improved, if that is the word, in the age of the computer. Many of these organizations already exchange their information in a routine manner; others are prevented by law from doing so, or have simply not yet realized the potential gains they could derive from such exchanges. In any case, it does not take a great deal of sociological imagination to realize that these are social control mechanisms that could acquire enormous potency, especially when they are centrally coordinated. Stalin once was referred to as Genghis Khan with a telegraph. But a Genghis Khan with a computer would still be vastly more effective in exercising total control over the citizenry.

American advocates of computer control and cybernetic regulative systems are usually at pains to show that such controls can readily be reconciled with pluralistic decision making and the active participation of citizens in public affairs. Soviet social scientists, on the other hand, feel no need to provide lip service to such liberal notions. They feel free to defend the notion of total technical control and to attack the obsolete claims of mere subjectivism. Thus writes V. G. Afanasyev, in a book entitled, *The Scientific Management of Society* (1971: 198-199):

> Any system has internal and external social conditions which the subjective factor has to reckon with. By itself, however, the subjective factor does not coincide with the conscious activities of all those belonging to one system or another but is the expression of the activities of those who fulfill control functions. In other words, with respect to control the subjective factor is the activity of the subject of control in providing for the optimal functioning and development of the system, it is the activities of those who are competent and authorized to make decisions.
>
> Subjectivism is a very dangerous thing. It leads to hollow arbitrary decisions that cannot possibly be fulfilled. It entails an overstrain on material human, financial resources, causes disorganization and undermines confidence in the government. In effect, subjectivism interferes with the normal let alone optimal functioning of society, breeding disproportions, giving rise to a tendency to make out that things are better than they are, and so on.

In the beginning of this chapter I discussed early American theorists of social control who largely assumed a pregiven human nature or personality when they discussed the ways in which social control over component actors was exercised by the community. I then moved to consider a group of theorists who argued that human personality or the self was not pregiven but slowly matured in the social intercourse that all human beings continually establish with their fellows. Here the problem of social control involved the key notion of internalization, the idea that social controls largely depend on the incorporation of societal norms within the structure of the psyche. In this somewhat oversocialized conceptualization it was assumed that most people most of the time like to do the things they have to do. Yet, in all of these conceptions it was tacitly or explicitly assumed that, no matter how it came to be constituted, the self possessed at least a measure of autonomy and that actors retained some freedom to make choices. I now wish to raise the question of whether even the notion of the self might be obliterated in some totalitarian nightmare of the future. Discussing the dystopian fiction of Zamiatin, Orwell, and Huxley, the literary critic Irving Howe evocates just such a nightmare when he writes:

> The idea of the personal self, which for us has become an indispensable assumption of existence, is seen by [these writers] as a *cultural* idea. It is a fact within history, the product of the liberal

era, and because it is susceptible to historical growth and decline, it may also be susceptible to historical destruction. All three of our antiutopian novels are dominated by an overwhelming question: Can human nature be manufactured? Not transformed or manipulated or debased, since these obviously can be; but manufactured by will and decision [Howe 1963: 178].

What these dystopian writers provide in their terrifying vision is a depiction of the principle of social control gone mad. All of them, or so it would seem to me, have built their nightmarish picture on Dostoevski's powerful parable "The Grand Inquisitor," where the great novelist evokes imaginatively one of the central questions of human life in society: Do human beings strive for freedom or do they not rather flee from freedom in order to gain controlled security? I fervently believe that the human urge for freedom is ineradicable, but I must also admit that this belief will be thoroughly tested in the times to come.

REFERENCES

Afanasyev, V. G. 1971. *The Scientific Management of Society.* Moscow: Progress Publishers, as quoted in Manfred Stanley, *The Technological Conscience.* New York: Free Press, 1978, p. 162.

Coser, Rose Laub. 1961. "Insulation form Observability and Types of Social Conformity." *American Sociological Review* 26:28-39.

Dealey, James Quayle. 1920. *Sociology: Its Development and Application.* New York: Appleton, as quoted in William W. Wentworth, *Context and Understanding.* New York: Elsevier-North Holland, 1980, p. 17.

Durkheim, Emile. 1933. *The Division of Labor in Society.* New York: Macmillan.

Etzioni, Amitai. 1961. *A Comparative Analysis of Complex Organizations.* New York: Free Press.

Gerth, Hans and Charles Wright Mills. 1953. *Character and Social Structure.* New York: Harcourt Brace.

Howe, Irving. 1963. "The Fiction of Anti-Utopia." Pp. 176-80 in *Orwell's Nineteen Eighty-Four,* edited by Irving Howe. New York: Harcourt Brace.

Merton, Robert K. 1969. "Conformity, Deviation and Opportunity Structures." *American Sociological Review* 24: 177-88.

Parsons, Talcott. 1964. *Social Structure and Personality.* New York: Free Press.

Piaget, Jean. 1948. *The Moral Judgment of the Child.* New York: Free Press.

Ross, E. A. 1896. "Social Control." *American Journal of Sociology* 1:513-35.

Ross, E. A. 1901. *Social Control.* New York: Macmillan.

Rule, James B. 1974. *Private Lives and Public Surveillance.* London: Allen Lane.

Stinchcombe, Arthur L. 1975. "Merton's Theory of Social Structure." Pp. 11-33 in *The Idea of Social Structure: Papers in Honor of Robert K. Merton,* edited by Lewis Coser. New York: Harcourt Brace.

Sumner, William Graham. 1906. *Folkways.* Boston: Ginn.

Wrong, Dennis. 1961. "The Oversocialized Conception of Man." *American Sociological Review* 26:184-93.

2

The Notion of Control in Psychological Theory

EUGENE BURNSTEIN

In the early seventeenth century one group of theoretical physicists, the *horror vacui* school, explained why water could not be pumped above 34 feet by postulating that nature's repugnance of a vacuum vanished beyond this height. Another school, the tensility theorists, took as their model for the behavior of a column of water the breaking point of a filament, such as a length of copper wire, and concluded that water could not extend beyond 34 feet because at this point the column broke of its own weight. Hydraulic engineers had no theory. They knew that they could pump water above 34 feet whenever necessary by constructing several 34 feet pumps in a vertical series. Similarly, the psychological practitioner has more useful advice to give about control than the psychological theorist. Nonetheless, there have been a variety of efforts to explain why the practice of control works. I take it as my task to outline these efforts and their future direction. I do this with every expectation that present theories will provide the same amusement to twenty-first-century readers that the *horror vacui* and tensile strength models do today.

Virtually every theory of mental life assumes that human action is purposive. Individuals thus have plans, that is, goals and procedures for accomplishing them. For the psychologist, the problem of control arises when an individual plan is incompatible with the collective one. How conflicts of this kind are resolved has been studied in two different areas of my discipline—developmental psychology and social psychology. For our purposes developmental psychologists are mainly concerned with *self*-control. They study how knowledge about values, standards, and rules is internalized and represented by individuals at different stages in their socialization. The term of reference for studies in this area is *moral development.* Social psychologists, on the other hand, are concerned with *social* control. They focus on the pressure the majority brings to bear on a minority to resolve a disagreement. Studies in this area have to do with *conformity.* We will consider the current state of knowledge in these two areas and then suggest what the future holds.

Control from the Point of View of Developmental Psychology

The classical *psychoanalytic* approach dominated conceptions of moral development until Piaget (1964) and Kohlberg (1969). That approach depicts the internalization of moral standards as a consequence of resolving certain basic social conflicts, namely, the conflict between relatively powerful, sophisticated, older group members (e.g., parents, teachers, bosses) and relatively powerless, callow, younger members (e.g., children, students, workers). The conflicts are postulated to stem from inborn predispositions, incestuous in nature, that have evolved over the history of the human species. These conflicts are strongest in the family during infancy, where they are known as the oedipal crisis. Most significantly, the unfolding of this crisis is assumed to generalize to, or serve as a model for, the person's later relationships with authority.

Psychoanalysis

The oedipal crisis occurs between three and four when, it is said, the desire in the male child for an exclusive erotic relationship with the mother increases markedly. It follows, under these conditions, that interaction with the father is characterized from the male child's view by a sense of mounting rivalry and the possibility of paternal violence. The theory assumes, further, that at some point during this period the child feels so threatened that he renounces his incestuous goals and internalizes the image of his father, an anxiety reducing mechanism commonly known as *defensive identification* or *identification with the aggressor* (A. Freud 1946). That is to say, the child attributes to himself, among other parental characteristics, a crude representation of the moral standards he believes are held by the father. In the mind of the child, being *like* this powerful person means having the *capacity* to exert rather than suffer his power. Defensive identification, in short, serves to reduce the perceived threat of parental violence (castration anxiety, in particular). Some claimed to have observed the comparable process among adults, particularly concentration camp prisoners (e.g., Bettelheim 1943). The theoretical rationale is that the adult who is totally helpless in the face of an all-powerful, malevolent, and violent system of authority will regress psychologically and escape in fantasy by adopting the attitudes and mannerisms of those who run the system.

The male child also takes on characteristics of the mother. The theory assumes that by internalizing certain maternal characteristics, he feels in possession of what is most valuable in the mother. These are aspects of the mother that the child dreads losing when he renounces an exclusive maternal tie. Unlike defensive identification, this form of internalization, called *anaclitic identification*, is based on the affectionate and nurturant elements in the child's relations with parents and surrogates. The knowledge about the self as an ideal state or entity that stems from these two forms of identification is represented for the most part unconsciously. Hence, it is virtually impossible for the child to assess how he acquired certain standards or what these standards signify about relations with the parents during the oedipal crisis. Since Sigmund Freud, this system of moral knowledge is called the *superego*.

Perhaps the most important assumption of psychoanalytic theory for the analysis of control is that the conflict with parents during the oedipal period serves as a model for later relations with individuals in positions of authority. This implies that processes analogous to defensive and anaclitic identification explain how persons adopt the standards of authority figures in adult society. As in the family, when persons violate these standards, they experience a form of anxiety called *guilt*. To diminish their anxiety, the thought or action is inhibited, restitution is made, punishment is inflicted on the self, and so on. From the point of view of psychoanalytic theory, therefore, the social engineering of control is primarily a matter of devising the appropriate institutions for inducing *and* for mitigating guilt.

On the whole, identification is assumed to proceed in a similar fashion for female children, who between three and five perceive themselves to be engaged in an increasingly rivalrous and threatening relationship with the mother. Here, internalization is based on fear of rejection, a fear that causes the female child to renounce and repress her wish for an exclusive affectionate relationship with the father. There is, however, one important difference between the situation confronting the female and the male child—psychoanalytic theory assumes that the threat of maternal violence is relatively weak compared to castration anxiety in the case of the male child. Hence, there is less need for defensive identification, and the female superego presumably is more lenient and complaisant than that of the male.

Given the foregoing assumptions, it follows that conflict between children and their opposite-sex parent is inevitable; and that the pattern of discipline and affection characteristic of the family "authorities" determines the child's attitude toward figures and symbols of social power incurred throughout its life. Individuals who have not resolved the oedipal conflict (usually when discipline has been inconsistent) and hence have not acquired a highly differentiated and well-organized superego, will continue to display hostility toward individuals and institutions symbolizing authority. By contrast, individuals who have "overresolved" the issue by internalizing a rigid and unforgiving representation of their parents (usually when discipline has been severe and unbending) will be overly compliant and unquestioning with the demands of authority. At the same time, however, they tend to be moralistic, inhibited, and cold in their relations with peers or the lower orders.

Consistent with the psychoanalytic formulation, Glueck and Glueck (1950) found that antisocial delinquents tend to have had parents who were exceptionally lax and erratic or overly severe disciplinarians, whereas nondelinquents had parents that were firm and consistent but not unbending (also see Bandura and Walters 1959; Moulton et al., 1966). For comparable reasons, relatively passive sons tend to appear in families where the father was absent during early socialization (Bach 1946; Sears et al. 1946). Other studies, however, find a less straightforward effect: The absence of the father during the first several years produces extraordinarily aggressive sons (Bacon et al. 1963; Burton and Whiting 1961). The latter association usually is explained in terms of overcompensation or the "reactive masculinity" of males whose primary identification is feminine. Furthermore, the consistent use of psychological or "love-oriented" techniques (e.g., when parents attempt to control the child by giving or withholding affection), rather than physical disciplinary practices, produces individuals who experience strong guilt when tempted to perform a deviant act and who suppress such temptations in order to reduce this guilt. The universal nature of this phenomenon is suggested by findings of cross-cultural studies (e.g., Whiting and Child 1953) indicating that societies in which love-oriented discipline prevails seem to have a more guilt-prone adult population than societies in which physical discipline is the prevalent technique of socialization.

Although research has failed to confirm psychoanalytic theory at numerous points (e.g., Miller and Swanson 1958), it is fair to say that two general implications of this approach for control are reasonably well-established truths. First, identification with parental figures is an important condition for experiencing guilt as a reaction to incipient deviance. And, second, such identification is fostered by the consistent use of psychological or love-oriented rearing practices rather than physical reward and punishment.

Social Learning Theories

During the 1950s, behavioristic theories of learning came to dominate psychology. Inevitably these theories were applied to complex forms of learning, in particular, the learning of moral standards (e.g., Bandura 1971; Dollard and Miller 1950; Miller and Dollard 1941; Mischel 1968; Skinner 1953). According to learning theorists, psychoanalysis implies that moral behavior, because it reflects internalized parental standards, will be consistent across situations. This they knew was untenable (e.g., Hartshorne and May 1928, but see Burton 1963). As a matter of fact, psychoanalysis as well as most other psychological theories are too imprecise to have *necessary* implications. Thus, for instance, psychoanalysis is not required to argue for complete cross-situational consistency. A theorist who wants to explain social actions in terms of stable individual traits can with good reason assume that the trait must be activated by specific features of the situation. Since these features will vary in salience across situations, such an assumption would allow for occasions in which behavior is inconsistent with a trait. Nonetheless, the learning theorists do have a point, given the tone of the psychoanalytic explanation if not its logic.

The various versions of learning theory, whether inductive and empirical (e.g., Skinner 1938; Ferster and Skinner 1957), deductive and formal (Hull 1943; Spence 1956, 1960), or eclectic and cognitive (Tolman 1932, 1948), handle cross-situational consistency by assuming that individuals learn to differentiate settings in which an action will produce a positive, negative, or indifferent outcome. That is to say, experience tells the person whether in this context a particular plan will be rewarded or punished.

The distinction made between reward and punishment is one of the more important contributions of learning theory to the analysis of control. This point is made most emphatically by radical behaviorists, such as Skinner. They note that while the occurrence of reflexlike acts (respondent behavior) is primarily determined by the frequency of certain environmental events that precede and *elicit* it (conditioned and unconditioned stimuli), the frequency of a purposive act (operant behavior) is mainly determined by its consequences (environmental events produced by the act). When the act leads to the introduction of an object or to the onset of an event that increases the likelihood of the act being performed again, the outcome of the action is *positively* reinforcing. When the action leads to the removal of an object or the cessation of an event, and this outcome also increases the likelihood of the act being performed again, then the outcome is *negatively* reinforcing. We commonly think of the former situation as presenting something that is rewarding or attractive to the person and the latter as terminating something that is aversive or punishing. Aversive control or punishment is often used to inhibit an action and, as noted earlier, may take a physical or psychological form. For example, a child who comes home late from visiting a friend may be spanked, have his or her "visiting rights" suspended for a period, or be told that his or her action worried and angered his parents. Punishment in most forms, however, is inefficient inasmuch as its benefits—the capacity to suppress action—endure only for a short time (except when traumatic levels of punishment are reached; see Solomon and Wynne 1954; Seligman, 1975). Its drawbacks, on the other hand, are long lasting.

Punishment controls by suppressing performance; it does nothing to diminish the tendency to engage in the performance, and under the threat of punishment persons are likely to suppress an action only while being monitored. Indeed, when punishment is discontinued, the suppressed act reappears in even more vigorous form (Church 1963; Holz and Azrin 1963; Kelleher et al., 1963). This effect is comparable to what psychoanalytic theory predicts when tendencies unacceptable to the superego are unconsciously repressed. In any case, punishment works only by producing a state of conflict; the to-be-suppressed tendency is forced to compete with other tendencies (e.g., escape) to determine behavior. There are many circumstances in which the relative strengths of the competing tendencies alternate rapidly or mix confusedly so that ongoing thought and action are interrupted. Thus, the conflict inherent in the punishment mechanism may lead to chronic disruptions in ordinary mental activities.

The suppression that punishment produces has a frustrating effect similar to that associated with physical restraint. Hence, it incites anger or rage. In all likelihood the increased vigor with which persons tend to perform an act upon cessation of punishment reflects the energizing effects of the anger or rage that remains (Amsel 1962). If this state of suppression and frustration is chronic, psychosomatic pathologies appear. Or in Skinner's language, such effects will occur when "the variables responsible for these emotional patterns are generated by the organism itself [and hence] no appropriate escape behavior is available" (1953: 191). In this connection it should be noted that many acts have emotional or interpretive components that are elicited in a reflexlike or automatic fashion by the social context, even though the action as a whole is voluntary, planned, and deliberate. Automatic processes are virtually impossible to block by means of punishment. Hence, punishment may prevent individuals from carrying out their plan, but it is unable to suppress the feelings and perceptions underlying the plan.

The most influential application of learning theory to moral development, called social learning theory (Bandura 1971; Bandura and Walters 1963; Mischel 1973), follows Tolman's approach more than Skinner or the Spence-Hull school (for examples of the latter two, see Skinner, 1953; Dollard and Miller, 1950). This is evident from the emphasis on the comprehension or interpretation (encoding) and the storage (representation) of information, especially information about the contingencies of action. Individuals supposedly gain such information by observing what a model does and what consequences follow therefrom. Notice is also taken of how consequences change with the context of action. As a result, individuals learn to discriminate the conditions under which an act leads to a positive, a negative, or an indifferent outcome. These observations are encoded, integrated, and stored in memory. The representation of such knowledge has been called a schema (Bartlett 1932; Rumelhart and Ortony 1977), a script (Schank and Abelson 1977), or a plan (Miller et al., 1960).

From the point of view of social learning theory, the first step in explaining control is to understand how individuals choose among competing models. We know that models will be imitated as a function of their status, prestige, or power (e.g., Bandura et al., 1963; Burnstein et al., 1961; Lippitt et al., 1952). These seem to be characteristics that make their possessors salient to others. The power structure of a group is reflected, therefore, in the "attention structure" (i.e., the distribution of attention, say, as indicated by visual regard) of its members (Chance 1967; Chance and Jolly 1970; Chance and Larsen 1976). Together these findings indicate that the likelihood of a member serving as a model for others depends on the amount of attention directed toward him or her, and this in turn is related to his or her status, prestige, or power (Abramovitch and Grusec 1978).

Serving as a model, having power, and receiving attention are mutually interdependent phenomena. This is suggested by an interesting series of studies demonstrating that the power attributed to members—the extent to which they are seen as the "causal locus" of events in the group— increases with their salience. Moreover, this effect occurs even though, first, the basis for their salience is arbitrary, totally unrelated to their "true" social position in the group; and, second, their actual behavior is no different from that of nonsalient members (Taylor and Fiske 1978). For instance, because of the seating arrangements, one member of a socially homogeneous discussion group may monopolize the visual regard of the other members; as a result, this individual would be perceived as controlling the discussion and "causing" others to behave as they did (McArthur and Post 1977; Taylor and Fiske 1975). Unless there are social stereotypes that imply that the person is unlikely to have power in this context (e.g., a child in a group of adults, a woman in a mostly male group, or a black in a mostly white group), a member who gains our attention will be perceived as socially powerful, which causes us to select him or her as a model; then he or she will gain still more attention from us, and so on.

That a model's actions are observed and learned does not mean that they will be performed. The observer may be quite capable of imitating the model but will avoid doing so if the results to the model are undesirable. Enactment is thus controlled by the desirability of the outcome. Desirability has its complications, however. For instance, physical rewards decrease in desirability and symbolic rewards increase in desirability as the person matures. Hence, a young child is more influenced by observing the model receive candy or toys than an older child, whereas the latter is more influenced by expressions of approval or praise. A more intriguing complication has to do with the fact that control and the desirability of an outcome are not linearly related. Excessive reward can actually reduce the tendency to perform the rewarded act (see Lepper and Greene 1978). When a desirable outcome is presented continuously on each and every occasion an act is performed, after many occasions *satiation* is obtained; the incentive value of the outcome, and thus its capacity to control action, decreases. As an illustration of this principle, children who initially are eager to gain approval from an adult eventually grow indifferent to such rewards when they have been delivered continuously (Gewirtz and Baer 1958). Therefore, once a plan has been formed the most effective control over the rate and the persistence with which it is enacted is obtained by rewarding enactment intermittently rather than continuously (see Ferster and Skinner, 1957, for observations on the effectiveness of different types of intermittent reinforcement schedules).

Satiation concerns the decrease in incentive value of a continuously given reward. There is a comparable effect, called *overjustification,* that occurs when there is an egregiously large reward for an act that the person rarely has had occasion to perform before, although he or she is perfectly capable of doing so. After such an outcome occurs, individuals have less desire to perform the act and their tendency to engage in it decreases (Lepper and Greene 1978; Lepper et al., 1973). It seems that the *intrinsic* value of the activity decreases as its *extrinsic* value increases. This may reflect a common judgmental bias whereby individuals infer that an activity must be inherently unpleasant when large incentives have to be offered for its performance (e.g., Carlsmith et al., 1966). Finally, recall that if an act is strongly suppressed, once punishment ceases there is an increase in the tendency to perform it. Together these findings suggest that when extrinsic incentives (i.e., the pressures from others to enact or avoid enactment) greatly exceed the intrinsic incentives (i.e., the person's own desire to enact or avoid enactment), the former will be unproductive, even counterproductive, in respect to control.

Social learning theory assumes that individuals recognize some consequences to be generally more desirable than others. At the same time, however, they will develop standards peculiar to specific contexts. Whereas an outcome may be desirable in general, to a particular person performing a certain task it may be inadequate. Think of the value of the grade B to the average student and its value to an anxious pre-med. We might conceive of these context-specific standards, especially when the context is that very common one of the self wanting to perform a task proficiently, as classical levels of aspiration (Lewin et al., 1944). In any case, standards for the self often operate unconsciously and automatically. What is experienced is the affect, as when an action has shameful consequences or makes the actor feel proud.

When individuals prepare to enact a plan, they become self-critical; in terms of social learning theory, a "self-monitoring reinforcement system develops." As a result, "anticipatory self-reproach ... provides an important motivating influence to keep behavior in line with adopted standards in the face of [temptation]. . . . There is no more devastating punishment than self-contempt" (Bandura 1971:28). For social learning theory, the "self-monitoring reinforcement system" is the key to moral development, and thus, to control, just as the superego is in psychoanalytic theory. The nature of this system depends, of course, on the models provided by the environment. Its standards will be stringent, for example, if during socialization, individuals observe prestigeful others who make difficult demands on themselves and who are rewarded for so doing; whereas lax standards will be acquired if prestigeful others make easy demands on themselves with rewarding consequences.

Lax or stringent, those standards for evaluating the self will be maintained that are reinforced by significant individuals or groups. From the point of view of social learning theory, procedures for encouraging socially desirable actions or suppressing those that are socially undesirable are no different than those for controlling other behavior. Deviants are simply less capable of exerting self-control; their "self-monitoring reinforcement system" is deficient. Thus, whatever form deviance takes, the underlying cause, according to this approach, is simply that a minority of members have somehow acquired more lax or different standards for evaluating the consequences of their actions than the majority of their fellows. Because social learning theory is silent about constraints imposed by the nature of human mental operations, it must beg off explaining the variation in effectiveness of different control processes with maturation (e.g., Why does the incentive value of some outcomes decrease and that of other outcomes increase with age?) or the variation in the prevalence with which different actions are controlled (e.g., Why are certain actions universally proscribed while others are proscribed only in a particular context?).

Moral Planning Theory

The final class of theories that view control primarily as a process of moral development in principle does address itself to the preceding questions. Indeed, the main concern of these theorists is to explain variations in moral development, particularly, the planning of moral action, as a function of mental and social development.

Perhaps the most influential psychological analysis of moral plans is that of Kohlberg (1969, 1978). This work is an extension of Piaget (1964) on moral judgment and moral reasoning. Its key assumption is similar to that of psychoanalysis, namely, that there are distinct stages in the psychological development of the person. Each stage has peculiar to it a set of mental operations relevant to moral planning, and the operations characteristic of a later stage supersede those the person was capable of performing at an earlier stage. In general, the moral planning peculiar to the later stages requires more empathy with, and thus, greater understanding of others. In this sense they can be said to constitute a "higher" morality. The Kohlberg-Piaget model concentrates on how people represent and think about moral issues rather than on motives and affect as in psychoanalysis or on learning and performance as in social learning theory. Most importantly, this approach assumes that there are stages in moral reasoning that do not appear until adolescence and early adulthood, rather than that moral judgments remain fundamentally unchanged after childhood as is suggested by the concept of superego in psychoanalysis and that of the self-monitoring reinforcement system in social learning theory.

The first two stages in Kohlberg's formulation are considered "preconventional," meaning that moral planning is relatively unrefined and brutish; adherence to a socially prescribed course of action depends on the power of the "prescriber" or on the immediate hedonic consequences of so doing. During State 1 (*heteronomous morality*), an action is evaluated according to its topographic (physical) similarity to that specified by authoritative individuals. Thus, under heteronomous morality, if the person's preferred plan conflicts with that demanded by another, the person will think it proper to comply only when the other is more powerful. Stage 2 (*individualism, instrumental purpose, and exchange*) is concerned with conflicts in which the participants have equal power. At this point individuals think they and others should do whatever is possible to accomplish their personal goals; propriety is based on the outcome of the action rather than on the relative power of the actor.

The next two stages are said to involve *conventional* morality, indicating that the actor begins to understand more fully and give greater weight to the socially desirable, to plans advocated by the majority of other group members. More specifically, in Stage 3 (*mutual interpersonal expectations, relationships, and conformity*) proper action is that which benefits the ingroup—others that are similar and close to oneself. Judgments are based on stereotypes of the conventionally nice, virtuous person. Ingroup cooperation, reciprocity, loyalty, and sympathy are inherently esteemed without regard to their instrumental value. During Stage 4 (*social system and conscience*) social approval ceases to be a major factor. Actions are judged proper to the extent that they support fundamental group standards. Note that these standards do not involve any particular ingroup member; rather, they refer to generalized authority; they are concerned with the good of the group as a whole and are typically embodied in its law, religion, and other institutions.

The final two stages, *principled* (or postconventional) *morality*, consider "higher" or more sophisticated issues, namely, that laws or institutions often conflict. For instance, there may be good and bad laws, and outgroup members may have a different interpretation of ingroup laws and institutions. In Stage 5 (*social contract or utility and individual rights*) individual action is perceived to take place in a social context that is inherently, even rightly, pluralistic. Ingroup standards and their embodiment in the law are recognized as relative, the product of an arbitrary history. As a consequence, according to the moral planning model, individuals are concerned with fairness. They believe they should reconcile divergent interests and achieve consensus among those likely to be affected by a plan before actually enacting the plan. This mode of reasoning is said to imply the acceptance of a social contract that protects individual rights while maintaining social order and unity in the face of conflicting interests. In other words, members recognize the need for standard procedures for making collective decisions and achieving group consensus that are rational and equitable.

Whatever conflicts remain are assumed to be solved in Stage 6 (*universal ethical principles*). At this point the person is supposed to have abstracted a system of moral plans that is not only comprehensive, consistent, and universal, but also demonstrably superior to any alternative system. These include unconditional respect for the individual and human life as well as the moral equality of every individual.

Although this sequence of operations would seem normative and merely a statement about optimum morality given certain cognitive capacities, Kohlberg holds that it is an *empirical* analysis of the development of moral reasoning. For him this development reflects the interaction between common conflicts in socialization and the maturation of basic mental capacities. Hence, the sequence of stages must be taken as necessary, fixed, and universal. In all likelihood there are conflicts between children and adults that occur in every society, especially if one describes these altercations sufficiently abstractly. Nonetheless, it is unclear that these are the universal social dilemmas that Kohlberg assumes spur on moral development. Nor are there findings from cross-cultural research that point to a common sequence of stages (Simpson 1974). Finally, an important reason for the absence of evidence for universality is that the prerequisite for obtaining such, namely, measuring the stages, is extraordinarily difficult (Kurtines and Greif 1974).

Still and all, considering the magnitude of the task, there is impressive support for a stagelike model. For example, Rest et al. (1969) and Turiel and Rothman (1972) found that arguments about proper behavior couched in terms appropriate to the person's level of development were more persuasive than those that use ideas appropriate to an earlier level; arguments appropriate to a later stage were quite difficult to comprehend. Moreover, there is interesting evidence that the explanations individuals give for social conflict do vary systematically with their level of moral development. Haan et al. (1968) observed that student activists as a group were not uniformly distributed over the six Kohlbergian levels, nor did they cluster within a single level; rather, they were either in Stage 2 or Stages 5 and 6. That is to say, some of these individuals indicated that they were rebelling against a particular institution on hedonic grounds, because the demands it made were overly onerous; whereas others indicated that they were rebelling because the institution had violated the social contract and thereby lost its legitimacy (also see Haan 1975).

Control from the Point of View of Social Psychology

For the social psychologist control has to do with the interaction between the many and the few, the majority and a minority, with the pressures each exerts on the other to alter its position. Rather than focusing on events in the person having to do with the acquisition and enactment of a plan, they concentrate on events that occur in a group whereby some members impose their plan on other members, namely, persuasion and conformity.

The traditional distinction in this area is between informational and normative influence (Deutsch and Gerard 1955; Gerard 1953). Informational influence refers to a process of persuasion in which one side, the minority or majority, changes its plan because the other side demonstrates that the plan is invalid—that it will not accomplish what it is supposed to, but an alternative plan will. With normative influence the process of persuasion consists in one side convincing the other not that there is a better plan, but instead that there are additional outcomes different from that intended in the plan and that the other side should take these into account. These additional outcomes usually involve a change in the relationship between the members on one side and those on the other. The minority members, for instance, are informed that if they persist in pursuing a course of action they will be ostracized by the majority. In sum, the group regulates individual choice either by providing knowledge about whether a course of action is valid, accurate, and true, or by providing knowledge about whether it is desirable, proper, and worthy of a member.

Either form of influence requires communication, implicit or explicit, and this requirement in turn assumes a common conceptual system, a system of *mutually shared* concepts, operations, and propositions about a domain of events. Let us call such a conceptual system *group knowledge*. When group knowledge is *complete* and *precise*, the members (i.e., the individuals who share it) will make the same judgments about events falling within that domain. Speakers will readily agree about the meaning of most words and sentences within their language, as will mathematicians about problems within a specific mathematics, or engineers about many problems of engineering within a certain physical or chemical system. People will even automatically make the same judgment about political, religious, moral, or esthetic issues to the extent that they share a complete and precise political philosophy, religion, moral code, or system of esthetics.

When group knowledge is complete, precise, and *accessible*, members will agree by means of implicit rather than explicit communication. That is to say, without discussing the matter, each confidently anticipates the position of the other members and the pressures they would apply were one inclined to disagree. Suppose, for instance, in a discussion with fellow members of the Ann Arbor Republican Club, Igor is asked his opinion of a statement misattributed to V. I. Lenin, to the effect that a little revolution every twenty years is a good thing. Virtually without thinking, certainly without consulting others, Igor immediately and automatically *knows* the statement to be invalid, since revolutions are destructive and therefore not a good thing, that his fellow members also know this, and that supporting Lenin's position would be improper on their part. If he himself were so inclined, he would certainly be asked by others to resign. Implicit communication, in short, is sufficient to control action when group knowledge is complete and precise—Igor in his mind's ear is certain about what the group says regarding Lenin and revolutions.

Often, however, group knowledge is inaccessible and what is accessible is ambiguous or only partially shared. As a result the information members possess in common may not clearly imply a particular course of action and important pieces of information may be available only to a few. Under these conditions each member might initially prefer a different plan (or some a similar plan for different reasons) whose superiority is difficult to demonstrate. Most important group functions, however, require uniformity of opinion or action. A division of labor requires agreement about the coordination of activities. Sometimes agreement is necessary simply for validation, that is, to legitimize, justify, or reduce uncertainty about a collective decision in the absence of objective criteria for choice. When disagreement occurs uniformity can be achieved only if members *explicitly* communicate about the matter. However, the underlying process of persuasion will depend on whether the issue is intellective or judgmental (Laughlin 1980). Intellective issues have to do with domains of events in which group knowledge is complete, precise, and accessible; members clearly sense that the choice that would best resolve such an issue is *demonstrable* within their shared conceptual system. Ordinarily intellective issues are seen simply as matters of fact or logic. A judgmental issue, however, is associated with a domain of events in which group knowledge is partial, ambiguous, or inaccessible; since there is no mutually shared conceptual system for the domain, members do not expect to have demonstrated which choice is best. Judgmental issues, therefore, are felt to be matters of taste or values. To the extent that the relative merit of alternative plans is demonstrable (i.e., an intellective issue) then disagreement will be controlled by means of informational influence. When relative merit is not demonstrable (i.e., a judgmental issue), then by definition the matter requires consensual validation and disagreement is controlled by normative influence.

According to this analysis, under conditions of an intellective task the members who advocate the more valid plan will dominate others. In the extreme case where the correct solution is immediately and automatically recognized as such once it is proposed by a member (a eureka-type problem), a minority of one can carry the day. Hence, when "truth wins" is the common procedure for achieving agreement, it means that disagreement in the group will be resolved once *any* member comes up with the right course of action—the problem is mainly one of search or retrieval (Davis 1973; Laughlin et al. 1975; Lorge and Solomon 1955). As the relative merit of alternative plans becomes less easily demonstrable so that a variety of arguments are needed to resolve disagreements, then a single member of the group is unlikely to be persuasive. Instead of "truth wins," "truth supported wins" comes to prevail; two or more members must argue for the valid course in order to gain the acceptance of others. When the relative merit of alternative plans becomes extremely difficult to demonstrate (i.e., the group is faced with a judgmental task), a minority of two or more loses its capacity to produce agreement. In these circumstances normative influence dominates, which implies a "majority rules" decision scheme. Finally, this also suggests that if there is no majority/minority split (about half the group favors one alternative and half the other), the likelihood of the two factions coming to an agreement will be considerably greater when the matter constitutes an intellective task rather than a judgmental task (Vinokur and Burnstein 1978).

The position members take under conditions of implicit communication is unlikely to be the same as under that of explicit communication. This is because members tend to represent the position of others in a biased fashion. They see others as being on the "right" side of the issue, as similarly inclined as themselves, but less extreme or committed: While Igor is confident that other Republicans disagree with Lenin on revolution, he is likely to feel that he disagrees somewhat more strongly than most (e.g., Codol 1980). There are several explanations for this bias. Researchers that concentrate on informational influence as a mechanism of persuasion note that a bias of this kind is typical whenever individuals are more certain about one judgment than another. Thus, they represent their own position as more extreme than that held by most others merely because they know more or are more certain about the former than the latter (Burnstein et al. 1974). On the other hand, researchers who are concerned with normative influence as the vehicle for persuasion assume that a member's position is a tactic in self-presentation. According to this point of view, people try to appear relatively extreme so that they will be considered as more truly embodying group values and, thus, more deserving of approval, status, and the like than other members (Sanders and Baron 1977). Given this approach, the normative influence theorists have a ready-made explanation of how control is exerted by the group via explicit communication. For instance, in group discussion some members inevitably discover that their plan is in fact *less* extreme, less truly an embodiment of group values, than that of others, and thus less worthy of approval from the group. In order to regain this approval they shift toward a more extreme course of action (Myers and Lamm 1976).

Minorities can also influence majorities. This occurs even when group knowledge implies that the majority plan is more valid. Minority influence depends on two sets of conditions: First, the group is short-lived, the members of the majority are strangers, cannot communicate explicitly, and will have no further contact afterward. Second, the minority members consistently and without exception support their position whenever there is occasion to manifest this support (Moscovici and Faucheux 1972; Nemeth et al. 1974). In other words, an *anomic* and *unorganized majority* is confronted with what appears to be a *unified* and *determined minority*. Individuals in the majority, under these conditions, will think extensively about the minority plan, elaborate on it, and search for contexts in which it has validity. Therefore, if the majority changes at all, it is most likely to shift toward the minority point of view. Normally, however, social situations are not so anomic, nor is individual thought so autistic. Groups are relatively cohesive entities, membership has appreciable value, and members can communicate freely and explicitly. Consequently, if the disagreement obtains on a judgmental rather than an intellective task, the majority is much more likely to impose its plan on the minority than the reverse.

The power of the majority to control the minority depends on the cohesiveness of the group and the importance of the plan. How this power is exerted is reasonably well agreed upon (Festinger 1950; Schachter 1951), but there is not an overwhelming amount of empirical support (see Berkowitz 1971, and a thorough review of this literature in Levine 1980). When group cohesion is high, so that members want very much to belong, and the issue in question is important, there will be a rapid increase in the efforts the majority makes to persuade the minority. The amount of pressure that can be exerted on minority members to conform depends on their attraction to the group (Cartwright and Zander 1968, especially chapter 7). The majority, thus, has power over the minority to the degree that membership is attractive. It will have the incentive to use this power to the degree that the issue in dispute is important. This implies that if the minority resists, these pressures will increase rapidly until they are equal to or greater than those acting on the minority to remain group members, at which point the boundaries of group are redefined so that the minority is rejected or defects and is considered as an outgroup (Festinger 1950; Newcomb, 1953; Thibaut and Kelley, 1959).

Evidence is reasonably strong that cohesive groups redefine their boundaries to "include out" a recalcitrant minority (Emerson 1954; Festinger et al. 1950; Schachter 1951). However, there is only mixed support for the argument that conformity pressures (as measured by the amount of explicit communication) peak more rapidly and at a higher level as the cohesion of the group and the importance of the issue increase (Emerson

1954; Festinger and Thibaut 1951; Festinger et al. 1952; Schachter, 1951). This in part stems from assuming, first, that conformity pressures will vary primarily with the *degree of deviance* and, second, that these pressures are reflected primarily in the *amount of communication* to the deviant. Orcutt (1973) has pointed out that a minority position should be distinguished from that of the majority not only quantitatively (i.e., in terms of extent of the difference, its pervasiveness, and its resistance to change) but also qualitatively. In the latter case, this means distinguishing between disagreements regarding group knowledge and those regarding opinions and judgments derived from this knowledge. The minority may disagree because it rejects certain fundamental propositions accepted by the majority or, while agreeing on these fundamentals, the minority rejects certain inferences made from these propositions by the majority. If the minority position constitutes a rejection of group knowledge, the majority is likely to react in an *exclusive* fashion, namely, to categorize the minority as an outgroup. This implies that the minority is fundamentally different from the majority and that there are no grounds for communication. Once the minority is perceived as unamenable to influence, there will be little or no attempt on the part of the majority to communicate and exert pressure. On the other hand, if the minority position constitutes a rejection of an opinion and does not imply the rejection of group knowledge, then the majority is likely to react in an *inclusive* fashion, namely, to continue to represent the minority as ingroup members with whom there are considerable common grounds for understanding. The majority, therefore, perceives the minority as amenable to persuasion and communicates intensively with it to this end.

To illustrate, in an experiment by Sampson and Brandon (1964) groups were assigned the task of choosing a course of treatment for a juvenile delinquent who was black. It was contrived that a member either agree or disagree with the group's assumptions about race. In the former condition this member was called a *role conformist*, in the latter, a *role deviant*. Whatever his or her role, the member at the same time was an *opinion conformist* or an *opinion deviant*, that is, the member either agreed or disagreed with the group's treatment plan. Note that their explicit goal was to decide on treatment. Dissent on this issue, therefore, was not unimportant compared to rejecting group knowledge regarding race. Nonetheless, the members probably recognized that the treatment plan was merely one of a large number of judgments that might follow from their assumptions about race, that differences about treatment were relatively narrow and resolvable while differences about race were relatively broad and obstinate, and so on. Whatever their thoughts, the upshot was that the majority responded to the spurning of group knowledge quite differently than to dissenting from a particular opinion. It engaged the role conformist/ opinion deviant in much more and in much franker discussion than the role deviant/opinion conformist. In fact, communication to the opinion deviant was like that that would be predicted by Festinger's model: At the outset it increased rapidly, reaching a relatively high level, remaining at this level until just prior to the close of discussion when it began slowly to decline. Communication to the role deviant, on the other hand, did not fit the model. Here the minority received less than half the amount of communication sent to the opinion deviant, and what there was of it was considerably less frank. In short, Sampson and Brandon found no great effort made to persuade the role deviant to change, whereas there was considerable effort made to this end with the opinion deviant. Indeed, ratings of liking and similarity indicate that the role deviant, but not the opinion deviant, was perceived as different from the others and, thus, no longer a member of the group. Therefore, the form of control elicited by deviance seems to depend on whether the act reflects a general principle *or* a judgment about a specific application of these principles.

A roughly similar pattern of findings emerges from studies that observe changes in a majority's reaction to minorities as a function of their extremity, direction, and stability. Note that each of these dimensions is useful in categorizing a minority as ingroup or outgroup as fundamentally similar or fundamentally different from the majority. Suppose, for instance, after wide and frank discussion the habitues of our Republican Club discover that the vast majority of them disagree with Lenin's advice about revolutions. Disagreement with the statement is thus the culturally approved or demonstrably valid direction. Independent of which side of the issue they are on, there are moderate and extreme minorities—a few on the "wrong" side who were undecided and a few who actually agreed with Lenin; and a few on the "right" side who were deviant in that they disagreed with the Lenin statement more strongly than the majority, as well as some who disagreed with it violently. Finally, each of these minorities contained stable and unstable members, that is, individuals who are firmly committed and individuals who can be persuaded to change toward, if not to totally agree with, the majority.

Taken together the evidence (e.g., Hensley and Duval 1976; Kiesler and Pallak 1975; Levine and Ranelli 1978; Levine et al. 1976; Levine et al. 1977) suggests a minority firmly committed to a position that is not only extremely different from the position of the majority but also on the "wrong" side of an issue will be seen as constituting an outgroup, whereas a minority weakly committed to a position that is moderately different from that of the majority, yet on the "right" side of the issue, will continue to be seen as an ingroup. It might be noted that categorizing others as outgroup or ingroup is a common operation in social cognition, with fairly uniform implications for action. When, for instance, individuals have the power to allocate resources to others, they typically behave so as to advantage ingroup members and to disadvantage outgroup members (see Tajfel 1978). In any case, when deviance is an issue, a minority that is perceived as ingroup is likely to be treated in an *inclusive* manner; whereas a minority perceived as outgroup is likely to be treated in an *exclusive* manner.

There are, to be sure, exceptions to such a general rule (see Levine 1980). These seem to occur because the minority's position is given an atypical interpretation, one rarely used in most other contexts. In general it is true that the greater the difference between the majority and a minority, the greater the majority will dislike the minority. Consider, however, the minority of Republicans who are undecided about Lenin's statement. Although less distant from the majority, they may be more disliked by them than those that actually agreed with Lenin because being undecided may be construed by the majority as weak-kneed. The problem of interpretation and comprehension, however, is not peculiar to the psychological analysis of control. Rather, it is inherent to any analysis of social action that is based on a model of human information processing. Within these models it is a truism that we do not recognize or perceive action (i.e., purposive behavior) *prior* to its interpretation.

Future Developments

Research in two areas of psychology seems to foreshadow important developments in our understanding of the mechanisms of control. The first, behavior genetics, is tangential to the work discussed earlier; it should be mentioned, but to avoid going far afield we will do so only briefly. The second, human information processing, is closely linked to this work and will be discussed at more length.

Behavior Genetics

We are accustomed to think that the susceptibility to certain psychoses, particularly schizophrenia, is in part genetically controlled. Somehow one set of genes constructs a neurophysiological system that is predisposed to psychoses, whereas another set constructs a system that is relatively immune (Gottesman and Shields 1982; Zerbin-Rudin 1980). We are not so accustomed to think in this fashion about sociopathic or criminal behavior. Nonetheless, some years ago Schachter and Latané (1963) presented a number of striking findings on differences in neurophysiological functioning between sociopaths and normals. For instance, sociopaths and normals are equally capable of learning to behave appropriately under positive reinforcement but not under negative reinforcement: While normals learn in order to avoid pain, sociopaths do not. On the other hand, sociopaths do improve markedly under negative reinforcement when injected with the sympathomimetic agent adrenalin, while normals do not. These researchers concluded that a combination of psychological (i.e., cognitive) and biological factors are needed to explain individual differences in criminality. More recently, Mednick and Christiansen (1977) have demonstrated that to a significant degree predispositions toward criminality are inherited, at least in Denmark. Despite the political dangers, this line of work is likely to stimulate new research on how human biology facilitates or hinders the process of control. To be sure, once the genetic and neurophysiological determinants of socially significant forms of deviance can be specified with reasonable precision (say, so that susceptible individuals can be identified ahead of time), there will be a radical change in the practice as well as in the theory of control.

Human Information Processing

The second development has to do with an increase in our understanding of encoding processes. This means that a good deal more will be learned about how social actions are interpreted, so that eventually it will be possible to foresee, say, when a disagreement will elicit an exclusive reaction or an inclusive one. To grasp how this might be done, note that the majority's reaction to a minority depends on the goals the former attributes to the latter. The meaning of the statement about a revolution every twenty years being a good thing would change dramatically if members of the Republican Club believed Ronald Reagan was its author. Knowledge of his goals, compared with those of Lenin, makes it clear what is intended is a "revolutionary" reduction in governmental control, or a "revolutionary" increase in individual initiative, and so on. Given such interpretations members probably would have no problem agreeing with it.

Effects of this kind have been repeatedly demonstrated in research on conformity (Allen and Wilder 1980; Asch 1948; Lewis 1941). Even in the classical studies by Asch (1956), where the experimenter has an unanimous majority indicate under optimal viewing conditions that, say, a 6-inch line is equal to an 8-inch line, the naive minority will uniformly reject its judgment and remain independent only when a context exists that explains why the majority would be likely to make this kind of mistake. If the naive minority discovers or is provided with such a context, then what is an atypical and unexpected judgment by the majority in most other situations becomes typical and expected in the present setting. Otherwise there is an amazing amount of conformity to the majority judgment (about 33 percent of the time) considering the blatant nature of the error. This implies that in the absence of a useful encoding structure it is difficult for naive members to understand how the majority can be incorrect, and they perceive themselves to have little choice but to agree (Ross et al. 1976).

We also touched on the issue of interpretation earlier in pointing out that the majority members will respond to a disagreement about general principles differently than they respond to a disagreement over some limited judgment. In fact it has been clear for considerable time that how they respond will depend on the intentions they attribute to the minority. For example, about thirty years ago researchers tried to determine the conditions under which frustration would produce aggression. They discovered that a member who is perceived to *intentionally* frustrate the group is subject to a greater amount of hostility than a member who causes the identical frustration but is believed to do so *unintentionally* (e.g., Pastore 1952; Cohen 1955; Berkowitz 1969). The important point these studies make is that virtually the identical behavior will be perceived by the majority in one case as part of a plan whose goal is inimical to the group and in the other case as part of a plan with benign goals.

Our present understanding of how this occurs derives from recent research on the perception of causation—when is an effect due to the actor and when is it due to the situation? To begin with we should note that there are stable individual differences in how people locate the cause for events in their lives. Research on the *locus of control* demonstrates that some individuals are generally inclined to believe in *internal* causation, that in the main they themselves control events; while other individuals believe in external causation, that events in their lives are primarily controlled by the people and things around them (Rotter 1966, 1975; Strickland 1977). Moreover, the general belief in an internal or an external locus of control has been shown to subsume a large number of specific attitudes about causation. For instance, some who hold to external control might do so because they think that what happens to them is determined either by fate, an uncaring social order, or powerful others (Collins 1974; Gurin et al. 1969). However, we have learned only a few facts about how differences in locus of control affect action. From the point of view of a theory of control, one of the more interesting of these is that externals, but not internals, perform as if they have little incentive to avoid punishment. This is said to reflect the tendency of an external to believe that the administration of punishment is regulated by others and that he or she is incapable of influencing them (Gregory 1978).

On the other hand, there is a good deal that has come to be known about when behavior will be interpreted as internally caused or as externally caused. Currently we think that if the act has low *distinctiveness*, meaning it is directed toward a large number of entities rather than to one particular entity, if it has low *consensus*, meaning only a very small proportion of people act this way in the same situation rather than a large proportion, and if it has high *consistency*, meaning the person displays the same form of behavior in other situations, rather than different forms of behavior, then an observer will be relatively confident that the action is internally caused or intentional. However, high distinctiveness, high consensus, and high consistency will lead observers to infer with equal confidence that the action is externally caused or unintentional (Kelley 1973; McArthur 1972).

At the same time we must take into account that actors and observers, figuratively and literally, have different perspectives (Storms 1973; Taylor and Fiske 1978). Actors, in the main, focus on their environment. They tend to be prepared to encode information about external events, the positive and negative incentives in the situation. Observers, on the other hand, attend to the actor. They are more prepared to encode information about the internal state of these individuals, their motives and beliefs. As a result, external events are more salient to actors and internal events are more salient to observers. Therefore, because each activates different encoding structures observers are inclined to interpret an action as reflecting the intentions of the actor while the actors themselves are predisposed to interpret the same event as reflecting situational forces. Needless to say, this "fundamental attribution error" (Ross 1977) suggests that majorities, as "observers," and minorities, as "actors," are preordained to make incompatible interpretations of deviant behavior. Hence, other conflicts between majority and minority are quite likely. For example, the magnitude and type of control (e.g., whether the majority reacts in an exclusive or inclusive fashion) anticipated by a minority will differ systematically from the magnitude and type actually exercised by the majority.

In many everyday social situations interpretations are made automatically and effortlessly rather than deliberately and laboriously. The importance of the automatic versus deliberate distinction for understanding social behavior in general and control in particular is just being recognized (e.g., Higgins and Kling 1981; Langer 1978; although see Bartlett 1932). Keep in mind that any encoding structure contains "default knowledge" (Rumelhart and Ortony 1977). These are features that are typically associated with the class of events that activates the structure. During encoding, if the event in question does not actually possess some of these features, this knowledge will be called from memory to fill them in by default. In ordinary circumstances "filling in" occurs outside of awareness and, thus, is not subject to self-monitoring or self-control. Hence, to the extent that encoding is automatic, an observer will not bother to think whether his or her understanding of an action is based on "default knowledge" or on the actual properties of the action itself. For this reason automaticity has been called "mindlessness" (Langer 1978).

To be sure, the reason persons do not think about what they are seeing or doing is that their attention is elsewhere, usually on a less practiced activity that can only be performed with deliberation. To illustrate, we may expect a stranger who requests a favor to give a reason. This expectation will serve as "default knowledge" and automatically control reactions in the appropriate social situation. Langer (1978) had confederates ask people who were about to use a copying machine in the library of a university in New York City to let them use it first. The request was made in three different ways: *Alone,* "Excuse me, I have five pages. May I use the Xerox machine?"; with an *explanation,* "Excuse me, I have five pages. May I use the Xerox machine because I'm in a rush?"; or with a *redundant phrase* in place of the explanation, "Excuse me, I have five pages. May I use the Xerox machine because I have to make copies?" The request alone got 60 percent of the people to comply; the request plus an explanation, however, produced 94 percent compliance; but the request plus a redundant phrase in place of the explanation had virtually the same effect as the request with explanation, that is, 93 percent complied. This suggests that in common situations, when there are grounds (i.e., the redundant phrase being located where an explanation typically is) an objectively incomplete attempt to control will automatically be interpreted as complete (i.e., "filled in" by default). Naturally, the person is preoccupied with his or her own task and is unaware that the other's action is incomplete; he or she perceives instead that it *is* complete and responds appropriately without deliberation.

It would seem then that if a contextual element typically associated with a plan of action (e.g., the explanation for a request) is in fact absent, under automatic encoding the plan is more likely to accomplish its purpose than under deliberate encoding. In the former case the observer does not notice its absence by virtue of the "default knowledge." In the latter case, the observer is eminently aware of its absence and is perplexed; in principle, no appropriate reaction is possible unless an encoding structure is found within which the absence is explicable.

Automaticity, to be sure, usually develops from long practice. This means that the observer and actor either have had a longstanding role relationship or that their roles are so constrained by well-established rules that the observer, in effect, has complete, precise, and immediately accessible knowledge about what the actor is likely to do. Otherwise, according to this analysis, the role system will be endangered because the occupants' encoding of each other's behavior will be effortful and problematic. Hence, under conditions sufficiently "noisy" that only a very small amount of information can be communicated, individuals would have great trouble understanding what the other has in mind *unless* they have a certain role relationship (e.g., if they are old friends or on the same football team). Right now reliable knowledge about automatic processing is confined to encoding and performance in nonsocial tasks (Anderson 1980: 26-32, 226-235; Spelke et al. 1976). Langer's work, however, suggests that there are many common role relationships in which the actions are highly practiced and thereby lend themselves to automatization. Thus, it would be surprising if in coming years we do not begin to learn about the function of automaticity in social settings.

REFERENCES

Abramovitch, R. and J. Grusec. 1978. "Peer Imitation in a Natural Setting." *Child Development* 49:60-65.
Allen, V. L. and D. A. Wilder, 1980. "Impact of Group Consensus and Social Support on Stimulus Meaning: Mediation of Conformity by Cognitive Restructuring." *Journal of Personality and Social Psychology* 39:1116-24.
Amsel, A. 1962. "Frustrative Nonreward in Partial Reinforcement and Discrimination Learning." *Psychological Review* 69:306-28.
Anderson, J. R. 1980. *Cognitive Psychology and Its Implications.* San Francisco: W. H. Freeman.
Asch, S. E. 1948. "The Doctrine of Suggestion, Prestige, and Imitation in Social Psychology." *Psychological Review* 55:250-76.
Asch, S. E. 1956. "Studies of Independence and Submission to Group Pressure: 1. On Minority of One against a Unanimous Majority." *Psychological Monographs* 70 (9 Whole No. 417).
Bach, G. R. 1946. "Father-Fantasies and Father-Typing in Father-Separated Children." *Child Development* 17:63-80.
Bacon, M. K., I. L. Child, and H. Barry. 1963. "A Cross-Cultural Study of Correlates of Crime." *Journal of Abnormal and Social Psychology* 66:291-300.
Bandura, A. 1971. "Analysis of Modelling Processes." Pp. 1-62 in *Psychological Modelling: Conflicting Theories,* edited by A. Bandura. Chicago: Aldine-Atherton.
Bandura, A. and R. H. Walters. 1959. *Adolescent Aggression.* New York: Ronald Press.
Bandura, A. and R. H. Walters. 1963. *Social Learning and Personality Development.* New York: Holt, Rinehart & Winston.
Bandura, A., D. Ross, and S. A. Ross. 1963. "A Comparative Test of the Status Envy, Social Power, and Secondary Reinforcement of Identifactory Learning." *Journal of Abnormal and Social Psychology* 67:527-34.
Bartlett, F. C. 1932. *Remembering: A Study in Experimental and Social Psychology.* Cambridge: Cambridge University Press.

Berkowitz, L. 1969. "The Frustration-Aggression Hypothesis Revisited." Pp. 1-28 in *Roots of Aggression,* edited by L. Berkowitz. New York: Atherton.

Berkowitz, L. 1971. "Reporting an Experiment: A Case Study in Leveling, Sharpening, and Assimilation." *Journal of Experimental Social Psychology* 7:237-43.

Bettelheim, B. 1943. "Individual and Mass Behavior in Extreme Situations." *Journal of Abnormal and Social Psychology* 38:417-52.

Burnstein, E., E. Stotland, and A. Zander. 1961. "Similarity to a Model and Self-Evaluation." *Journal of Abnormal and Social Psychology* 62:257-64.

Burnstein, E., A. Vinokur, and M. F. Pichevin. 1974. "What Do Differences between Own, Admired, and Attributed Choices Have to Do with Group Induced Shifts in Choice?" *Journal of Experimental Social Psychology* 10:428-43.

Burton, R. V. (1963. "Generality of Honesty Reconsidered." *Psychological Review* 70:481-99.

Burton, R. V. and J.W.M. Whiting. 1961. "The Absent Father and Cross-Sex Identity." *Merrill-Palmer Quarterly* 7:85-95.

Carlsmith, J. M., B. E. Collins, and R. L. Helmreich. 1966. "Studies in Forced Compliance: 1. The Effect of Pressure for Compliance on Attitude Change Produced by Face-to-Face Role-Playing and Anonymous Essay Writing." *Journal of Personality and Social Psychology* 4:1-13.

Cartwright, D. and A. Zander, eds. 1968. *Group Dynamics:Research and Theory,* 3rd ed. New York: Harper & Row.

Chance, M.R.A. 1967. "Attention Structure as the Basis of Primate Rank Orders." *Man* (new series) 2:503-18.

Chance, M.R.A. and C. Jolly. 1970. *Social Groups of Monkeys, Apes, and Men.* New York: Dutton.

Chance, M.R.A. and R. R. Larsen, eds. 1976. *The Social Structure of Attention.* London: John Wiley.

Church, R. M. 1963. "The Varied Effects of Punishment on Behavior." *Psychological Review* 70:369-402.

Codol, J. P. 1980. "On the So-Called 'Superior Conformity of the Self' Behavior: Twenty Experimental Investigations." *European Journal of Social Psychology* 5:457-501.

Cohen, A. R. 1955. "Social Norms, Arbitrariness of Frustration, and Status of the Agent of Frustration in the Frustration-Aggression Hypothesis." *Journal of Abnormal Social Psychology* 51:222-26.

Collins, B. E. 1974. "Four Components of the Rotter Internal-External Scale: Belief in a Difficult World, a Just World, a Predictable World, and a Politically Responsive World." *Journal of Personality and Social Psychology* 29:381-91.

Davis, J. H. 1973. "Group Decision and Social Interaction: A Theory of Social Decision Schemes." *Psychological Review* 80:97-125.

Deutsch, M. and H. B. Gerard. 1955. "A Study of Normative and Informational Social Influences upon Individual Judgment." *Journal of Abnormal and Social Psychology* 51:629-33.

Dollard, J. and N. E. Miller. 1950. *Personality and Psychotherapy.* New York: McGraw-Hill.

Emerson, R. M. 1954. "Deviation and Rejection: An Experimental Replication." *American Sociological Review* 19:688-93.

Ferster, C. B. and B. F. Skinner. 1957. *Schedules of Reinforcement.* New York: Appleton-Century-Crofts.

Festinger, L. 1950. "Informal Social Communication." *Psychological Review* 57:271-92.

Festinger, L. and J. Thibaut. 1951. "Interpersonal Communication in Small Groups." *Journal of Abnormal and Social Psychology* 46:92-99.

Festinger, L., H. B. Gerard, B. Hymovitch, and B. H. Raven. 1952. "The Influence Process in the Presence of Extreme Deviates." *Human Relations* 5:327-46.

Festiner, L., S. Schachter, and K. Back. 1950. *Social Pressures in Informal Groups: A Study of Human Factors in Housing.* New York: Harper & Row.

Freud, A. 1946. *The Ego and the Mechanisms of Defense.* New York: International Universities Press.

Gerard, H. B. 1953. "The Effect of Different Dimensions of Disagreement on the Communication Process in Groups." *Human Relations* 6:249-71.

Gewirtz, J. L. and D. M. Baer. 1958. "Deprivation and Satiation of Social Reinforcers as Drive Conditions." *Journal of Abnormal and Social Psychology* 57:165-72.

Glueck, S. and E. Glueck. 1950. *Unraveling Juvenile Delinquency.* New York: Commonwealth Fund.

Gottesman, I. and I. Shields. 1982. *The Schizophrenia Puzzle.* New York: Cambridge University Press.

Gregory, W. L. 1978. "Locus of Control for Positive and Negative Outcomes." *Journal of Personality and Social Psychology* 36:840-9.

Gurin, P., G. Gurin, R. C. Lao, and M. Beattie. 1969. "Internal-External Control in the Motivational Dynamics of Negro Youth." *Journal of Social Issues* 25(3):29-53.

Haan, N. 1975. "Hypothetical and Actual Moral Reasoning in a Situation of Civil Disobedience." *Journal of Personality and Social Psychology* 32:255-70.

Haan, N., M. B. Smith, and J. Block. 1968. "Moral Reasoning of Young Adults." *Journal of Personality and Social Psychology* 10:183-201.

Hartshorne, H. and M. A. May. 1928. *Studies in Deceipt.* New York: Macmillan.

Hensley, V. and S. Duval. 1976. "Some Perceptual Determinants of Perceived Similarity, Liking, a Similarity, Liking, and Correctness." *Journal of Personality and Social Psychology* 34:159-68.

Higgins, E. T. and G. King. 1981. "Accessibility of Social Constructs: Information Processing Consequences of Individual and Contextual Variability." Pp. 69-121 in *Personality, Cognition, and Social Interaction,* edited by N. Cantor and J. F. Kihlstrom. Hillsdale, NJ: Erlbaum.

Holz, W. C. and N. H. Azrin. 1963. "A Comparison of Several Procedures for Eliminating Behavior." *Journal of the Experimental Analysis of Behavior* 6:399-406.

Hull, C. L. 1943. *Principles of Behavior.* New York: Appleton.

Kelleher, R. T., W. C. Riddle, and L. Cook. 1963. "Persistent Behavior Maintained by Unavoidable Shocks." *Journal of the Experimental Analysis of Behavior* 6:507-17.

Kelley, H. H. 1973. "The Process of Causal Attribution." *American Psychologist* 28:107-28.

Kiesler, C. A. and M. S. Pallak. 1975. "Minority Influence: The Effect of Majority Reactionaries and Defectors, and Minority and Majority Compromisers, upon Majority Opinion and Attraction." *European Journal of Social Psychology* 5:237-56.

Kohlberg, L. 1969. "Stage and Sequence: The Cognitive-Developmental Approach to Socialization." Pp. 347-480 in *Handbook of Socialization Theory and Research,* edited by D. A. Goslin. Chicago: Rand-McNally.

Kohlberg, L. 1978. "Moral Stages and Moralization: The Cognitive-Developmental Approach." Pp. 31-53 in *Moral Development and Behavior: Theory, Research, and Social Issues*, edited by T. Lickona. New York: Holt, Rinehart & Winston.

Kurtines, W. and E. B. Greif. 1974. "The Development of Moral Thought: Review and Evaluation of Kohlberg's Approach." *Psychological Bulletin* 81: 453-70.

Langer, E. J. 1978. "Rethinking the Role of Thought in Social Interaction." Pp. 35-58 in *New Directions in Attribution Research*, edited by J. H. Harvey, W. J. Ickes, and R. F. Kidd. Hillsdale, NJ: Erlbaum.

Laughlin, P. R. 1980. "Social Combination Processes of Cooperative Problem-Solving on Verbal Intellective Tasks." Pp. 127-155 in *Progress in Social Psychology*, Vol. 1, edited by M. Fishbein. Hillsdale, NJ: Erlbaum.

Laughlin, P. R., N. L. Kerr, J. H. Davis, H. M. Halff and K. A. Marciniak. 1975. "Group Size, Member Ability, and Social Decision Schemes on an Intellective Task." *Journal of Personality and Social Psychology* 31:522-35.

Lepper, M. R. and D. Greene, eds. 1978. *The Hidden Costs of Reward*. Hillsdale, NJ: Erlbaum.

Lepper, M. R., D. Greene, and R. E. Nisbett. 1973. "Undermining Children's Intrinsic Interest with Extrinsic Reward: A Test of the Overjustification Hypothesis." *Journal of Abnormal and Social Psychology* 28:129-37.

Levine, J. M. 1980. "Reaction to Opinion Deviance in Small Groups." Pp. 375-429 in *Psychology of Group Influence*, edited by P. B. Paulus. Hillsdale, NJ: Erlbaum.

Levine, J. M. and C. J. Ranelli. 1978. "Majority Reaction to Shifting and Stable Attitudinal Deviates." *European Journal of Social Psychology* 8:55-70.

Levine, J. M., L. Saxe, and H. J. Harris. 1976. "Reaction to Attitudinal Deviance: Impact of Deviate's Direction and Distance of Movement." *Sociometry* 39:97-107.

Levine, J. M., K. R. Sroka, and H. N. Snyder. 1977. "Group Support and Reaction to Stable and Shifting Agreement/Disagreement." *Sociometry* 40:214-24.

Lewin, K., T. Dembo, L. Festinger, and P. Sears. 1944. "Level of Aspiration." Pp. 333-378 in *Personality and the Behavior Disorders*, Vol. 1, edited by J. McV. Hunt. New York: Ronald Press.

Lewis, H. B. 1941. "Studies in the Principles of Judgment and Attitudes: IV. The Operation of 'Prestige Suggestion.' " *Journal of Social Psychology* 14:229-56.

Lippitt, R., N. Polansky, F. Redl, and S. Rosen. 1952. "The Dynamics of Power." *Human Relations* 5:37-64.

Lorge, I. and H. Solomon. 1955. "Two Models of Group Behavior in the Solution of Eureka-Type Problems." *Psychometrika* 20:139-148.

McArthur, L. 1972. "The How and What of Why: Some Determinants and Consequences of Causal Attribution." *Journal of Personality and Social Psychology* 22:171-93.

McArthur, L. Z. and D. L. Post. 1977. "Figural Emphasis and Person Perception." *Journal of Experimental Social Psychology* 13:520-35.

Mednick, S. A. and K. O. Christiansen, eds. 1977. *Biosocial Bases of Criminal Behavior*. New York: Gardner.

Miller, D. R. and G. E. Swanson. 1958. *Inner Conflict and Defense*. New York: Schocken.

Miller, G. A., E. Galanter, and K. H. Pribram. 1960. *Plans and the Structure of Behavior*. New York: Holt, Rinehart, & Winston.

Miller, N. E. and J. Dollard. 1941. *Social Learning and Imitation*. New Haven, CT: Yale University Press.

Mischel, W. 1968. *Personality and Assessment.* New York: John Wiley.

Mischel, W. 1973. "Toward a Cognitive Social Learning Reconceptualization of Personality." *Psychological Review* 80:252-83.

Moscovici, S. and C. Faucheux. 1972. "Social Influence, Conformity Bias, and the Study of Active Minorities." Pp. 150-202 in *Advances in Experimental Social Psychology*, Vol. 6, edited by L. Berkowitz. New York: Academic.

Moulton, R. W., E. Burnstein, P. G. Liberty, Jr., and N. Altucher. 1966. "Patterning of Parental Affection and Disciplinary Dominance as a Determinant of Guilt and Sex Typing." *Journal of Personality and Social Psychology* 4:356-63.

Myers, D. C. and H. Lamm. 1976. "The Group Polarization Phenomenon." *Psychological Bulletin* 83:602-27.

Nemeth, C., M. Swedlund, and B. Kanki. 1974. "Patterning of the Minority's Responses and their Influence on the Majority." *European Journal of Social Psychology* 4:53-64.

Newcomb, T. 1953. "An Approach to the Study of Communicative Acts." *Psychological Review* 60:393-404.

Orcutt, J. D. 1973. "Societal Reaction and the Response to Deviation in Small Groups." *Social Forces* 52:259-67.

Pastore, N. 1952. "The Role of Arbitrariness in the Frustration-Aggression Hypothesis." *Journal of Abnormal and Social Psychology* 47:728-31.

Piaget, J. 1964. *The Moral Judgement of the Child.* New York: Free Press.

Rest, J., E. Turiel, and L. Kohlberg. 1969. "Relations between Level of Moral Judgment and Comprehension of the Moral Judgment of Others." *Journal of Personality,* 37:225-52.

Ross, L. 1977. "The Intuitive Psychologist and His Shortcomings: Distortions in the Attribution Process." Pp. 177-220 in *Advances in Experimental Social Psychology*, Vol. 10, edited by L. Berkowitz. New York: Academic.

Ross, L., G. Bierbrauer, and S. Hoffman. 1976. "The Role of Attribution Processes in Conformity and Dissent: Revisiting the Asch Situation." *American Psychologist* 31:148-57.

Rotter, J. B. 1966. "Generalized Expectancies for Internal Versus External Control of Reinforcement." *Psychological Monographs* 80(1, Whole No. 609).

Rotter, J. B. 1975. "Some Problems and Misconceptions Related to the Construct of Internal Versus External Control of Reinforcement." *Journal of Consulting and Clinical Psychology* 43:56-67.

Rumelhart, D. E. and A. Ortony. 1977. "The Representation of Knowledge in Memory." Pp. 99-135 in *Schooling and the Acquisition of Knowledge,* edited by R. C. Anderson, R. J. Spiro, and W. E. Montague. Hillsdale, NJ: Erlbaum.

Sampson, E. E. and A. C. Brandon. 1964. "The Effects of Role and Opinion Deviation on Small Group Behavior." *Sociometry* 27:261-81.

Sanders, G. and R. S. Baron. 1977. "Is Social Comparison Irrelevant for Producing Choice Shifts?" *Journal of Experimental Social Psychology* 13:303-14.

Schachter, S. 1951. "Deviation, Rejection, and Communication." *Journal of Abnormal and Social Psychology* 46:190-207.

Schachter, S. and B. Latane. 1963. "Crime, Cognition, and the Autonomic Nervous System." Pp. 221-273 in *Nebraska Symposium on Motivation,* edited by D. Levine. Lincoln: University of Nebraska Press.

Schank, R. and R. Abelson. 1977. *Scripts, Plans, Goals and Understanding.* Hillsdale, NJ: Erlbaum.

Sears, R. R., M. M. Pintler, and P. S. Sears. 1946. "Effect of Father Separation on Preschool Children's Doll Play Aggression." *Child Development* 17:219-43.

Seligman, M.E.P. 1975. *Helplessness.* San Francisco: Freeman.

Simpson, E. L. 1974. "Moral Development Research: A Case of Scientific Cultural Bias." *Human Development* 17:81-106.

Skinner, B. F. 1938. *The Behavior of Organisms.* New York: Appleton-Century-Crofts.

Skinner, B. F. 1953. *Science and Human Behavior.* New York: Macmillan.

Skinner, B. F. 1957. *Verbal Behavior.* New York: Appleton-Century-Crofts.

Solomon, R. L. and L. C. Wynne. 1954. "Traumatic Avoidance Learning: The Principles of Anxiety Conservation and Partial Irreversibility." *Psychological Review* 61:353-85.

Spelke, E., W. Hirst, and U. Neisser. 1976. "Skills of Divided Attention." *Cognition* 4:215-30.

Spence, K. W. 1956. *Behavior Theory and Conditioning.* New Haven, CT: Yale University Press.

Spence, K. W. 1960. *Behavior Theory and Learning.* Englewood Cliffs, NJ: Prentice Hall.

Storms, M. D. 1973. "Videotape and the Attribution Process: Reversing Actors' and Observers' Points of View." *Journal of Personality and Social Psychology* 27(2):165-75.

Strickland, B. R. 1977. "Internal-External Control of Reinforcement." Pp. 219-279 in *Personality Variables in Social Behaviors,* edited by T. Blass. Hillsdale, NJ: Erlbaum.

Tajfel, H., ed. 1978. *Differentiation between Social Groups: Studies in the Social Psychology of Intergroup Relations.* London: Academic Press.

Taylor, S. E. and S. T. Fiske. 1975. "Point of View and Perceptions of Causality." *Journal of Personality and Social Psychology* 32:439-45.

Taylor, S. E. and S. T. Fiske. 1978. "Salience, Attention, and Attribution: Top of the Head Phenomena." Pp. 249-288 in *Advances in Experimental Social Psychology,* Vol. 11, edited by L. Berkowitz. New York: Academic.

Thibaut, J. W. and H. H. Kelley. 1959. *The Social Psychology of Groups.* New York: John Wiley.

Tolman, E. C. 1932. *Purposive Behavior in Animals and Men.* New York: Appleton.

Tolman, E. C. 1948. "Cognitive Maps in Rats and Men." *Psychological Review* 55:189-208.

Turiel, E. and G. R. Rothman. 1972. "The Influence of Reasoning on Behavioral Choices at Different Stages of Moral Development." *Child Development* 43:741-56.

Vinokur, A. and E. Burnstein. 1978. "Depolarization of Attitudes in Groups." *Journal of Personality and Social Psychology* 36:872-85.

Whiting, J.W.M. and I. L. Child. 1953. *Child Training and Personality.* New Haven, CT: Yale University Press.

Zerbin-Rudin, E. 1980. "Genetics of Affective Disorders." Pp. 35-57 in *Handbook of Biological Psychiatry,* edited by H. von Praog, M. H. Lader, O. J. Rafaelson, and E. J. Sachar. New York: Dekker.

PART II

Where Control Is
the Name of the Game

Extensive efforts to conceptualize social control have been restricted primarily to sociology. Prior to the 1950s, the prevailing sociological conception of social control stemmed largely from E. A. Ross, who virtually defined social control as any human institution that contributes to social order. The objection is not just that such a definition denies or belittles any necessary intentional quality of social control; additionally, since institutions are themselves components of social order, it is as though social order explains social order. Stating the matter in the way of a question: If institutions are the *sources* of social control, what of social control within and over institutions? To illustrate, assume that in predominantly Catholic countries the religious practice of confession somehow contributes to social order. Even so, what promotes participation in the confessional? Surely participation is not instinctive.

Commencing with Talcott Parsons' theoretical perspective (especially *The Social System,* 1951), the prevailing sociological conception of social control shifted to something like this: any social process or mechanism that counteracts deviant tendencies. Appearances to the contrary, Parson's conception of social control is not fundamentally different from the older conception (i.e., that promoted by Ross). Since social order is commonly thought of as conformity to norms, counteraction of deviance promotes social order. The two conceptions are also similar in that both deny the relevance of intention in social control. Nonetheless, despite widespread acceptance of the Parsonian conception, the older conception is more relevant in contemplating something that few scholars would dispute: Social control is especially conspicuous in two institutions, government and law. Since control is virtually the "name of the game" in those two institutions, they have been accorded special recognition in this volume.

For better or for worse, government and law have yet to be appreciably influenced by theories or research in the social and behavioral sciences. Perhaps that is the case because those sciences seemingly have little to offer when it comes to furthering the effectiveness of human control over human behavior. Nonetheless, some lines of work in the social and behavioral sciences appear to have implications for human control over human behavior, and in recent decades one such line of work has been loosely designated as "behavior modification." Social and behavioral scientists (primarily psychologists) who engage in that work may deny that they are really concerned with furthering the effectiveness of human control over human behavior, but to deny that the work has implications in that direction is naive and dangerous.

Although Sam Krislov (Chapter 3) does not make the point, political scientists seldom use the term social control; and there are two possible interpretations. First, virtually everything in the subject matter of political science pertains to social control; hence, the term has no particular descriptive utility. Or, second, political scientists use another term in lieu of social control. Krislov's chapter lends credence to the second interpretation, and the term is *power*. However, few writers suggest that power is a means or type of social control, and it could be argued that power must be conceptualized in terms of social control. The argument takes on significance in light of Krislov's suggestion that the preoccupation of social scientists with power is matched only by their trouble in conceptualizing the notion and studying the phenomena. However, in conceptualizing power in terms of social control one must confront this question: What kinds of social control, what scope of social control, and what effectiveness of social control are *logically* necessary corollaries of power? Krislov's survey indicates that the control correlates of power vary so much among individuals (e.g., Hitler versus Castro) and among regimes that such conventional designations as dictator and totalitarian state have little meaning. Moreover, as Krislov indicates, it appears that the control correlates of power depend on sociocultural conditions and perhaps unique historical circumstances. For that reason alone, it is extremely difficult to *define* power in terms of attributes of social control; and more than a definition (even a defensible definition) is needed. In the absence of a compelling theory about the way in which the relation between control and power is contingent on sociocultural conditions, speculation about the future character of power in any society cannot be little more than conjecture. Hence, Krislov's reluctance to indulge in prophecies is surely sensible.

As emphasized in Chapter 4, there is widespread agreement that law is a means or type of social control: but disagreements as to the appropriate definition of law and social control make the exact nature of the logical (conceptual) relation between those two phenomena debatable. That relation is all the more important because of the idea that legal control and extralegal control do not change independently; rather, as the major structural features of a society (e.g., division of labor, urbanization) change, one of those two principal classes of social control tends to be substituted for the other. Casual observations indicate an evolutionary trend toward the expansion of legal control and the relative diminution of extralegal controls. However, even if that trend is not questioned, its extrapolation to, say, 2000 is not really informative. For that matter, the atheoretical character of contemporary sociology of law is not conducive to speculation about the future of law, and the validity of well-known nineteenth-century theories (Durkheim's theory and Marxist theory) is dubious at best. Nonetheless, a forecast is made in Chapter 4—that the future will be one of increasing departures from "the rule of law." Appearances to the contrary, the forecast does not preclude an expansion of regulatory law; but the forecast is conditional, as all should be. Briefly, if there is a decline in the use of inanimate energy and a concomitant decline in the division of labor, the forecast of trends in law will not hold.

Rightly or wrongly, Orwell did not describe the control apparatus in *1984* as the product of evil or compliant social and behavioral scientists. Perhaps Orwell thought of those scientists as inept, and even today the knowledge of the behavioral and social sciences scarcely provides an effective basis for anything akin to Orwell's *1984* or Huxley's *Brave New World*. Yet a rare mentality would be required to deny the prospects of such knowledge. Indeed, social critics often point to what is now a traditional line of work in the behavioral sciences (psychology in particular) as a dreadful harbinger. That line of work is identified as "behavioral modification," and it is treated in Chaper 5 by Leonard Krasner.

Krasner is not concerned with techniques, research findings, or theories; rather, he focuses largely on ethical and legal issues entailed in behavior modification. That focus is particularly appropriate for a volume on social control, and the issues are the central consideration in contemplating the future of behavior modification. While the effectiveness of contemporary techniques of behavior modification is debatable, especially with a view to their use in social control on a massive scale, the possibility of clearly effective techniques should not be dismissed as "science fiction." What could or will prevent the extensive and effective use of behavior modification techniques or principles in social control on a massive scale? Krasner suggests that the future of behavior modification depends on the values of those engaged in that line of work. Note, however, that another but not contradictory argument can be made. Briefly, the potential use of behavior modification techniques in social control depends on the social control of the behavior modifiers. Throughout the history of behavior modification, the practitioners have worked under all manner of legal and extralegal restraints, many self-imposed or readily accepted by the practitioners; and it is likely that there will be no major turning point in the future of behavior modification until those restraints are substantially loosened.

3

The Politics of Control and the Control of Politics

SAMUEL KRISLOV

In the light of the obvious centrality of the concept of power—by whatever name currently fashionable—to the field of political science, it is remarkable how little literature actually exists within the discipline on the subject. It is usual to attribute this to the baneful effect of the concept of sovereignty and the role that normative discussion has had in dominating the field of political theory. The notion of sovereignty, which locates power solely in one central source and assumes obedience on the part of all others, reduces the problem of social control to the rather banal one of maintaining or losing power. As one plunges from absolute monarch to discredited tyrant there is no need for scientific or other analysis; occupation of the throne is succeeded by being cast out into darkness. Traditionally such notions are obvious examples of political folklore: "Treason never prospers; for if it prosper none dare call it treason."

The preoccupation with legalistic and monolithic control survived long past the time when analysts really believed in the existence of such a phenomenon as sovereignty. Surprisingly, even Woodrow Wilson, in his marvelous discussion of *Congressional Government* (1885), sees the task of political science as discovering the one true and central institution that wields ultimate power. Since he was writing in twentieth-century Federalist America, which hardly had one unitary institution capable of complete control, the statement in itself seems rather ostrich-like. Since the book is concerned with a careful and minute dissection of the disintegration of authority within the Congress itself, such an idea emerges as almost perverse. It indicates the beguiling effect that preoccupation with false concepts can have on a persisting basis in any field of inquiry.

There are traditional names who were preoccupied with something quite different. Thus, Hobbes saw the problem of sovereignty in terms of precisely the lack of power of the central government. The necessity of an absolute ruler was based on the dreaded fear of *"imperium in imperio."* Lest the government disintegrate into the true natural constituents of authority, everyone must promise obedience. Without such a pledge even greater costs would be borne by each citizen. The resting of the pledge of cooperation upon fear of social disintegration makes Hobbes's point of view more socially realistic than most discussions of sovereignty. Earlier, too, Machiavelli had written a mordant volume outlining the tasks of the ruler who wished to maintain power. Such guidebooks in the tradition of, for example, Henry Taylor's *The Statesman* (1836) were fairly common; the understanding of the means of manipulation and the sources of social division of authority also constitute a major change in approaches in political theory. The attribution of modernism to the work of Machiavelli and Hobbes—occasionally writers also include Locke in what is essentially an indictment—suggests a fully developed break with the concept of sovereignty that is certainly not to be found in these writers. Rather it is argued that ideas that are begun in their writing (most clearly with Hobbes) must ultimately lead to a sharp departure from tradition. Indeed it was not, as we have indicated with the example of Wilson, until the twentieth century that there was much of a break.

Perhaps surprisingly, one of the first areas in which a departure from clear notions of sovereignty took place was in the field of international relations. Close examination of the notion of "nation-state" showed that beneath the monolithic surface there were cross-currents and cross-pressures. Nations might gain in power and their citizens decline. Groups within any society had transnational connections. Others might question the posture of a militaristic or evangelizing nation. Even in considering the capabilities of a nation to make war, the relative unity of the country, the extent to which it could expect not just political obedience but loyalty and service, constituted a major analytic problem. The French Revolution and the Napoleonic era emphasized not just the question of availability of resources but the ability to marshal and to concentrate the resources.

In another area puzzling evidence brought out new problems and suggested new approaches. In many ways this was a major contribution to political science of political sociologists, economists dealing with broadly sociological questions, and legal theorists, who began to look realistically at the role of leadership in societies. James Burnham has analyzed this school of thought under the name, *The Machiavellians* (1943); but while he makes the case that their tradition was that of Machiavelli, he brings forward very little evidence that the influence was a direct one. In any event, the work of Michels on political parties, of Mosca on the ruling class, and of Pareto on elites generally is so well known that there is no need to elaborate here. Their influence on political science, however, was at least as great as on sociology. It forced some recognition of the interactional process that is really the source of political loyalty and affiliation. It suggested that leadership was largely self-starting and purposive, and that it required certain resources, techniques, and advantages to maintain itself.

From a more benign viewpoint, somewhat similar arguments were brought forward by group theorists of various sorts. Corporationists who advocated societies based on such quaint-seeming notions as Guild Socialism (e.g., G.D.H. Cole), legal pluralists (e.g., Harold Laski), and pluralistic idealists such as Mary Parket Follett, made arguments for the need for the maintenance of balance in the society through the creation of numerous power centers. These power centers would maintain societal relations with at least a diminution of the use of force, if not, as in various forms of syndicalism or anarchism, eliminating it altogether as a factor in human life. In their semi-utopian writings they suggested not only that sovereignty ought not to exist; they often veered into the argument that it did not. They substituted for notions of blind allegiance the notion of social bonds, primary and secondary controls, and many other aspects of political relationships that seem to the modern analyst more realistic or more appropriate than traditional political science.

The emergence of an alternative to the notion of sovereignty was also attributable to nonprofessionals. After World War I it is not surprising that support for a subnational state should exist, as well as for a supernational state. We find in efforts, such as that of Bertrand Russell, to project a realistic view of power in society and to advocate dispersion of authority a perfectly natural reaction to the collision of the great nations in a disastrous world war. Lippman's *Public Opinion* (1922) challenged central notions of public concern, attention, and understanding. The popularity of such writings was to provide the foundation for the first really professional emergence of questioning of sovereignty as a concept and of moralizing or legal analysis as the prime concerns of the field.

The Chicago department of political science was the first to explore these notions professionally. The dominant figure in the development of the school was Charles Merriam. Merriam's work was apparently less impressive than his presence; little of the former is regarded today as important in its own right. Nevertheless, Merriam developed his notions of political science in a plea for systematic political theory centered upon work on political power.

The notion of "systematic political theory" was parallel to the role that theory plays in economics and to a lesser degree (though in intention to an equal degree) in sociology. Merriam attempted to systematize emprical generalizations as opposed to normative ones. And in that approach and in his other writings, political power seems to him to be a focus. For the first time there was concentration of a notion of what could be effective in leadership and in manipulation. Lasswell was to pick up those concerns and, by and large, outstrip Merriam, but his indebtedness is clear. At the same time, British political science under the influence of various forms of group theory and Fabianism picked up some of this emphasis, as we find in idiosyncratic writing such as that of A. E. Lindsay.

Under Merriam's influence, the Chicago school had something of a central concern for the subject of power, though it was not a monopolistic one. Neither Quincy Wright, nor Harold Gosnell, nor Leonard White, in the field of public administration, embraced the central core of Merriam's approach. To Wright and Gosnell, the essence of Merriam's approach was scientific method, experimentation, and data collection; and they applied this to international relations and voting studies, respectively. White centered on Merriam's preoccupation with public administration. To this day White's various volumes remain an outstanding treasure of American administrative development, carefully recorded in the minute description of past histories. His history, however, gives us mostly information; White, by and large, left it to others to weave generalizations.

That part of the Chicago tradition that is most relevant to understanding social control was exemplified in the work of Harold Lasswell. The preeminent political scientist of his day, Lasswell easily outstripped his master, Merriam. To Lasswell the notion of power was not merely an organizing concept. It was something of an obsession. But in truth, Lasswell was at least as fascinated by the powerful as he was by the concept of power. Much of his early work is on the psychology of the powerful, and particularly the abnormal psychology of political leaders. (While Almond was still under the influence of Lasswell he wrote his study of the "New York Rich" and their political ideas.)

In the field of international relations, Lasswell extended the idea of power in the analysis of international events. The now fashionable study of irrational responses by powerful decision makers is a direct projection of Lasswellian notions. Elite analysis, as exemplified by the Hoover Institute's RADAR studies, also reflects Lasswellian influence. Lasswell later emphasized the study of the type of elites that were likely to achieve and maintain power. In order to pursue this, Lasswell largely invented the notion of futuristic scenarios in the form of "developmental constructs," and thus made one of his many contributions to other fields. The final major phase of his thinking was dominated by his exploration of the psychic needs of the powerful, and the characteristics that they wish to project through their behaviors. While Lasswell regarded this as his major contribution, the effect was to create a cult that divided those who accepted these notions—who became Lasswellians—and the rest of the community. During this phase he was rather impatient with those who would not accept his schema, unlike earlier times when one could, with his blessing, adopt some of his ideas and use them in a nonsystematic fashion.

Two remaining contributions of Lasswell's are of great importance to us here. One was his formalization of notions of politics under the rubric *Power and Society* (1950) with Abraham Kaplan, the well-known philosopher and formal logician. This is an important book in that it attempts to develop axiomatic formulations for the understanding of power, which, they project, is the central concept in society. It is interesting that the book has few imitators and virtually no followers. Perhaps it was premature simply in that it did not develop a group of scholars that could benefit from it; perhaps it was also premature in the sense that the material was not there to create a body of findings commensurate with the complexity of the apparatus.

Second, in cooperation with a law professor, Richard Arens, Lasswell wrote *In Defense of Public Order: The Emerging Study of Sanctioning Law* (1961). This volume, which is extremely uneven in quality, unsystematically brings together a great deal of material on the effects on behavior of penalties and rewards. In particular it rests upon work such as that of the World War II Office of Price Administration staff and that of subsequent scholars such as Clinard on punishment and behavior. The bulk of this work was sociological, and its follow-up remains in the main the concern of sociologists, such as Gibbs and Skolnick. However, law professors such as Packer and Arens were clearly influenced by Lasswell, as were a number of political scientists.

The first area of political science to be permeated by the notion of power and control was the field of judicial behavior. Jack Peltason had called for a restructuring of the field of constitutional law in his seminal monograph, *Federal Courts in the Political Process* (1955). More forcefully than most who had had this insight, Peltason called for concern with the effects of a court decision, rather than concentration on its content, as part of a broadening of the field from simple doctrinal analysis. His chapter on consequences is somewhat brief, and the concept that he uses to call for attention to such phenomena—"after-math"—is also not very helpful. The attention to postdecision behavior was important and persuasive. It was one of his students, Gordon Patric, who did perhaps the first study of consequences in the Prayer decision (1957). This study was followed independently by a more thorough effort by Frank Sorauf. A number of such studies took shape in the light of key Supreme Court decisions, most notably the desegregation decision. In 1956, I formulated this concern into a theoretical paper given at the American Political Science Association under the title, "The Perimeters of Power" (1963). This called for greater attention to the acceptance of decisions and suggested that the concept "compliance" would open up new dimensions not only for the study of judicial behavior, but equally for other aspects of political science as well. Indeed, I called for reversal of the famous Lasswellian motto, "Politics is the study of power and the powerful," and suggested that the time had come to devote attention to the study of powerlessness and the effects of decisions on those who were the objects rather than the originators of power. While the paper was influential in promoting compliance studies and in formulating a rationale for such efforts, the rubric under which such studies have continued to be undertaken has not been, in general, that of compliance, but rather "impact." I have argued against the utility of that concept, but to no avail. The formulation of most of the work in the field, at least at the time of the compilation by Stephen Wasby, reflects that point and triumph of the "impact" notion (1970). The advantage of "impact" is that it avoids many of the judgments and evaluations that would be necessary in a compliance model. That allows discussion without a great deal of thinking or proof and can embrace anything that happens subsequent to the event. Thus it is, of course, much easier for the observer to detail, and it requires less defense than the attribution of causation. Of course, it is precisely for those reasons that I advocate the much tougher standard.

The type of study exemplified has now radiated out to the arena of public administration. Here the efforts of Aaron Wildavsky and Jeffery Pressman (1973) have led to an entire school of researchers who are concerned with the subject matter of "implementation." Most prominent are Eugene Bardach, also at Berkeley, and the school includes others, such as Martin Levin and Gordon Chase at Brandeis. Here the emphasis· is sometimes instrumental—How does the bureaucrat get to implement what he wishes to implement?—and at other times it is descriptive of a general process. While this has some connections with work such as that of Chester Barnard, who insisted that implementation was in fact more difficult than invention, there is little in the Simon-March tradition that deals with the general phenomena. Nevertheless, it is easily absorbable into that tradition. After all, the Simon-Thompson-Smithburg and the Simon-March approaches emphasize that clientele groups are in fact invisibly attached to the organization. Thus, change and control become a question not just for "employees," but for the general community—users, buyers, and sellers as well. The implementation question, both as a strategy and the scientifically observable phenomenon, thus becomes part of the general pattern of organization theory.

It is interesting to note that these connections with the concept of social control are indirect and not central to most areas of political science. There is almost a reluctance on the part of the analysts, who use related concerns and problems that could benefit from direct central assumptions of social control and its methodologies, to employ it at all. There are, of course, exceptions, such as those who deal with the media or those who are specialists in the study of violence. These are very unusual concerns for political scientists, and the tendency is for students of such phenomena to drift into sociological circles. Thus we have the paradox of a profession that avoids its own central concern.

Controlling Politics

At one level there is a decisive explanation for the disconcerting array of projections of the future of social control as developed by social scientists. As if they were the most untutored of seers, their predictions run the gamut from utopian expectations to despair. And the sovereign explanation of this is the same for the specialist as for those blessed with invincible ignorance. On a matter so fundamental, one that amounts to a vision of the future of mankind, the true determinant of the conclusion is the preconception. Over such antinomies temperament, not logic, prevails.

Errors ensue from perfectly reasonable deductions or extrapolations. Experts, perhaps even more than others, view trend-lines as inexorable. They extrapolate technical feasibility into implementation. Functional theorists and Marxist theorists, among others, convert an essentially probabilistic argument into one of inevitability. There is inadequate appreciation of societies' tolerance of inefficiency, of their abilities to spread costs so widely, to the point of invisibility and, therefore, to acceptance. Along the same line of argument, I would suggest that developments occur in significant measure because of sequencing as well as because of import. Spelling that out, it means that not only does control ebb-and-flow as technology and social invention interact, but their different ordering in time will affect practice in different societies in demonstrably separable ways.

Political scientists have understandably concentrated upon those processes of social control involved in regime maintenance. They note, though different analysts have different vocabularies, two aspects of political control. On the one hand, there is the degree of monopoly of power, the absolute or nonabsolute right to rule and direct the state. The other dimension relates to the extent to which those political organs influence others and extend into society. The concept of "penetration" was developed by the SSRC Committee on the Study of Comparative Government to explain a repeated phenomenon in former colonial governments in the post-World War II liberation era. The bureaucracies continued to function with the same nominal efficiency as before. But with the removal of the mystique and might of the imperial power, their authority tended to atrophy.   .

In this light, Lipset's differentiation of right-wing authoritarianism from left-wing absolutism becomes clearer (1960). Left-wing regimes legitimize their right to penetrate all aspects of life by conferring new benefits (e.g. free rent as in Cuba) in exchange for destruction of older relationships (e.g., encouragement of betrayal of one's family for political disloyalty). Right-wing regimes wedded to history and traditional institutions have the practical power to abuse and destroy, but they do it extralegitimately and under the table. In this sense, the Nazis never completely lost some of the left-wing impulse in the sense of reconstruction of society from the ground up.

Wittfogel's important book, *Oriental Despotism* (1957), would have benefited immensely from this distinction. It discusses the two-dimensional problem in one-dimensional form, to its detriment. The mode of Asiatic authority is complete and sweeping, even when underneath it is consultative and consensual. What the "hydraulic society" (i.e., a "totalitarian" society with an overriding purpose, such as finding water in arid areas) created were the conditions under which the authoritarian impulses could penetrate into the very being of a society's institutions. This penetration, in turn, insured that the absoluteness of form would, over time, also become absoluteness in fact.

In the modern world, the modalities of power are disguised, though often barely. Absolute regimes proclaim martial law for extended emergencies—some have perdured over a decade already—or look forward to an imminent election. (Some have been imminent for more than a score of years.) Today all regimes are "democratic," though perhaps modified by an adjective rendering the term oxymoron (e.g., "guided" or "directed" democracy).

The pace of modern society makes it impossible to recreate the "night watchman" limited state, if it ever existed. Because any relationship, economic or social, may threaten the workings of society, all regimes assert their right to intervene indiscriminately over all aspects of life. My own view is that it was always thus, but that the need to change objects and forms of relationships was formerly sufficiently infrequent to permit the fiction of constancy. In any event, even "liberal" regimes are interventionist in fact, though they may not be so in principle. Their attitude toward other institutions is that they are licensees or franchise holders subject to significant change. Of course, totalitarian regimes see even the family or religion as tenants at sufferance. These are highly significant differences of attitude, though in essence differences of degree only.

The essential questions become regime capability and regime intention. It is clear as to the latter that a number of societies have secure regimes whose style is to impose minimum constraints upon individuals and institutions. These societies, for shorthand called "democracies," tend to be Western advanced societies. While some societies move from democratic to nondemocratic forms of government, new recruits into the "club" are seldom drawn from outside that group, and those that are seldom maintain those forms for long periods—say, over five to ten years.

There was a period in which it was fashionable to attempt to isolate differences between such societies and others in terms of social patterns. The well-known efforts of Lipset (1960) and Cutright (1963) were probably most salient. In the face of constructive critiques such as those of Marsh (1967), Rustow (1970), and Lijphart (1977), work of this type has been largely abandoned. Essentially it was found that the different social patterns did not hold up on diachronic analysis, that indeed cross-sectional and diachronic results were incompatible. Thus it seems likely that prerequisites and requisites for democracy are very different. Furthermore, such countries as Syria and Lebanon, where conditions seemed ripe, did not seem impelled to move in predicted directions. Thus the approach emerges, at best, as stating necessary but not sufficient causes. This may be interpreted as simply incompleteness—the need for classifying cultural variables, for example—or it may indicate a genuine aleatory element involved.

Notions of evolutionary development in power distribution were fashionable in the 1960s and fell into disfavor in the light of incongruity of results derived from diachronic versus historical method. The culmination of the approach in Brzezinski and Huntington's work (1964) suggesting American and Soviet congruence has been a source of embarrassment to the approach as well as to the authors. Their reputation as hard-line anti-Soviet thinkers and policymakers makes its ingenuity and their unabashed commitment to playing out the logic of an idea particularly charming to read today.

A revival of these notions with quite different policy implications has been pressed by Jeanne Kirkpatrick (1979), writing as publicist and political scientist, and acting as policymaker. Reasoning along Lipset's neo-Aristotelian lines (1960), the approach leans heavily on his distinction between authoritarian and totalitarian regimes. Conservative upper-class autocracy, even at its most ruthless, has a certain noblesse oblige that is a source of vulnerability when legitimacy begins to wane. (The Shah's reluctance to order firing on mass protests on the grounds that he would cease to be the father of his people comes to mind.) Left-wing totalitarianism also aggressively deinstitutionalizes and delegitimizes other social structures and thus preserves itself effectively. Right-wing totalitarianism is unlikely (as in Nazism) because radical change and conservatism is a difficult blend to sell, requiring both acute crisis and exceptional demagoguery. Furthermore, right-wing power is often exercised by those already entrenched who have little motivation to displace their peers and supporters.

The standard forms, then, of dictatorship are analyzed as right-wing autocracy and left-wing totalitarianism. An asymmetry exists as to the future. With some luck, both tend to persist to the death of their perpetrators. But authoritarian regimes, preserving a basic pluralism, can evolve to democracy; totalitarian structures survive everything but crushing defeat.

On this analysis Kirkpatrick argues for careful appraisal of withdrawal of support from right-wing allies. They may even be morally reprehensible; but if the new regime proves as repressive (e.g., Khomeini) or avowedly totalitarian (as with Castro, and, in the view of this school, ultimately the Sandinistas) nothing is gained morally while allies are lost. But where the new regime is clearly totalitarian left, something is lost—the possibility of change. The marked differences in probability of desirable change are so great that we would be morally wrong in upsetting an authoritarian regime.

The alleged pattern will not stand up to scientific or rigorous analysis. The "rescue terms" needed to keep the theory even plausible are so extreme that it is of doubtful validity for policy guidance. A simpler, alternative approach—simple continuity, or reversion to an earlier state—has fewer problems, in any event.

The examples of Czechoslovakia (under Dubcek) and Poland clearly indicate that in the absence of external pressures, quite democratic and pluralistic structures would have evolved. The considerable pluralism achieved in both countries is impressive. Furthermore, Hungary had also made moves along these lines. And Poland's cycle of throwing out repressive leaders also suggests that communist regimes are quite vulnerable (Gittleman 1981).

These are not fly-specking objections based on municipal or provincial communist regimes or those of negligible mountain republics. Their composite history is at least as impressive as the shaky emergence of democratic regimes in the Iberian peninsula.

The counter to this argument is a strained one. It is to suggest that the external imposition of the regime imposes special strains and limits on effectiveness of the total control. Nationalism can resist totalitarianism while religion, family, and the like, cannot. While this has some validity, it reduces the number of regimes subject to the rule of cycles to a literal handful, with some like Cuba yet to experience the crisis of leadership transition. To develop historical laws based upon China, Yugoslavia, the USSR, Cuba, and, arguably, Korea, Albania, and Ethiopia seems strange and decidedly beyond any reasonable accumulation of information. The possibility of "right-wing authoritarianism" evolving into democracy would have had virtually no support prior to 1978 (except for countries like Germany, Italy, and Japan, which experienced massive foreign intervention, or France, if one took the Vichy regime seriously).

In short, to eliminate half or more of the left-wing authoritarian regimes of the world from generalization weakens any conclusion derived from experience. Relegating the phenomenon to the realm of such small numbers as to suggest that the result is a product of chance is bad enough; *ex post facto* reclassification is doubly suspect.

In any event, as suggested earlier, the simple prediction that recently democratic authoritarian regimes of any stripe may slip back into that column (and its converse about once-authoritarian governments) turns out to be the parsimonious and more comprehensive explanation. Only Japan requires more detailed explanation, while Eastern Europe is easily comprehended. While explanations based upon simple or complex extrapolations are not much more helpful for scientific purposes than weather predictions that suggest tomorrow's weather will be identical with today's, they are, however, quite adequate for day-to-day policy, especially when taken as a rule of thumb meant not too seriously. And such modest trend-projection is preferable to a rigid ideology not rooted in reasonable evidence.

The Future of Technologically Created Power

As to the prognosis of regime capability to control society, equal and opposite approaches can be identified—again a common phenomenon.

(1) Given the Weberian definition of the state as the monopolizer of ultimate force, most see the pattern of technology as augmenting the position of the establishment. However, some see that monopoly sorely threatened for much the same reasons.

(2) Recognizing that moral authority, not military power, is the basis for governance, some view the emergence of surveillance potentiality and social techniques of opinion manipulation as continuously advancing control and power. Others find in the need for social differences an imperative toward less control. Both of those approaches require elaboration.

Governor Earl Long sidled over one day to Leander Perez, segregationist boss of Plaquemines Parish and asked, *sotto voce*, "What'cha gonna do, Leander, now the Feds got the H-bomb?" With this mischievous inquiry Long epitomized an entire approach to politics.

In this view the evolution of weaponry is the key to politics. Ballistics is destiny. The emergence of the gun, requiring little skill and training, brought on democracy. The sword, like the bow and arrow, required practice and Samurai-like apprenticeship. The gun was politically what its colloquial name implied—the "great equalizer." It is this philosophy that is enshrined in the Fourth Amendment's equation of a republic with the right to bear arms.

Arguably, this was a prerequisite of a certain kind of order. Certainly in this century a rifle has become a highly anachronistic weapon in the face of advanced weaponry. Thus modernity comes to Syria, as it did to Turkey, with submachine guns and tanks, leaving not the bourgeoisie but the military in control of the premises.

If we extend this argument, the "wave of the future" suggests that an even more restricted technocratic-military elite will emerge. A scientific research grouping, allied with a highly proficient military, will inherit the earth. The Harold Browns and the Alexander Haigs, arms in arms, will march into the sunlight.

But the proliferation and availability of those weapons has, it is also suggested, moved society in another and contradictory fashion. Development and maintenance of military technology is always complex. But logic and efficiency aim at deployment and use in simpler and simpler fashions. The ultimate—push-button or pull-trigger—is one adaptable to nontrained use. This means that there are increasingly present in modern society dangerous modalities of destruction readily available for the taking. Knowledge of how to seize them is rarer and more complex than knowledge of how to use them once available.

Those who continuously warn us of the dangers from brigands or dissidents are also implicitly arguing for a check upon armed might from the instruments that are available. Regimes that live by the sword are blunt instruments; living by the sword, they die by the sword. Firmly established external occupiers bear some of this cost, but if they represent truly overwhelming force they manage to deter or overcome such risks.

The absence of seizures of such instruments to date, it is argued, is accidental and fortuitous. Perhaps so, though the argument becomes less plausible with the passage of time. The high probability that even "free" societies will pursue abusers of such opportunities even after initial appeasement is no doubt a heavy deterrent. The high cost of information and the fear that the unexpected will occur has resulted in a preference for the simple and known. Limited technological force applied to a concrete situation is generally all that has been needed, and it requires less conspicuous inquiry and therefore less risk. To date, the evidence supports those who see technology as aiding the powers-that-be, not those who would be. Desperate people are likely to be disparate people whose efforts are identifiable and therefore preventable.

Regime Maintenance and Popular Freedom

The availability of means of surveillance has increased at an awesome pace. The cost of complete recording has moved from five or so person-years for one year of observation to the trivial cost of mechanical recording. To be sure, these means fail from time to time, but so do people in such roles.

· It was once argued that precisely this efficiency was the protection; the redundancy of information made analysis impossible. Modern retrieval methods, however, permit drastic reduction of redundancy, permitting key words or phrases to serve as signs, to print up or otherwise call to attention contexts desired. To be sure, the observed may use Aesopian language, but there are limits to ingenuity. The subject has no idea of the extent to which the authorities engage in surveillance or the degree to which they scan for euphemistic language or sample recorded observations. The advantage with respect to any small number of targets is clearly with the authorities.

Combined with known social techniques of control, such as registration by place of residence and close control by residential groupings and associations of co-workers, together with forms of collective responsibility, these methods have been effective in deterrence of much opposition. Ruthlessness in fact and in advertisement have kept the public cowed, while, in most systems, making much of that ruthlessness unnecessary. It was the Polish government, not the Soviets, that brandished under various code names Russian might in an attempt to achieve limited compliance from the strikers. "We must be aware that there are limits." The Russians under such circumstances *always* announce *non*intervention; in the Czechoslovakian crisis such an announcement was the *prelude* to invasion. Past behavior is well established and can be escalated to extremes. What can we make of a system where the prime minister offers to shoot, *on the tarmac,* his minister of aviation, because the plane supplied to a visiting foreign minister will not fly? Somewhat dreadfully, Mr. Kissinger tells this story, as an example of Mr. Kosygin's lack of humor. There is an alternative explanation, that Kissinger exaggerates the nuances. Quite obviously, Kosygin would have been at least surprised if Kissinger had taken up the offer. But the resort to brutality under any embarrassment is a real fact of life that dissidents—let along high functionaries who experience a breakdown—know they have to cope with.

In socialist societies, social control is in point of fact more nearly total than that achieved in private-enterprise, right-wing Nazi Germany. In Russia the party power over all major means of livelihood is not only legally and factually self-evident; but a regime of over sixty years' duration has purged and repurged its operations. There are no Admiral Canaris' or Junker's islands of opposition, though individual and principled opposition is, of course, present. While church or nationalist networks are to some degree tolerated, these are, so far as we can tell, well penetrated, kept at arm's length from the ruling circles, and must operate as a kind of counter-culture, avoiding political connotations. Even this represents an advance in tolerance and sophistication on the part of the rulers.

It is argued that such advance—and progressive advance—is predictable as required by modern social functioning. This equal-and-opposite approach emphasizes the growth of political freedom as a functional requisite for carrying out industrial and scientific development.

The reasoning is neither elaborate nor very specific. Habits of creativity, it is suggested, are clearly needed in a rapidly developing scientific world. Closed societies prevent development: (1) by compartmentalizing knowledge and cutting off vital information while drying up the juices; (2) by transferring key decisions to trusted but ignorant individuals; (3) by emphasizing irrelevant criteria for decision; and (4) by inevitably corrupting the reward system. Thus inefficiencies abound. Inevitably, reform sets in. Modern technology penetrates internally as radio and television from abroad penetrate from the outside.

Certainly this analysis is essentially correct. It is only the conclusion (and even more, the thrust and bite of the conclusion) that is suspect. What the Soviet system does, for example, is to grant exemption from many of the restrictions imposed on the masses to selected elites. Much as some select few can buy goods in closed-to-the-public stores, there are gradations of access to forbidden information. In addition to sanctioned exemption from restrictions, illegal activity will be allowed. Thus, suitcases of the privileged coming in from abroad will not be searched, precisely so that a mathematician, let us say, might be able to smuggle through a copy of *Playboy*, or even a political novel. Idiosyncracy points, then, are "given," though those can be easily revoked or their use punished after the fact.

All of the inefficiencies noted above have occurred, but they have caused drastic failure, mostly in areas of low-level concern to the leadership—e.g., art and psychology. An exception was in the field of botany-biology. In areas important to the Soviets they have bargained and accommodated to achieve, e.g., the mathematics and physics they know they need. In effect, they minimize in rather precise fashion the concessions made by legal or illegal permissiveness in those domains necessary for external rivalries. They eschew efficiencies even, e.g., in agriculture, that would threaten the system, but these are merely costly, not seminal threats.

There are small thaws. There are now phone books, though in small quantity. Weather reports are published and are not secret. Visitors are welcomed for their *valuta,* and censorship has become no more efficient than most aspects of Soviet life. There is even an interofficial effort to get crime rates published and declassified. We are left with the question: How many swallows make a spring?

Where we end, then, depends on where we start. By concentrating on what is technically feasible (as well as the elaboration of social techniques of control that are also continuously embellished), some would project the decline of individual autonomy. By looking at the need for skills and the lack of fungibility of trained people in the modern world, others argue that the bargaining power of skill elites is enhanced and must be recognized.

It is difficult to accept either sovereign theory on contemporary evidence. Given the incredible power of complete triumph, the Kampucheans reduced virtually *all* city dwellers to something approaching the Nazi concept of *Untermenschen.* Rural dwellers were not treated much better. To be sure, the policy was functionally inefficient, but that price *was* paid until the Vietnamese invasion. Had the policy been within normal limits of social atrocities—aimed at a stratum of society rather than its bulk—the invasion might have been delayed. If Kampuchea had been an island community, easily defended, generations might have passed before any regime change would have been possible. Certainly it would have required interelite struggle.

What, too, do we make of China? The costs of the game of total New Society, played by inexperienced and deliberately ill-educated youths, were self-evident before the Thermidorian regime detailed them. That Mao was his own Stalin and Lenin combined tempts one to accept the Solzhenitsyn notion that it was a dynamic of the system, not personality, that dictated Soviet development.

In both instances deaths of top leaders were required to effect changes, modifying the extremes. Such deaths, too, were needed to push Spain and Portugal into quite different states from those of their uncommon dominators. Of course, the death of leaders is inexorable, though it can be hastened or, as with France, suspended for quite some time.

The essence of my argument is that these things are much more dicey than we pretend. The tolerance of a society for inefficiency is much higher than is assumed. We have been amazed at the ability of societies to cope with incredible rates of inflation and crime. Much depends upon the perceived alternative, the pace, and the circumstances. War production can be kept at normal rates in devastatingly bombed cities, given the proper expectations and reinforced values.

In projecting control or freedom as inevitable, futurists err as they would if asked whether the offense or defense will prevail in war (or in sports). Both proceed interactively. In societies where virtually all means of control are assumed to be available and legitimate, it is difficult to develop the concept of limitation. Inasmuch as some notions of autonomy of person exist in all modern societies, this can be embellished. It is difficult to change key decisions on appropriateness, and this inertial force persists. (Often the legal nominal decision masks a different practice.) The meaning of deviation from legal norms also has different meaning in different societies, but has potential for change in either direction. Thus, the timing of a technological or cultural invention has impact easily ignored. Restraints on wiretapping in the United States have much to do with the emergence of the technique just at a time when a desire to control an obtrusive and unsophisticated locally based police became manifest, and the legal doctrine to control states was unfolding. Had the FBI been a full-blown organization with its 1930s mystique, legal restraints might have been much more limited. The Soviet police power rests not only upon the historic base of czarist methods, but upon its old revolutionary role as a principal fighting tool. In an essentially frozen political situation, such power deposits function much as Soviet research laboratories continue to evolve their basic inventions and retain functions. In a more free-floating society, differing methods of securing the same services are constantly being evaluated (as again, on analogy, military and other research procurement).

The implication of Solzhenitsyn on the Gulag enterprise is also clear. The closing of most of the camps was a very serious step for the Soviets, and some of their plans for the East were drastically altered; substitutes for slave labor have not been found. However socially efficient we may see that decision—and they probably also so view it—there have been costs.

In any society program costs are highly controversial and subject to debate. Thus the bureaucratic structure of decision impinges on the evidence of decision and the process by which facts are evaluated.

All of this is hardly to gainsay the thrust of tendency or functional desirability. Thinkers working independently on the same problem usually come up independently with similar solutions. Razors are more alike than different, and not only Detroit cars but cars world wide are really distressingly similar. To run society like the Kampucheans is to court disaster, but reckless, foolish individuals often die rich. The argument of tendencies and underlying forces say that, independent of perturbations, societies would operate thus and so. But real societies have continuous perturbations. And, as we are interested in projecting real worlds, not ideal, we must recognize the inherently probabilistic, nondeterministic, nature of those statements.

We must also recognize the protean nature of societies and the artificiality of our analytic terminology. Societies that consistently operate on the margin of current control possibilities, carefully meting out accommodations, are almost as capable of mutating forms of relationships as avowedly free-floating, newly anarchistic governments. The expectation that "free" societies, with their historically accidental balances on control and license are pure and just, suffers from the historical evolutionary fallacy that assumes the survival of the perfectly fit, not merely the fittest. Evolution has its logical and empirical support, but all physiologists tell us that men could have emerged with less vulnerability to hernias.

The strong evidence is that it is as possible to evolve functioning nonoptimal autocracies as it is possible to have nonoptimal open societies. We can project conditions in Western society with reasonable confidence that they will survive. The overcoming of urban terrorism in Western Europe was as impressive a demonstration as one might seek. In the United States at the height of the cold war, the McCarthy period, John Roche wrote his series, "We Never Had More Freedom" (1963). The institutionalized tolerance of Vietnam war opposition transcended two presidents' attempts at brow beating and worse. There does not seem much in normal evolution to top those strains.

In all of this we have assumed means of communication constant or irrelevant, and that "technology" is the basic industrial structure. It is striking that modern television centralizes communication as never before. In American society attitudes are incredibly and rapidly transformed, shaped and molded on many issues. Is this the wave of the future? Could not seizure of these concentrated modes of communication completely centralize attitudes?

It appears not. (1) Proliferation, not concentration, seems in order. Maximum influence has probably been experienced. (2) Impact seems much greater in the more open, less centralized systems of the West. Indeed, the political impact of television is noticeably much greater in the United States than in, e.g., the controlled system of France, let alone Eastern Europe.

In the sum, barring catastrophic developments, we need not anticipate major changes in the coercive relations of modern societies. Surges in economic conditions will have definite, but comparatively mild, consequences in both directions. War could produce even more severe changes.

But the impetus should not in this analysis come from random political change or known trends generated by our basic technologies.

The Politics of Control

We assume that politically salient deviance can be controlled from a technical standpoint, and that counter-pressure in the form of organized political strength would be necessary to constrain rulers who wish to use such powers to the hilt. That is to say, political deviance persists because of structured support for it.

On the other hand, low-level deviance, a problem, but not a threat to the regime, is flourishing in all systems, though specific rates will vary depending upon specific conditions—definition of crime, age cohorts, and the like. But powerful forces are impelling greater deviance and the likelihood of tolerance of it in most systems. Even bearing in mind Sorokin's notions of the cyclical nature of many of these influences, trends here seem both logically and empirically evident.

Throughout the world it is apparent that "crime" has been increasing. The explanation that age cohorts were the cause had considerable power, as we all know. But, as we also know, wherever the data permit close analysis, such an explanation accounts for a fraction (less than a majority) of such an increase. Detected increases in rates of women's deviance as a product of changes in sex roles are evident. Furthermore, expectations of declines, at least in the rate of increase because of age distribution have so far been disappointed. Something more is at work here.

The explanation seems quite correctly to be decline of traditional institutions of primary control as instruments of shared fate. The need for flexibility and mobility of large segments of the population renders much of conformity nonhabitual, nontraditional, and personal and utilitarian in nature. Such calculation induces less than invariant obedience.

Though this change in values is less precipitous than appears in looking at the rise in crime rates, it seems to inhere in the nature of contemporary society. The toleration for minor property theft is quite great in relatively affluent societies where possessions are seen as temporary, and where the costs of processing complaints are higher than the loss, both from the vantage point of the complainer and the agents of society.

This process is less advanced among less mobile, and therefore, less productive, societies. That is, some of the effects of group liability (e.g., the punishment of families and strata for individual behavior) and the intrusion of neighborhood and work groups into individual affairs (both arrangements being maintained for political policy) affect low-level deviancy as well. As regimes become secure, as they rely more on technological surveillance, and as they permit freer breaking away of family units, they "catch up" on other societies in their crime levels, though at rates usually kept secret. The theoretical possibilities for fascinating studies are empirically nonexistent. Probably, though, the data would not result in a neat pattern and we would be frustrated in a different way if we had the information.

The discussion assumes the regime views such activities as nonthreatening, but that is oversimplified. If the rate is excessive, rulers might find their prestige is impaired, or that such crimes seem to encourage political deviancy as well. In socialist regimes, embezzlement and other crimes against enterprises are the taking of public property. They thus have an ambiguous standing. In general they are not that much more vigorously detected than in bourgeois countries, but are much more vigorously punished, particularly for first convictions.

Regulation Pro and Con

I have now touched upon the less sensational problem suggested by the topic: What can we expect as to the future of regulation, both in regard to its nature and extent? No doubt there is some mutual relationship between the factors affecting criminal latitude and normal business regulation, but that relationship is shrouded.

The Argument for Increased Regulation.

This argument has both cogency and pedigree. It is rather less fashionable today, and it has become a cliché that it is a cliché. I will outline only two varieties of arguments but there are many more.

Arguments Based on Market Failures

These' arguments constitute a classic line from mercantilist thought to the present. (1) Conceptually it is quite easy to conjure up situations in which voluntary or contractual arrangements will not yield desired results, but an agreement to abide by a decision will. Thus volunteering in a war is not a sound, rational choice for those who abhor war but are patriots. Since there is no guarantee of adequate response and little likelihood one would be the precisely needed last volunteer, it is rational not to go at all. A vote for a draft is quite rational since a calculated choice of numbers and types will be made. Essentially Prisoner's-Dilemma-like puzzles are resolved by political contrivances. (This insight—the foundation of welfare economics—is now the basis of the modification of the common law of consideration as it relates to charitable giving. Pledges are enforceable in court as the consideration is the mutual liability assumed, making realization of the project. possible.) (2) Market and contract societies have difficulty vindicating third-party rights in a two-party decision process. While such costs are normally ignored, they may become so socially dysfunctional as to require intervention. Environmental issues are almost ideal-type examples of this type of issue requiring regulation. (It has been suggested that a substitute would be to expand tort liability in such areas, but conceptually that is mostly a preference for one type of regulation over another.) (3) Closely related, but even more compelling a push toward regulation, is the problem of public goods or collective costs. The indivisibility of some benefits or costs (e.g., parks or a nuclear plant) makes party bargaining an inefficient solution. Also, since parties do not have equal bargaining power under such conditions, as well as little means to estimate costs, the solution may not be socially acceptable.

In recent years the most vigorous voice for such arguments has been that of Charles Lindblom. A man who has followed the academic path that parallels the stock market strategy of buying contracyclically, Lindblom was anti-union in the 1940s and "greened" in the late 1970s. Lindblom has also an established position arguing against holistic approaches, vigorously defending "disjointed incrementalism." His review-article, "The Science of Muddling Through," (1957) gave wide currency to both the "muddling" and "incrementalist" terms. In his award-winning *Politics and Markets* (1977), Lindblom now contrasts synoptic planning (largely isomorphic with Soviet efforts), market socialism (Yugoslavian), and strategic planning (United States). He predicts and urges further convergence of U.S. practice in the direction of corporation coordinated planning. Yugoslav practice occupies in the volume much the same place as that of Sweden in discussions of the 1950s. Essentially Lindblom sees regulation and its growth as concomitant to growth of industrial units, the nature of economic problems, and the complexity generated by their growing interdependence. A move toward planning and centralization is a rational response to the domain of the problem.

Such arguments are quite common in the social sciences of this century. A classic in point is Lester Ward's concept of telic evolution, which, on the one hand, suggests planning is an evolutionary stage of mankind, but also posits its necessity. Bell's contemporary discussions of centralization do emphasize the diversity of a society and the contradictory nature of centralization and disarray in various components of the social order, but expert technology will require more, rather than less ordering. Lindblom's book with its ellipses and the sketch of an argument (rather than the argument itself) represented a distinctive personal view, but also, in many ways, a common one.

Arguments for Equality

A second strand of impetus was anticipated by Max Weber. Our contemporary emphasis on egalitarian standards was seen by him as a logical extension of demands for the bureaucracy to perform in universalistic fashion. Such arguments radiated new-type demands, constantly generating claims requiring action as well as abstention. This can be expressed in abstruse terms, such as T. H. Green's call for "positive freedom," or direct ones, as with Tawney's claim that equality was the essence of the Labor party program, or Rawls's identification of equalization with striving for justice.

This radiating, almost insatiable, nature of claims for equality has not escaped the eagle eye of our contemporary school of revisionism, the *Public Interest* neoconservatives. Irving Kristol has argued that contemporary emphasis on equality is a guise under which middle-class intellectuals try to do in middle-class businessmen (1972). This is a cultural as well as political clash, and "equality" is a demagogic expression of envy used by the intellectuals in an attempt to curry popularity with the masses. The greater the actual equality, the bitterer the rhetoric. In Scandinavian society the impetus is toward control of more and more minutia. (The spanking law had not been passed when Kristol wrote but would well illustrate his argument.) Society will plunge in deeper and deeper to less avail.

The positive basis of these efforts is clearly and preeminently the theme of John Rawls's *magnum opus, A Theory of Justice* (1971). It is enough to note here that Rawls not only clearly provides a strong undergirding for "normal" welfare programs, but has been interpreted to argue for augmented programs such as highly intensive education for the retarded and extraordinary expenditure for potential use of transportation by the handicapped. It is too much by far to say that the existence of kneeling buses—Has anyone ever seen a kneeling bus actually kneel?—are tributes to Rawls; rather they show the practical power of the people who think the way he does. (Or perhaps they only think they think the way he does. For our purposes it does not matter.)

Such social regulation seldom is the cheap way to do things. In its initial stages equalization is the elimination of artificial badges of degradation. Desegregation also saved the taxpayers money, and, by opening up professional schools to women and minorities, expanded the pool of talent in the society, thus reducing the waste of such talents through archaic attitudes. The "affirmative action" phases dynamically generated invariably involve a stage of social dysfunction. (The best and most sensitive treatment is Arthur Okun's *Equality and Inefficiency* [1975]). This is a second driving force then toward regulation.

The Case for Deregulation

To those living in the Reagan era the case for reduction of governmental intervention is not a novelty.

Theoretical Arguments

The theoretical arguments involve demonstrations that centralized systems of decision making are not as efficient as individual action. There are many variations on this theme. Traditional University of Chicago economists such as Sam Peltzman elaborately demonstrate the unprofitability of specific regulatory schemes, abstract schemes, or regulation in principle. Somewhat less predictably, the late Michael Polanyi published a mathematical proof of the same proposition (1948).

These demonstrations are closely related to proofs by communication theorists that any communication requires more energy than it can create, and ultimately, they are related to the Law of Thermodynamics that so frightened Henry Adams. Because they prove so much, of course, they convince one of so little. After all, all mechanical contrivances are also "inefficient" and equally demonstrate that "there is no such thing as a free lunch." While in some sense there is truth in those formulations, they are "long-run" arguments of the type speared by Keynes. Perhaps they offer a cautionary note supporting political mistrust of centralization and the general societal attitude that problems should be solved at the lowest feasible level.

Empirical Evidence

The empirical evidence has become almost faddish as to the failures of many regulatory schemes. These failures and/or the sense of failure are experienced throughout welfare state countries. (The sense of disillusion is sharpened by the colossal inefficiency and *immobilisme* of Eastern European economies.) Economists and other social scientists have examined these tendencies and are well on their way to developing concepts of "regulatory failure" analogous to market failure. Those have resulted in a political backlash of a limited nature. (In some Scandinavian countries the swing back left has apparently begun. Mrs. Thatcher's less than awesome results may have similar political consequences.)

(1) Some of these regulatory failures are products of human error and overload. These, of course, increase with centralization. Horror stories abound. A prolonged conflict between the Federal Trade Commission (FTC) and Control Data was resolved after ten years of conflict on the basis of a promise that CDC would behave in accordance with behavior it had already adopted before the complaint. The case would have been

settled four years earlier if the FTC had not unaccountably failed to transmit acceptance of an offer to settle. (2) In the absence of the market, or other natural point of equilibrium, decisions will be arbitrary or "political." This argument, developed by von Mises and von Hayek, is also the essence of a left-oriented critique of the administrative state by Theodore Lowi (1969). (3) Once a sector is regulated, vested interests not only distort and produce results incongruent with the original reasons for regulation; they also cling to the regulatory scheme well beyond any reason for its existence. Railroads are a conspicuous example. (4) Regulation tends to encourage noneconomic competition on matters other than price and thus produces overly expensive service. (5) Regulatory schemes generate officiousness and regulation for its own sake.

Under various auspices, the process of deregulation has started in a number of societies. In the United States, an interesting collaboration between the Carter administration and Kennedy produced decontrol in transportation, banking, and, to some degree, in communication. Some of these regulations—e.g., prohibiting savings and loans from issuing checks—seem trivial beyond logic. The first venture—encouragement of competition in the airline industry—was a general but not universal success. (Cities like Louisville maintain the expected small craft replacement of big-plane service has not occurred.) Enthusiasm has sustained these efforts and promises continuation of the policy. On net, support is surprisingly high.

There is also significant movement in the nature of regulation. In the environment field, for example, user's fees—virtually schedules of penalties—are in favor over prohibitory regulations. The overload in administrative capacity has forced reexamination of means. Kenneth Davis has extolled administrative rule making over administrative *ad hoc* conclusions, arguing it is not only more flexible as to situations and more workable, but also more likely to be reviewed and discarded when unnecessary (1969). This flexibility of means is probably the most important development in regulation today.

It will be noted that regulation for equality does not fall under those rubrics. The societies heavily into these matters do not encourage us to believe that such programs ever end or solve the problems they address. Thus India, a half-century after initiating its program for equality, has more groups and a much higher percentage of the population registered as backward and underprivileged. Elaborate structures have developed at the state level as well as the national. The rate of structured change in the basic problem has seldom been impressive either abroad or at home. (The only exception I am aware of is the very high rate of employment of French phones in Canadian federal government. A coincidental near doubling of the service made this possible.)

Generally very complex social relations are being tackled. Assumptions about the cause of the problem and *á priori* solutions have generally proven naive. Programs proliferate and new stages at which regulation is necessary become apparent. Thus, in Washington and Boston efforts to control race discrimination have required complex court orders on salaries of teachers, specific assignment of officials, the nature of programs (including extracurricular activities and sports), number and race of children in particular activities, and even the furnace arrangement in the schools. This insatiable nature of such issues is directly addressed by Kristol and documented by Horowitz (1977).

In sum, economic, technocratic regulation is likely to wax and wane. New areas will be controlled and others decontrolled. More flexible and looser concepts of regulation, sampling, and control are likely to develop. Regulations for social motives are likely to proliferate in number and in heavy-handedness unless and until the same spirit of flexibility and level of intelligence is applied to that type of regulation as well.

Conclusions

We have reviewed several types of power and control relations in society and have reluctantly rejected efforts to project future balances between freedom and power as inadequate or unconvincing. Only with regard to a continued increase in crime rates (based upon sex-ratios and other demographic factors) does a trend seem clear. On regulation of economic, political, and social life, rival factors leading to centralization and individuation are likely to continue to produce cyclic events. Broad social patterns seem to set the limits for the societies that have the potential for maintaining reasonably democratic systems. The club of democratic societies is apparently not likely to expand appreciably in the near future. Within that group of potential democracies, basic historical attitudes toward political power rather than objective social forces seem determinative.

The zone of possible social and political relationships that can sustain a modern society (and be sustained by it in turn) is manifestly wider than functionalists of the 1960s believed. The functionalists were accused of being social conservatives, but this argument suggests societies will tolerate dysfunctional political (or other) subsystems out of habit far beyond limits Parsonians projected. At the same time, our expectations and arguments suggest much more leeway for volunteerism and other existentialist approaches than is commonly believed to exist. Societies may have sharp constraints on power distributions, but social scientists have yet to demonstrate that argument in any conclusive fashion.

REFERENCES

Arens, Richard, and Harold Lasswell. 1961. *In Defense of Public Order.* New York: Columbia University Press.

Brzezinski, Zbigniew, and Samuel P. Huntington. 1964. *Political Power: USA/USSR.* New York: Viking.

Burnham, James. 1943. *The Machiavellians.* New York: John Day.

Cutright, Phillips. 1963. In Nelson Polsby, Robert Dentler and Paul Smith. *Politics and Society.* Boston: Houghton Mifflin.

Davis, Kenneth. 1969. *Discretionary Justice.* Baton Rouge: Louisiana State University Press.

Gittleman, Zvi. 1981. "The Politics of Socialist Restoration in Hungary and Czechoslovakia." *Comparative Politics* 13:187-211.

Horowitz, Donald. 1977. *The Courts and Social Policy.* Washington, DC: Brookings.

Kirkpatrick, Jeanne. 1979. "Dictatorships and Double Standards." *Commentary* 68:34-45.

Krislov, Samuel. 1963. "The Perimeters of Power." Reprinted in Krislov et al. 1973. *Compliance and the Law.* Beverly Hills, CA: Sage.

Kristol, Irving. 1972. "About Equality." Reprinted in Burkhart et al. 1978. *The Clash of Issues.* Englewood Cliffs, NJ: Prentice-Hall.

Lasswell, Harold, and Abraham Kaplan. 1950. *Power and Society.* New Haven, CT: Yale University Press.

Lijphart, Arend. 1977. *Democracy and Plural Society.* New Haven, CT: Yale University Press.

Lindblom, Charles. 1957. "The Science of Muddling Through." *Public Administration Review* 29:79-88.

Lindblom, Charles. 1977. *Politics and Markets.* New York: Basic Books.

Lippmann, Walter. 1922. *Public Opinion.* New York: Harcourt Brace.

Lipset, Seymour Martin. 1960. *Political Man.* New York: Doubleday.

Lowi, Theodore. 1969. *The End of Liberalism.* New York: Norton.

Marsh, Robert. 1967. *Comparative Sociology.* New York: Harcourt, Brace, Jovanovich.

Okun, Arthur. 1975. *Equality and Efficiency: The Big Trade-off.* Washington, DC: Brookings.

Patric, Gordon. 1957. "The Impact of a Court Decision: Aftermath of the McCollum Case." *Journal of Public Law* 6:455-69.

Peltason, Jack. 1955. *Federal Courts in the Political Process.* New York: Doubleday.

Polanyi, Michael. 1948. "The Span of Central Direction." Reprinted in Polanyi. 1958. *The Logic of Liberty.* Chicago: University of Chicago Press.

Rawls, John. 1971. *A Theory of Justice.* Cambridge, MA: Harvard University Press.

Roche, John P. 1963. *The Quest for the Dream.* New York: Macmillan.

Rustow, D. A. 1970. "Transitions to Democracy." *Comparative Politics* 2:337-46.

Taylor, Henry. [1836]. 1957. *The Statesman.* London: W. Heffer.

Wasby, Stephen. 1970. *The Impact of Supreme Court Decisions.* Homewood, IL: Dorsey.

Wildavsky, Aaron. 1973. *Implementation.* Berkeley: University of California Press.

Wilson, Woodrow. 1885, 1956. *Congressional Government.* New York: Meridian.

Wittfogel, Karl. 1957. *Oriental Despotism.* New Haven, CT: Yale University Press.

4

Law as a Means of Social Control

JACK P. GIBBS

Virtually all social scientists and legal scholars accept two ideas—law is a means of social control and laws are norms. Both ideas could serve to clarify the meaning of law, norms, and social control; and without clarification no related theory can be productive. Malinowski's work (1959) is illustrative. Since he did not emphasize a distinction between laws and other norms, or between *law* and other means of social control, the term law appears superfluous. As for legal evolution, there are these major possibilities: Law replaces extralegal social control and/or law is used to control kinds of behavior heretofore essentially uncontrolled. These possibilities loom large in several theoretical works (e.g., Black 1976), but they are meaningless without a defensible distinction between law and extralegal social control.

Conceptions of Social Control

The prevailing conception of social control is largely limited to sociology and anthropology, and it stems primarily from Talcott Parsons (1951:297, 321):

> The theory of social control is . . . the analysis of those processes in the social system which tend to counteract the deviant tendencies. . . . Every social system has . . . a complex system of unplanned and largely ,unconscious mechanisms which serve to counteract deviant tendencies.

Criticism of the Prevailing Conception

Parson's counteraction-of-deviance conception of social control makes intention irrelevant. Thus, should someone demonstrate that wearing wedding rings promotes marital fidelity and that adultery is deviant, then the custom is social control regardless of anyone's intention or perception. Yet it makes little sense to say (for example): "He is controlling her but does not know it." Perhaps the conception reflects the conviction that unanticipated behavioral consequences are the most important; but if sociological conceptualizations ignore the purposive quality of human behavior, the distinction between successful and unsuccessful social control is lost; and that distinction bears on this question: Why are some means of social control employed more than others? Finally, accepting the counteraction-of-deviance conception, it is illogical to ask: Does social control actually counteract deviant tendencies?

The Notion of Norms

The prevailing conception of social control presupposes norms, because deviance is traditionally defined as behavior contrary to a norm. Problems with the notion of norms are evident in two well-known definitions.

[A norm is] any standard or rule that states what human beings should or should not think, say, or do under given circumstances" [Blake and Davis 1964:456].

A *norm* is a statement made by a number of members of a group, not necessarily by all of them, that the members ought to behave in a certain way in certain circumstances" [Homans 1961:46].

The Blake-Davis definition promises little empirical applicability (i.e., agreement among independent investigators in identifying instances of norms) if only because the meaning of standard or rule is obscure, and the definition does not even suggest how to identify the norms of a social unit (be it a family, corporation, or country). By contrast, Homans's definition suggests the only systematic way to identify a social unit's norms—solicit responses of members to "evaluative" questions, such as: Do you approve or disapprove of smoking marijuana?

Despite its merits, Homans's definition does not stipulate a criterion of *sufficient normative consensus*. He indicates that all members need not make a statement for it to be a norm, which is far more realistic than assuming absolute normative consensus. But what proportion of members must make the statement? Any answer would be arbitrary.

The "consensus" problem takes on added significance in considering the idea that laws are norms. If a statement is not a norm unless made or subscribed to by most social unit members, then no statute is a law unless accepted by the majority of those to whom it applies. Even if all statements commonly identified as laws in Anglo-American countries are consistent with public opinion, some definitions of law (*infra*) make "organized coercion" the principal consideration, not public opinion. So definitions of norms and definitions of laws commonly contradict the idea that laws are norms.

Another conceptual problem stems from recognition that norms have a situational quality, and to illustrate its relevance suppose that 85 percent of community residents respond "disapprove" to the evaluative question about marijuana (*supra*). If the question had stipulated "smoking marijuana when prescribed by a physician to alleviate the discomfort of cancer treatment," introducing that contingency probably would have made an appreciable difference. Similarly, respondents who voice approval of smoking marijuana might balk at "conformity" by a child. The point is that evaluations of acts are markedly contingent, but normative questions cannot be worded so as to recognize *all* relevant contingencies.

Although "evaluations of conduct" are central in most definitions of a norm, it could be argued that the normative quality of an act is *best* revealed by *actual* reactions (e.g., whether punitive or rewarding). Then consider the conventional rationale for treating norms as important—they govern much of human behavior. Yet human behavior may be governed by *expectations* of conduct rather than evaluations. For that matter, individuals may govern their behavior not in accordance with their *personal* evaluations of expectations but, rather, in accordance with their perceptions of the evaluations and expectations of others. However, a definition of a norm that recognizes personal evaluations, personal expectations, perceived evaluations, perceived expectations, and actual reactions to acts would border on the incomprehensible.

Since the foregoing problems seem insoluble, the notion of norms should be replaced with the notion of normative properties, meaning any property of a *type of act* having to do with evaluations of it, expectations pertaining to it, or actual reactions to instances of it. Those properties are collective in that they pertain to a social unit; but each property would be treated as purely quantitative, which avoids the need for a criterion as to *sufficient* normative consensus or uniformities in behavior. All evaluative and expectational normative properties would pertain to responses of social unit members to normative questions, with the contingencies introduced in those questions determined by theoretical interests. The strategy is quite different from the conventional treatment, which depicts norms as simply "out there" and no less real than fireplugs.

Other Objections

Even if there were no problems in identifying deviant acts and the conditions that counteract deviance, the prevailing conception of social control excludes some manipulations of behavior on a vast scale. Contemplate contemporary American advertising, where thousands of individuals attempt to manipulate millions; yet it is not social control unless the advertisers are "counteracting deviance."

Then contemplate the activities of Nazis in Weimar Germany and American abolitionists prior to the Civil war. To say that those activities were social control because they "counteracted deviance" only generates sterile arguments about norms. But, apart from norms or deviance, what were those activities if not social control?

An Alternative

The counteraction-of-deviance conception does speak indirectly to an important question: What is social about social control? The *typical* American bank robber is engaged in control but not social control (i.e., not the counteraction of deviance), nor is someone when hailing a cab. Such illustrations suggest that social control has a normative quality and is distinct from everyday interaction. The trick, therefore, is to concep- tualize social control so as to recognize those two features but avoid reference to norms or deviance.

Social control is an attempt by one or more individuals (the first party in either case) to manipulate the behavior of one or more other individuals (the second party in either case) through still another individual or individuals (the third party in either case) by means other than a chain of command (Gibbs 1981). The definition excludes proximate control, mean- ing control *without* a third party, as when a customer requests something or a mother physically restrains her child; and it also excludes sequential control, as when X orders Y to order Z. Social control is not necessarily more important; rather, proximate and sequential control are conspicuous in everyday interaction, especially in bureaucratic or military social units. Yet the distinction does bear on this question: What happens when requests are ignored or commands disobeyed? People commonly resort to social control. Moreover, social control, so defined, is essential to manipu- late behavior on a large scale. As such, it is indispensable for the Ghandis, Hitlers, Khomenis, Maos, and Roosevelts of the world; and the point bears on Hart's argument (1961) that law is a means of controlling large numbers.

Types of Social Control

Should a child say to a sibling, "Give me back my candy or I will tell Mother!" that statement is *referential social control.* The first party (the child in this instance) attempts to manipulate the behavior of the second party (the sibling) by making reference to a third party (the mother). But referential social control may involve millions, as when Hitler (first party) berated Jews (third party) to gain the support of non-Jewish Germans (second party). Then observe that referential social control is a feature of adjudication in American law, as when a trial attorney makes reference to a Supreme Court ruling.

Another type of social control—allegative—is conspicuous in tort law. A plaintiff cannot command a judge or jury to compel the defendant to pay damages; rather, that goal is realized by allegations about the defendant (second party) that the judge and/or jury (third party) find credible and evaluate negatively. Yet allegative social control transcends law. Thus, rather than resort to referential social control, a child may make allegations about a sibling to their mother.

Vicarious social control is illustrated by an idea in the deterrence doctrine—when legal officials (the first party) punish accused criminals (third party), the punishment deters others (second party) from criminality. However, a judge may impose punishment, including an award of damages in a civil case, to placate the complainant or plaintiff. But vicarious social control is not limited to punishment or to the legal sphere. For example, an employer may ceremonially reward a very productive employee in the hope that other employees will strive for greater productivity.

Insofar as the *third* party has influence over the second party's behavior, the first party can manipulate that behavior by using or terminating the third party's influence; and such *modulative* social control does not entail an allegation about the second party. Thus, when a manufacturer (first party) pays a celebrity (third party) to extol some product on television, the manufacturer assumes that the celebrity has some influence over consumers (second party). Modulative social control in the legal sphere is the most likely when law is used to promote class or caste interests, as when teaching slaves to read is legally proscribed to reduce the influence of "agitators" on the slaves.

Without accurate knowledge as to what and whom prospective controllees hate, love, fear, value, and respect, the would-be controller cannot answer this question: Which kind of control would be the most effective? The question becomes an acute problem in controlling numerous individuals; and, given that goal, limited resources force controllers to confront another question: Who should be subject to special efforts at control? The first party may answer both questions by using a third party (1) to gather information on prospective second parties, including surveillance; (2) to conduct research on the relative effectiveness of alternative means of control; (3) to create conditions that facilitate control; or (4) to exclude particular kinds of second parties from certain social contexts, as in the case of immigration laws. Those uses of a third party are *prelusive* social control, the most highly organized type.

The Utility of the Conceptualization

Accepting the foregoing conceptualization, instances of social control can be identified *without* reference to norms and deviance. Moreover, social control is distinct from control over human behavior in general; and normative qualities, such as recognition of authority, can be identified in analyzing instances of social control without postulating identifiable norms. For that matter, an earlier question is no longer illogical: Does social control actually counteract deviant tendencies?

No conceptualization is true or false; rather, some conceptualizations may prove more useful than others in formulating theories. The present conceptualization has been used to that end (Gibbs 1981), and it also serves to describe law as a means of social control despite contending conceptions of law.

The Principal Contending Conceptions of Law

The three major schools of jurisprudence—analytical jurisprudence, legal realism, and natural law theory—are distinguished *primarily* by sharp contrasts in their definitions of law. Those contrasts are manifested in subsequent definitions of law, but observe that the English language tends to blur the distinction between *a* law and law. Whatever "law" may mean, it includes "laws"; hence, a defensible definition of law presupposes a defensible definition of *a* law, and for that reason the latter is the primary concern here.

Because of space limitations, some strategies in defining a law cannot be treated at length. For example, Friedman and Macaulay (1977:820) define a legal system as a "set of subsystems which, for one reason or another, people choose to call 'legal.'" If their strategy were extended to defining a law, then laws would be peculiar to English-speaking countries. Such a definition would be worthless in addressing the perennial question about the universality of law (Hoebel 1968), and to assume that in all languages there is a term equivalent to "a law" simply relegates the problem to students of non-English languages. For that matter, Friedman and Macauley's strategy is dubious even when applied to Anglo-American countries, if only because it assumes concensus among English-speaking people in identifying laws.

Analytical Jurisprudence and Coercive Definitions of Law

The following four definitions make coercive enforcement the essential feature of a law.

[A] law is a command which obliges a person or persons, and obliges *generally* to acts or forbearances of a *class*. ... A command is distinguished from other significations of desire ... by the power ... of the party commanding to inflict an evil or pain in case the desire be disregarded. ... The evil ... is frequently called a *sanction*. ... Every positive law ... is set, directly or circuitously, by a sovereign individual or body, to a member or members of the independent political society wherein its author is supreme [Austin 1954:24, 14, 15, 350].

An order will be called ... *law* if it is externally guaranteed by the probability that physical or psychological coercion will be applied by a *staff* of people in order to bring about compliance or avenge violation [Weber 1968:34].

A social norm is legal if its neglect or infraction is regularly met, in threat or in fact, by the application of physical force by an individual or group possessing the socially recognized privilege of so acting [Hoebel 1968:28].

Law is the primary norm, which stipulates the sanction. ... If "coercion" in the sense here defined is an essential element of law, then the norms which form a legal order must be norms stipulating a coercive act, i.e., a sanction [Kelsen 1945:61, 45].

Some Dubious Criticisms

The emphasis on coercion elicits vigorous objections. For example, Hart (1961) argues that people may heed laws without regard to the threat of punishment. Even so, it hardly follows that *no one* is ever deterred; and a "coercive" definition implies no claim about the efficacy of laws. So Hart is demanding something that no definition provides—answers to empirical questions (see Gibbs 1968, for elaboration).

Legal realists reject the "formalism" of analytical jurisprudence (i.e., laws constitute a logical system) and its preoccupation with the purely normative features of law rather than the actual behavior of legal officials. Criticisms of Austin and Kelsen along those lines may be justified; but the idea that laws are enforced coercively does not imply that laws constitute a logical system or necessarily emanate from a sovereign, and the definitions of Hoebel and Weber refer to actual behavior.

Accepting a coercive definition, laws have no connection with putative principles of justice and morality, for the definition makes the "content" of a law irrelevant. Consider the notorious Nuremberg Laws of Nazi Germany, which (*inter alia*) threatened Jews with punishment for practicing certain professions. The Nuremberg Laws may have been laws in light of a coercive definition; but advocates of natural law theory reject the implied "ethical neutrality." Since definitions are not demonstrably true or false, the issue cannot be resolved.

Some Defensible Criticisms

Reference to norms in defining a law reduces the definition's empirical applicability because of several problems with the notion of norms that have been described previously, and what has been said of norms applies also to rules. Coercive definitions would be improved by identifying laws as a subclass of "statements that imply an evaluation of a type of conduct." That terminology is not free of ambiguity, but it promises greater empirical applicability than does norm or rule.

Hart (1961) rightly points out that coercive definitions are especially dubious when extended beyond criminal law. While some Anglo-American statutes serve as guides or instructions for (*inter alia*) entering into marriage, disposal of property, and adoption, they do not *prescribe* those actions. Such "enabling functions" are not trivial incidents of law, and Kelsen's argument that the actions in question create a sanction potential borders on logomachy. It is more realistic to recognize that some laws are intended to facilitate particular kinds of behavior *without prescribing them*, but interference with that facilitation elicits a coercive threat.

Now contemplate this question: With what frequency must a statement be enforced coercively to qualify as a law? Austin and Kelsen provide no answer. Hoebel's term "regularly" is unrealistic if taken to mean all instances, and Weber's "probability" is extremely ambiguous.

Coercive definitions neither attribute normative consensus to laws nor speak to the question of "legitimacy." Critics of coercive definitions reject the idea that legitimacy *stems from laws*; but if legitimacy is something more than normative consensus, it appears to be metaphysical (i.e., it has no empirical applicability). Yet to argue that a law is necessarily accepted by at least the majority of subjects is to invoke an ethnocentric, democratic criterion. Nonetheless, coercive definitions do ignore a feature of statements that are commonly recognized as laws—the rarity of coercive resistance to, or coercive retaliation for, their enforcement. Yet isolated instances of resistance or retaliation do occur. So the crucial question is frequency; and while a defensible "maximum frequency" criterion is wanting, the phenomenon deserves recognition in defining a law.

Restatement of the Coercive Conception

Perhaps there is no solution to all problems in defining a law. The alternative to seeking solutions is to abandon the notion for all but casual purposes and to focus theory and research on certain quantitative variables, such as the degree of normative consensus, the frequency of coercive enforcement, and the frequency of coercive resistance. But since social scientists and legal scholars would reject such a radical strategy, efforts should be made to modify extant definitions of a law so as to blunt criticisms. Such a modified coercive definition follows.

A law exists in a society or other social unit if: (1) the majority of at least one socially recognized category of members (e.g., a legislative body) make or endorse a statement in a public manner; (2) the statement implies an evaluation of some type of conduct; (3) all members of at least one socially recognized category (e.g., the police) have by their public actions consistently indicated an intention to promote, facilitate, prevent, revenge, or rectify such conduct by all members of at least one socially recognized category (e.g., juveniles); (4) the intention extends to the use of unlimited coercion given coercive resistance or coercive retaliation; and (5) no socially recognized category of members is collectively engaged in such coercive resistance or coercive retaliation.

Legal Realism

The central argument of "legal realists" is suggested in the following definitions.

[P]rophecies of what the courts will do in fact, and nothing more pretentious, are what I mean by the law [Holmes 1897:461].

This doing of something about disputes . . . is the business of law. And the people who have the doing in charge, whether they be judges or sheriffs or clerks or jailers or lawyers, are officials of the law. *What these officials do about disputes is . . . the law itself. . . .* the theory that rules decide cases seems for a century to have fooled not only library-ridden recluses, but judges [Llewellyn 1951:12, 1934:7].

Rules, whether stated by judges or others, whether in statutes, opinions or text-books by learned authors, are not the Law, but are only some among many of the sources to which judges go in making the law of the cases tried before them. . . . The law . . . consists of *decisions,* not of rules. If so, then *whenever a judge decides a case he is making law* [Frank 1949:127-128].

Some Objections to Legal Realism

Advocates of analytical jurisprudence dismiss Holmes by arguing that a court cannot exist without law, and Holmes did not speak to several questions. Whose prophecy constitutes "law"? If a prophecy stems from recognition of some uniformity in court. rulings, why the uniformity? Since uniformities suggest something that constrains and guides judges in making decisions, what is that "something" if not law?

Unlike Holmes, later legal realists speak of decisions rather than prophecies. However, is any judge's decision "law"? If not, what kind of decision? If an American judge sentenced a defendant convicted of tax evasion to execution, the sentence would be a decision; but would it be "law"? If legal realists argue that the sentence is not law because it will be appealed and overruled, why the prediction?

The legal realists' conception of law is difficult to apply outside Anglo-American jurisdictions. If courts and judges are to be defined in terms that apply cross-culturally, reference must be made to the administration of laws; but legal realism implies that laws cannot be identified without first identifying courts and judges. Legal realists do not recognize the problem because they speak of judges and courts as they know them in Anglo-American jurisdictions; indeed, their conception of law grew out of a preoccupation with case law and appellant decisions.

Law and Social Control Reconsidered

In light of the three-party conceptualization of social control (*supra*), law is a means of social control despite the debate over analytical jurisprudence and legal realism. Austin's critics argue that not even a criminal statute is literally a command. The alternative interpretation depicts a criminal statute as an implied prediction as to what will happen given some type of act. However, whether construed as a command or a prediction, a criminal statute is referential social control by those who enacted it (the first party, whether a legislative body or a despot), for the statute is an implied reference as to what a third party (judges, police officers) will do given some type of act.

Now assume, along with legal realists, that law is "found" only in the actual behavior of judges. Even so, imagine a judge imposing a sentence or awarding damages *without regard* to promoting general deterrence, catering to public opinion, currying the favor of elites, and/or placating the complainant. Indeed, any court order is referential social control because it implies reference to what other legal officials will do should the order be violated.

Now reconsider Hart's "enabling functions of law" (not his term), such as legal instructions for marriage. While it distorts to argue that people follow those instructions to create the potential for a *particular* sanction, it is inconceivable that such instructions are formulated or followed without regard to the eventual manipulation of behavior. Elaborating briefly, compliance with legal instructions in legally *permissive* actions (e.g., making a will) furthers the influence of those who comply. Since both the second and third party in social control may be indefinite categories of individuals, officials who formulate such legal instructions are the first party in modulative social control, with one goal being the prevention or resolution of disputes.

. Finally, accepting the coercive conception of law, there are at least three differences between legal and extralegal social control. First, extralegal social control has no necessary connection with a socially recognized category of individuals or with making evaluative statements. Second, extralegal social control need not extend to the unlimited use of coercion. Third, extralegal social control may evoke widespread collective resistance or retaliation.

Natural Law Theory

Still another school of jurisprudence argues that positive law (laws actually enacted and enforced) must be or should be consistent with "natural law." That argument has been debated for centuries, and definitions of natural law intensify the debate. Those definitions are so divergent that only a very long list would be representative. Legal scholars have recognized eight meanings of natural law, and in a well-known work Patterson (1953:333-334) identifies six meanings:

(1) "Any critical or constructive theory of legal valuation, or of the ideals of law."
(2) "The use of reason in the making and administration of law."
(3) "Principles of human conduct that are discoverable by 'reason' from the basic inclinations of human nature, and that are absolute, immutable and of universal validity for all times and places."
(4) "A theory of natural rights based upon a supposed 'state' of nature, a pre-political society, and a supposed social compact in which men conferred limited powers on a political government, and in so doing reserved natural rights."
(5) "Norms of human conduct discoverable by experience and observation as prevalent and useful among different peoples."
(6) "The capacity to perceive, or any intuitive perception of, 'justice' or 'equity' in concrete situations."

Patterson's list is questionable because it excludes the idea that natural law is the will, command, or design of a supreme being, which further indicates marked divergence in conceptions of natural law.

The issues pertaining to the notion of natural law are not limited to divergent meanings. Critics depict the notion as metaphysical, and no well-known definition suggests criteria or procedures for identifying *particular* natural laws. Consider, for example, the "universality" criterion akin to numbers 3 and 5 in Patterson's list. If natural law is defined as comprising norms that are present in all societies, that definition would be fairly clear; but numerous social scientists doubt if there are any truly universal norms. True, Patterson's terminology suggests only a qualified universality, but such qualifications tend to be vague.

Fuller's Work

No American scholar has contributed more than Lon Fuller (1969) to natural law theory. If nothing else, his following eight *desiderata* of law could lead to an empirically applicable definition of natural law: (1) general, (2) promulgated, (3) clear, (4) free of contradictions, (5) not retroactive, (6) does not demand the impossible, (7) appreciable constancy over time, and (8) congruent with official actions.

Fuller (1969:96) characterized his work as a "procedural version of natural law"; and his *desiderata* scarcely constitute even a partial definition of positive law, especially given Fuller's statement (1969:106) that "law is the enterprise of subjecting human conduct to the governance of rules." All manner of such enterprises lack some of Fuller's *desiderata*. However, should Fuller's argument really be that such an enterprise is not law without the eight *desiderata*, then it is simply another chapter in the long and now sterile debate. The alternative interpretation is that Fuller's *desiderata* imply an empirical proposition about the efficacy of law—to the extent that a law (positive) lacks those *desiderata*, compliance is reduced. Yet the "generality" *desideratum* appears to be a partial *definition* of law, and Fuller's disciples do not treat his work as such a proposition.

While Fuller's work perhaps points the way to an empirically applicable definition of natural law, not even its realization would terminate the debate. The central issue is the insistence that a statement cannot be a positive law unless it is consistent with natural law (see, e.g., Olivecrona 1971:23); hence, critics regard any definition of natural law as value judgments about positive law (i.e., what it *should* be). So there are no prospects for resolution of the great issue.

Some Questions and Theories about Law

In posing questions for the sociology of law, text writers often speak of "the relation between law and society" or "the causes and consequences of law." Those questions provide little direction for research or theory, and they are unrealistic if construed as demanding answers about each particular law in each society. Yet the answers cannot take the form of generalizations without identifying analytical properties of laws. Thus, "punitiveness" once received considerable attention (Sutherland and Cressey 1974:336-346) on the assumption that all criminal laws can be described in terms of that property.

The Functions of Law

Concern with analytical properties seldom transcends the question: What are the functions of law? There are three reasons why that question has been unfruitful.

The Notion of Function

Evidential problems in demonstrating the *consequences* of a social phenomenon worsen when claims are made about functions. Social scientists tend to think of "a function" as not just any consequence of a phenomenon (e.g., a particular social institution) but one that contributes to the maintenance of the social unit (or social system) in which that phenomenon is present. Yet "maintenance" is a vague notion and a defensible method of *demonstration* is wanting.

Functionalism is inherently controversial because of the idea that *valid* claims about functions are somehow adequate explanations. A functional explanation of a social phenomenon is especially disputable if it does not claim that the phenomenon is both necessary *and* sufficient for social units to exist. Typically, it is not clear whether that claim is made. Thus, the idea that law provides individuals a basis for calculating the consequences of their behavior (Pepensky 1976:3) has a functional ring to it; but the claims are obscure. Even an explicit claim is questionable if it identifies only a *sufficient* condition for the survival of social units. Consider the conventional argument that the function of law is dispute settlement. One must surely wonder where the dispute is in cases of victimless crimes or, for that matter, in cases of armed robbery. In any event, there are clearly other means for settling disputes (perhaps even more effective means), and in some conditions law appears to generate disputes. However, if various social phenomena (institutions and so forth) can "perform" the function in question, a functional explanation of *any of them* is not adequate.

Endless Functions

All manner of functions have been attributed to law. For example, Parsons (especially 1980) postulates no less than five functions—integrative, interpretive, legitimizing, sanctioning, and jurisdictional. Perhaps so, but taking "functions of law" as the central question promotes glib answers.

Glibness is promoted because statements about the functions of law are rarely distinct from definitions of law; hence, they scarcely imply any empirical claim whatever. Thus, the argument that law has a "sanctioning" function borders on a trite tautology.

The Overgeneralization Problem

Most statements about functions are not limited to any particular law; but if construed as generalizations about *all laws in all societies,* they tax credulity. Regardless of the type of law, it is dubious to assume that its functions are even approximately universal. Illustrating briefly, there is surely reason to presume that the functions of criminal law in a society characterized by intense class conflict are markedly different from its functions elsewhere.

The "overgeneralization" problem stems from the glibness with which functions of law are identified. Specifically, writers commonly speak of the functions of law as though universal, whereas their knowledge of law is largely limited to one legal system. For example, Parsons' argument about the functions of law reflects his Anglo-American background, and even in that context he was indifferent to the exploitative features of law.

The Alternative

For reasons just described, little can be said for taking the "functions of law" as the central question. Glib answers, evidential problems, and parochial concerns can be more nearly avoided by pursuing these questions. First, what analytical properties of law should be recognized? And, second, what are the correlates of variation in those properties?

Neither question can be answered without a theoretical perspective, but the sociology of law is now predominantly atheoretical. Indeed, the two best-known theories are from the nineteenth century.

Durkheim's Theory

Because Durkheim stated his theory discursively over hundreds of pages (1949), a brief version of it is necessarily a *restatement.* This restatement is oriented around the diagram in Figure 4.1.

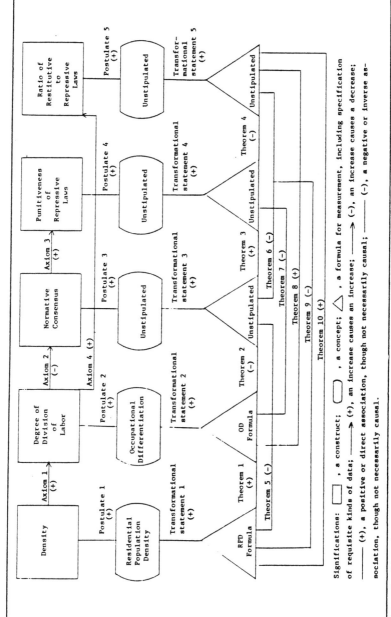

Significations: ▢ , a construct; ◠ , a concept; △ , a formula for measurement, including specification of requisite kinds of data; ——▶(+), an increase causes an increase; ——▶(-), an increase causes a decrease; —— (+), a positive or direct association, though not necessarily causal; —— (-), a negative or inverse association, though not necessarily causal.

Figure 4.1: Durkheim's Theory

97

Preliminary Considerations

Durkheim used the terms "mechanical solidarity" and "organic solidarity" to denote types of societies, with mechanical solidarity denoting the lowest degree of division of labor and, concomitantly, the greatest normative consensus (or "likeness"). Since those two variables are shown in Figure 4.1, also including mechanical solidarity and organic solidarity would be redundant and confusing.

Some terms in Figure 4.1 are identified as constructs to signify that the theorist's definition of the term is neither complete nor empirically applicable. In contrast, a concept is defined completely but becomes empirically applicable (if it denotes quantitative phenomena) only when linked to a formula that stipulates a measurement procedure and requisite data. Such distinctions are necessary to indicate the sense in which the theory is incomplete (i.e., several concepts and measurement formulas remain unstipulated).

Axioms

The first axiom (Figure 4.1) expresses two of Durkheim's ostensible assumptions: (1) that an increase in density leads to potentially lethal competition for land if agriculture continues as the predominant economic activity and (2) that the division of labor avoids such competition because people in different occupations (e.g., farmers, carpenters, priests) do not necessarily compete. Here we see Durkheim's "functionalism."

Axiom 2 expresses a murky line of reasoning by Durkheim. He evidently assumed that individuals agree in their evaluations of conduct (i.e., normative consensus) only insofar as they engage in the same kinds of economic activities (an essentially Marxist assumption, unacknowledged by Durkheim).

Durkheim described repressive law as an expression of the "collective conscience," meaning shared evaluations of conduct; but it is not clear why a decrease in normative consensus supposedly causes a decline in the punitiveness of legal sanctions (axiom 3). Durkheim evidently assumed that evaluations of conduct are intense only to the extent that they are shared (i.e., truly collective).

Since Durkheim spoke of punishment as the purpose of repressive law and equated it with penal law, the term "criminal law" might be more appropriate. Restitutive law is a more troublesome notion. Durkheim suggested that the function of restitutive law is to restore order or maintain cooperative relations, but he indicated (1949:122) that it encompasses all nonrepressive law (e.g., civil law, constitutional law). That residual character virtually precludes "counting" the number of restitutive laws, and it is difficult to state a coherent rationale for Durkheim's assertion that restitutive law appears and expands with increases in the division of labor. Restitutive law becomes a manageable notion only if thought of as regulatory; and the rationale for Durkheim's assertion becomes something like this: The division of labor creates problems (e.g., economic crises, strikes, unemployment, fraudulent occupational practices) that can be prevented or resolved only through regulatory law. Yet Durkheim did not claim that repressive law disappears; rather, it declines relative to restitutive law.

Postulates

Durkheim's use of the term "density" precludes a complete definition of it. He spoke of both material density and moral (social) density, which are quite different notions. Moral or social density evidently is the total amount of interaction in a population, and it defies measurement. Additionally, Durkheim's argument about the relation between density and the division of labor is more plausible if stated in terms of material density; and while Durkheim left the meaning of material density unclear, one can assume a close direct relation between it and residential population density. The latter term can be defined completely, and there is a conventional measurement procedure. That is the rationale for postulate 1.

Some dimensions of the division of labor (e.g., functional interdependence) are not subject to measurement; but occupational differentiation can be defined completely, and there is a related measurement procedure. Moreover, while Durkheim did not state postulate 2 as it is shown in Figure 4.1, that version is consistent with his observations on occupational specialization.

Postulates 3, 4, and 5 will remain incomplete until someone stipulates the appropriate concepts. Since there is no obvious mensurable correlate of normative consensus, postulate 3 stands "unfinished." The immediate problem with postulate 4 is that judgments of punitiveness tend to be subjective and ethnocentric. Finally, even if repressive law is equated with criminal law and restitutive law equated with regulatory law, computing the ratio in question (postulate 5) may not be feasible.

Transformational Statements

The conventional formula for measuring residential population density (transformational statement 1, Figure 4.1) is: $RPD = Nr/La$, where Nr is the number of residents in a territorial unit and La the amount of land area in that unit. The formula is readily applicable because census data provide the Nr and La values.

One simple formula for measuring occupational differentiation is: OD = $Nc(1 - [\Sigma X^2/(\Sigma X)^2])$, where Nc is the number of occupational categories and X the number of individuals in a particular category. While published census data on occupations are not sufficiently detailed and comparable over time, that problem could be solved by analyzing individual census schedules. As for the "missing" formulas (transformational statements 3-5), there is no immediate prospect of their formulation. That is the case because the related concepts remain unstipulated.

The Validity of the Theorems

On the whole, criticisms of Durkheim's theory can be based on little more than general observations (see Turkel 1979). Thus, so it could be argued, the punitiveness of criminal sanctions reflects the decisions of elites and not normative consensus in the total population; hence, the apolitical character of Durkheim's theory invalidates axiom 3. Then consider this *implied* axiom (not shown in Figure 4.1): The greater the degree of division of labor, the less punitive the repressive laws. General observations on nonliterate, historical, and contemporary societies suggest that if there is any relation at all, punitiveness is most pronounced when there is a moderate degree of division of labor. Yet such criticisms are a far cry from systematic tests, and only the theorems are testable in any direct sense.

Unfortunately, only theorem 1 can be tested systematically; and there have been few tests, perhaps because the requisite historical data on occupational composition are not readily available. Systematic evidence indicates that theorem 1 does not hold internationally. For example, residential population density (RPD) is much greater in India than in the United States, but all evidence indicates that occupational differentiation (OD) is much greater in the United States. However, there is evidence for numerous countries of a direct longitudinal relation between RPD and OD.

Marxist Theory

Stating the major premises of a Marxist theory of law is far more difficult than stating Durkheim's premises. Marx's arguments about law are scattered over hundreds of letters, essays, articles, and books; and for that reason alone even sympathetic critics doubt whether those arguments constitute a coherent theory. So the only realistic goal is to formulate a central Marxist proposition and assume that most Marxist arguments about law suggest or presuppose that proposition.

The Control of Law

The prime candidate is this proposition: In any society those individuals who own the predominant form of productive property also control law. The proposition does not assert that ownership and property exist independently of law, nor is it limited to capitalist societies. Nonetheless, critics may object that the proposition distorts Marx by introducing a volitional element, and they could quote Marx in refutation (1963:83): "Legislation, whether political or civil, never does more than proclaim, excpress in words, the will of economic relations." The statement could be construed as suggesting that economic relations determine law *directly*; yet surely laws are created by human action. Those actions may be determined totally by economic relations, but to deny that these actions are control is to imply that control must be purely volitional. Finally, the central proposition does not preclude the indirect control of laws, as when members of the propertied class manipulate legislators.

Avoiding Evidential Problems

Granted other candidates for the central Marxist proposition about law, attempts to test them will confront horrendous evidential problems. Examine this general proposition: Economic relations determine the features of a legal system. Unless extended to assertions about the particular types of laws or other specific features, the proposition is an empty formula. Nor will it do to state causal generalizations like this: The economic relations of capitalism give rise to bourgeois law; and in the absence of slavery, the concentration of control over access to land results in feudal law. The meaning of "bourgeois law" or "feudal law" is much too vaguely inclusive, and one must surely wonder about conspicuous *variation* in specific features of law among capitalist societies or among feudal societies. In any case, such generalizations are simply summaries of history; and they become something more than crude induction only when *deduced* from the premises of a Marxist theory. But the premises of Marxist theory remain obscure, and for that reason alone the very idea of testing the theory is an illusion. That is far less the case for the present central proposition. Insofar as owners of the predominant form of productive property (e.g., land, factories) in a particular society can be identified, there is only one question: To what extent do these owners control law?

Observe that the proposition does not speak to the "how" of control. Marxists do not claim that the propertied class control law in any particular, exclusive way; and there are various possibilities, including bribery, blackmail, coercive threats, selective promotion of political careers, alliances through marriage, and direct control, (i.e., members of the propertied class occupy political office). Eventually, the central proposition should be extended to generalizations about the association between types or features of economic relations and the specific means of control employed, but that is not necessary to bring evidence to bear on the central proposition.

The central proposition makes no reference to the *ultimate* goals of the propertied class in controlling law. Marxist writers use diverse terms to describe those goals—furthering economic interests, protection of property, repression of dissidents, and the like. That diversity alone creates an evidential problem; and while a propertied class may have several distinct ultimate goals, the meaning of terms commonly used to denote them is very vague. Consider, for example, the protection of economic interests. The immediate problem is whether the term denotes subjective interest or objective interest. In either case, the appropriate method of demonstration is disputable at best. Yet all such evidential problems are diminished in assessing the central proposition. Indeed, unless it can be shown that a propertied class does control law, there is no point in speculating about ultimate goals (or even consequences).

The Paucity of Evidence

There is little systematic evidence bearing on the central proposition, and advocates of Marxist theory are primarily responsible. When those advocates speak of the control exercised by a propertied class, they do not conceptualize control and stipulate a *method of demonstration.* Hence, critics of Marxist theory are in the forefront of research. Space limitations permit only a very brief summary of that research in connection with criminal law.

The legislative process by which criminal statutes are enacted, modified, or revoked has been studied to answer this question: Who attempts to influence the process? Surveys of U.S. studies (e.g., Hagan 1980) indicate that those who seek to influence the legislative process are markedly heterogeneous, with employers far outnumbered by professionals (e.g., physicians, professors) and career moral entrepreneurs. Perhaps the propertied class somehow "pulls the strings" from the wings; but what is the appropriate method of demonstration? Moreover, there is an alternative interpretation—the central proposition is an overgeneralization at best. Even granting a well-organized propertied class, why would that class attempt to control *all* laws? Specifically, why would that class concern itself with criminalizing or decriminalizing sexual relations between cousins? One strategy is to limit the central proposition to "laws having to do with economic relations," but that notion must be clarified for it to be constructive.

Another body of putative evidence comes from social surveys in which respondents express the extent to which they disapprove of particular types of criminal acts or regard them as "serious." The findings purportedly bear on the Marxist or conflict theory of criminal law; however, they are *inferential* evidence and relevant only if the theory encompasses this argument: Criminal law reflects evaluations of conduct by a propertied class, and those evaluations are peculiar to that class because they stem from economic relations. In any event, the findings (e.g., Rossi et al. 1974) show a remarkable amount of relative agreement among various subdivisions of the U.S. population (e.g., race, occupation, and income level). Moreover, numerous findings support this generalization about the United States: Those crimes that are harshest legal punishments (e.g., life imprisonment, death) are the very ones that the public ostensibly disapproves the most. In brief, the findings suggest that criminal law reflects appreciable *normative consensus* rather than evalutions of conduct peculiar to capitalists. One obvious conclusion is that Marxist arguments about criminal law are overgeneralizations. As a case in point, contemplate what is implied when statements are made about crimes in general without any qualification as to type. Since armed robbery was a crime in England long before capitalism, it taxes credulity to imply that its continued criminalization stems from evaluations of conduct peculiar to capitalists. So, again, Marxist arguments (including the present central propositions) would appear more credible if limited to certain types of laws and crimes.

Still other evidence pertains to the enforcement of criminal laws. Marxist writers often appear to make this argument: Since enforcement is controlled by capitalists, there is a class bias in sentencing. Yet the findings of numerous studies (see, e.g., Hagan's survey, 1974) do not show a substantial or consistent *inverse* relation between the presumptive severity of sentence (e.g., length of imprisonment) and the socioeconomic status of defendants. In light of such findings, Marxists should confront this question: Assuming that capitalists control the enforcement of criminal law, why do they risk intensifying class conflict *and* diminishing control over their own members by imposing more lenient sentences on those members *for all types of crimes?* There is surely an alternative strategy, with the harsher prescribed punishment of Aztec nobles for drunkenness being illustrative (Soustelle 1962:156).

Recapitulation

Any argument that a propertied class uses law to some end (whatever it may be) assumes that the class does control law. However, the present central proposition and Marxist arguments about law in general appear to be vast overgeneralizations.

Even if the central proposition is restated so as to recognize that the control of propertied classes over law is limited in various ways, *direct* evidence can be realized only by pursuing this question: If legislators do not own the predominant form of productive property, who controls their actions? The question cannot be answered defensibly without prior work on the conceptualization of control and related methods for demonstrating control. Contemporary Marxists eschew such work; and the theory suffers accordingly, because it is first and foremost a theory about control. That point is implicitly denied by the current practice of describing capitalism as a diffuse "cultural phenomena," a practice that creates insoluble evidential problems. Finally, if Marxist theory is taken as an ideological tool to "move people," it becomes all the more a theory of control.

Another Central Question: The Efficacy of Law

Systematic evidence on the effectiveness or efficiency of law as a means of social control is rare (Jones 1969), even though negative evidence would cast doubts on most ideas about the functions of law. Hence, from the outset the sociology of law should have focused on the efficacy of laws and not their supposed functions.

The Paucity of Research on Efficacy

, The paucity of systematic research on the efficacy question stems from horrendous investigative problems. When it comes to tort, contract, and regulatory law, the problems have precluded truly defensible research. Whereas statutory penalties in criminal law are a point of departure for deterrence research, there is nothing comparable in other branches of law. Then there is a special problem in dealing with regulatory law. Far more than contract, tort, or criminal law, compliance with a regulation is viewed by the "regulators" as only a means; and the end may not be realized regardless of compliance. Thus, experts may disagree as to whether a particular proposed regulation of energy use will prevent the biotic sterilization of lakes, even assuming full compliance; and cost-benefit considerations complicate matters further.

Granted doubts about the reliability of official crime statistics, there are no official statistics whatever on the incidence of torts, breaches of contract, or regulatory violations. Adjudicative incidence cannot be equated with actual incidence, and there is no feasible alternative procedure for gathering data on actual incidence. Concealment of regulatory violations and public ignorance of regulatory law caution against a "victim-ization" survey; and even if a meaningful victimization question could be formulated about torts or contract breaches, litigational outcome may well be the only objective basis for judging the validity of the answers. Finally, neither violation rates nor litigation is relevant when assessing efficacy in the most rapidly expanding sphere of law—control through positive incentives (e.g., stimulating the housing industry by permitting income tax deductions for mortgage interest).

Deterrence Research

For reasons just indicated, extensive efficacy research has been limited to criminal law. The research has been guided by the deterrence doctrine; but writers often distort the doctrine by suggesting that it reduces to a simple proposition, such as: Severe punishments deter criminality. That proposition ignores *eight* other possibly relevant properties of legal punishments (Gibbs 1975), and they can be recognized only by going beyond Beccaria or Bentham to a statement of the doctrine as a systematic theory. Space limits alone preclude that statement here, or even a survey of research findings. Only some reasons for inconclusive findings can be examined.

Studies of capital punishment in the 1950s led social scientists to reject the deterrence doctrine; but in comparing the homicide rates of capital states and abolitionist states the investigators considered *only one* property of punishment and a related *implicit* assumption—that potential murderers perceive execution as more severe or certain than life imprisonment. Recognition of that defect renewed deterrence research in the late 1960s, with a focus on *actual* punishments rather than statutory penalties. Two principal findings emerged. First, consistent with the doctrine, an inverse relation holds among states and also among types of crime between the objective certainty of punishment (e.g., the proportion of robberies that result in imprisonment) and the official crime rate. Second, contrary to the doctrine, an inverse relation does not hold among states between the average length of imprisonment and the official crime rate.

Because of numerous evidential problems, the findings are not compelling. Expanding the scope of research could solve some of these problems, such as the failure of investigators to consider more than two properties of legal punishments and insufficient attention to *change* in variables over time. But some problems can be solved only by abandoning conventional crime rates. Even if reliable, those rates cannot show the extent of restrictive deterrence (*curtailment* of criminal activity to reduce the risk of punishment); and it may well be that few potential offenders are deterred *absolutely*. Then there has never been a study of nonmarginal deterrence, a comparison of the incidence of some act (e.g., gambling) in a jurisdiction where it is a crime and in one where it is legal. The findings might sober critics of the deterrence doctrine.

Extensions of deterrence research may yield more defensible conclusions and perhaps explain why present findings are markedly inconsistent from one type of crime to the next and from one jurisdiction or period to the next. However, two evidential problems now appear beyond solution. One stems from the possibility that the crime rate is primarily a function of extralegal conditions, some of which (perhaps unemployment) generate criminality and others (perhaps social condemnation) inhibit criminality. Without an accepted theory to identify those conditions, there is no defensible strategy for controlling them in deterrence research.

The other seemingly insoluble problem is that legal punishments may prevent crimes through nondeterrent mechanisms. Incapacitation is one obvious possibility (e.g., automobile theft is difficult in prison), and it is difficult to distinguish evidence of such mechanisms from evidence of deterrence. While research could ignore such distinctions and purport to demonstrate the *general* preventive effects of punishment, the distinction does bear on penal policy. A deterrent penal policy is attractive because it appears "cheap," and reducing the crime rate through incapacitation is very costly.

Turning from general deterrence (the deterrence of potential offenders who have *not* been punished) to specific deterrence (the deterrence of those who have been punished), the official recidival rate is commonly greater for offenders who receive more severe sentences (e.g., imprisonment rather than probation). However, those studies have ignored changes in perceived certainty and perceived severity concomitant with actual punishment, and doubts about the reliability of official recidival rates are perennial. Then there is a seemingly insoluble problem. Offenders with the most extensive criminal history tend to receive the most severe sentences, and they are the very ones most likely to be repeaters with or without punishment. Randomization of actual legal punishments (with some much more severe than others) might solve the problem, but it would reek with injustice.

The Major Implication

Some theories about law, Durkheim's theory especially, virtually ignore the purposive quality of human behavior. In particular, they appear to presume that laws are enacted or abandoned without regard to efficacy.

Given the paucity of research on the efficacy question and the inconclusive findings, it may appear that the question has no bearing on legislation. The argument could be this: Since legislators scarcely have reliable knowledge about the efficacy of law, the subject has no bearing on their actions. While the enactment or continuance of laws without reliable knowledge is common (and astonishing), it does not follow that law in no way reflects beliefs about efficacy, however erroneous. Here we see a glaring gap in the literature—the paucity of research on beliefs about the efficacy of laws.

Orwell's *1984* and Beyond

Although George Orwell may become a discredited prophet, his work does pose an important question: Is *1984* a realistic possibility at any time? The answer hinges in large part on ideas about law as a means of social control.

Unless one is indifferent to human liberty, this theme is more important than any theory in the social sciences or jurisprudence: The rule of law is essential to prevent despotism. Moreover, the notion of rule of law is not hopelessly vague. Fuller's enduring contribution is that his eight *desiderata* of law could be the bases for defining the notion. Yet the theme has received little attention in systematic research. Thus, in the vast literature on the Nazi era there is no defensible answer to this question: To what *extent* was the rule of law abandoned in Hitler's Germany? Most authors create the impression that Nazi social control was absolutely "lawless"; but while the major Nazis ridiculed the rule of law, the extent to which it was actually abandoned is another question. Even admission that the Nazis relied on a vast bureaucracy would raise doubts.

By comparison, *1984* will function entirely without the rule of law. The last thing that Big Brother will want is the promulgation of evaluations of types of conduct. The use of torture by *1984* "officials" in itself will not negate the rule of law; rather, the citizenry (particularly Party members) will not know what *types of conduct* avoid torture, especially since "thought crime" will be the ultimate crime. Far from literary license, Orwell's depiction of control in *1984* is consistent with a terror principle: Fear and concomitant striving for conformity is engendered by uncertainty.

The terror principle is alien to the rule of law; but, unfortunately, efficacy is the central question in assessing the possibility of a *1984.* If Fuller's *desiderata* of law constitute an implicit but valid proposition about the efficacy of means of social control in general, then Big Brother's attempt to impose evaluations of conduct will not be efficacious. Those evaluations will lack virtually all of Fuller's *desiderata,* especially generality, promulgation, nonretroactivity, and commanding only the possible.

While studies of Nazism, Soviet Russia under Stalin, the People's Republic of China under Mao, and the United States in the McCarthy era would be relevant in assessing Orwell's prophecy, in none of those cases was there a departure from the rule of law remotely approaching *1984.* Even if the Hitlers, Stalins, Maos, and McCarthys of the world strive for total control, limited resources force them to leave several areas of life (e.g., conventions of work, leisure activities) far from *completely* controlled. That is still another reason for doubts about Orwell's prophecy. But there is a depressing implication—liberty survives only because Big Brothers lack the resources to end it. If so, an abiding fear of technological change is understandable; and Orwell's arming of Big Brother with an awesome surveillance technology precludes dismissing *1984* as a sociological impossibility.

Looking Beyond 1984

Speculation about law in, say, 2000 is a dubious enterprise. One reason is doubt as to whether the predominant form of social change is monotonic (as evolutionary theories suggest), and casual observations on the United States furthers doubt. Those observations indicate an expansion of regulatory law over the past century; but the increase has been very irregular, and deregulation in the 1980s appears likely. Similarly, criminal justice has followed a bewildering historical course from retribution to deterrence to rehabilitation, and now (1982) some combination of deterrance and retribution. So there are scarcely any monotonic trends in U.S. law that could be extrapolated to 2000. There are such trends in urbanization, the division of labor, inanimate energy consumption, and population density; but a correlative forecast about law in 2000 would reek with conjecture because there is no defensible theory about the relation between social change and change in law. In keeping with legal realism, the sociology of law in the United States long ago shifted to studies of the legal profession, the pursuit of facts that supposedly interest law professors or officials, and analyses of particular court rulings, thereby abandoning the grand tradition of Durkheim, Marx, and Weber. Donald Black (1976) has perpetuated the tradition, but his propositions are not particularly useful in speculating about the future of law. Consider this proposition (Black 1976:63): "The more culture, the more law: law varies directly with culture." Even if one is capable of thinking of culture and law as quantities, a feasible measurement procedure is inconceivable. Nonetheless, accept the proposition and assume that American culture "increases" between 1982 and 2000. The volume of American law would be expected to increase; but that prospect is scarcely informative, for it does not pertain to changes in the form and functions of law.

An informative speculation about law in 2000 must focus on some meaningful general property of law other than "volume," and the prime candidate is the rule of law. However, not even a precise conceptualization of that notion would be a substitute for a theory as a basis for speculation about the future. Despite their defects, Marx's theory and Durkheim's theory are the only viable candidates.

Law and the Control of Crime

Taking Durkheim's theory as valid and assuming that the division of labor continues to increase, by 2000 crime control in the United States will be a far cry from the rule of law. One predominant strategy will be "anticipatory prevention," meaning that (*inter alia*) individuals are incarcerated on the basis of alleged evidence of criminal propensity. Numerous laws and court rulings now hinder gathering such evidence through systematic surveillance (e.g., unlimited wiretapping), but within a generation those legal barriers will have eroded.

The kind of crime control envisioned is incompatible with mandatory definite prison sentences, and by 2000 it will be recognized that the amount of deterrence and incapacitation realized through long prison sentences does not justify the cost. The alternatives that will be pursued are the extensive use of drugs and psychosurgery to prevent recidivism, a return to indefinite prison sentences (e.g., not less than two years), and "correctional authorities" with enormous discretion.

All of the forecasts stem from an anticipated decline in normative consensus. Although not truly central in Durkheim's theory, it is assumed that the rate of deviance (crime or otherwise) is primarily an inverse function of the intensity of social disapproval; and there is some supporting evidence (e.g., Erickson and Gibbs 1978). However, the argument is not that criminality will destroy social order by 2000 (or ever). Like all other social problems, reactions will be determined by perceptions of the threat. For political purposes one faction or another will magnify the threat; but genuine attempts will be made to check crime, and the elites will not be totally blind to problems and failures.

One correlate of a high degree of division of labor—large concentrations of residentially mobile individuals—will preclude effective crime prevention through general deterrence. In that condition, the certainty of apprehension is not an awesome threat, and negligible normative consensus is not conducive to promoting deterrence through Draconian punishment. True, public concern with crime indicates some normative consensus and prompts preventive measures; but as normative consensus declines, reactions to crime will become more instrumental and less retributive. The instrumental quality is manifested today in the proliferation of private police and diverse extralegal measures (e.g., polygraph tests for prospective employees). That trend will accelerate.

The anticipated decline in normative consensus will be reflected in the decriminalization of victimless crimes, but a countertrend is anticipated. As normative consensus declines, conformity to extralegal evaluations of conduct pertaining to status relations (e.g., employer-employee, teacher-student, parent-child) and to everyday interaction will be perceived as so problematical that legislators will resort to statutory law, including the creation of agencies, to maintain order. Hence, despite decriminalization, the volume of law will expand; and it will be an extension of a long trend. The history of traffic regulation is illustrative, and it demonstrates how legal control comes to transcend tort and contract law. The general point is this: As normative consensus approaches the minimum, law becomes the only effective basis for status relations, everyday interaction, and collective action. However, since it will become increasingly difficult to control through deterrence, law will shift from negative incentives (e.g., punishment) to positive incentives, which will be a tacit recognition that greed has become the only viable kind of normative consensus.

Regulatory Law

Two correlates of a high degree of division of labor—large population concentrations and a technology powered by inanimate energy—pollute the environment and exhaust natural resources. Apart from the division of labor, legislators will continue to seek solutions to those problems through regulatory law. The argument does not contradict Durkheim's theory, but it does further justify forecasting an enormous expansion of regulatory law.

The forecast is consistent with the present general theme—erosion of the rule of law. Since regulatory law operates so much through *ad hoc* directives to particular organizations, Fuller's generality *desideratum* is sacrificed. Moreover, since survival of economic organizations in a competitive market is problematical, much criticism of regulatory law is that it commands the impossible. Finally, given the complexity of regulatory law and enforcement difficulties, clarity and congruence with official action are rarely realized in regulatory law.

The Energy Crisis

The forecasts are especially debatable because they appear contrary to *current* trends. Deregulation is now the stated goal of numerous politicians, and crime control is now sought through long mandatory prison sentences. However, even if the division of labor does increase more or less regularly, the related trend in *departures* from the rule of law could take the form of irregular cycles, with a net increase only over several decades. After all, law is a problem-solving institution, and humans rarely solve problems in a linear way. Rather, they grope for solutions, including retreats to previous practices. Nonetheless, the present forecasts do assume that before 2000 the current trend toward deregulation and mandatory definite prison sentences will be perceived by the elites as failures.

The most serious qualification of the forecast is that major sociocultural change can occur abruptly in conjunction with crises that could not have been anticipated by extrapolating long cycles or monotonic trends. Accordingly, since the United States may be approaching a crisis, the forecasts are especially dubious. The impending crisis stems from deceleration of the net energy yield: Ed/Ei, where Ei is the energy (human, animal, and inanimate) invested in acquiring inanimate energy sources (petroleum in particular) and Ed is the amount of energy actually provided by those sources. Various theories and findings indicate that major societal features depend on the Ed/Ei ratio; hence, a substantial decline in that ratio will generate an unprecedented crisis. In particular, a high degree of division of labor is both necessary for and requires a very efficient technology, one that substitutes inanimate energy for human energy. Accordingly, without a rapid shift before 2000 to some energy resource other than petroleum (e.g., coal, solar radiation, gravitational forces), the division of labor will cease increasing; and, if so, all bets are off.

Should a new energy source be utilized after 2000, the forecasts will be only premature. But take the grim view—no new energy source and substantial decline in Ed/Ei over several generations. It may appear that as the division of labor declines, the legal system will become more consistent with the rule of law. Yet there is surely reason to doubt that stages of sociocultural evolution are reversible. Imagine, for example, some 250 million Americans surviving a reversion to feudal technology. Of course, reversion would not take place suddenly; but unless it occurs very slowly, there will be lethal competition for land and an enormous increase in the death rate.

There is no body of theory to anticipate the sociocultural consequences of that "ultimate crisis." Despite Durkheim's sensitivity to the impact of the Industrial Revolution, his theory scarcely treats crises or conflict. Marx's theory of capitalism appears superior; but Marx did not remotely anticipate an energy crisis as the ultimate threat to capitalism, and he assumed an evolutionary trend in productivity. Hence, in speculating about the ultimate crisis one must turn to literary figures, such as Orwell.

But Orwell is of questionable relevance because he thought of *1984* as simply a manifestation of the insatiable human appetite for power rather than the outcome of an energy crisis.

So we reach an unhappy conclusion. Insofar as theories provide a credible basis for speculating about the future of law in the United States, they do so only insofar as one assumes no energy crisis. Nonetheless, that very limitation suggests a fertile line of work in the sociology of law—an examination of changes in regulatory law as correlates of changes in energy production and consumption.

REFERENCES

Austin, John. 1954. *The Province of Jurisprudence Determined.* New York: Noonday.

Black, Donald. 1976. *The Behavior of Law.* New York: Academic.

Blake, Judith and Kingsley Davis. 1964. "Norms, Values, and Sanctions." Pp. 456-484 in *Handbook of Modern Sociology,* edited by Robert E. L. Faris. Chicago: Rand McNally.

Durkheim, Emile. 1949. *The Division of Labor in Society.* New York: Free Press.

Erickson, Maynard L. and Jack P. Gibbs. 1978. "Objective and Perceptual Properties of Legal Punishment and the Deterrence Doctrine." *Social Problems* 25:253-64.

Frank, Jerome. 1949. *Law and the Modern Mind.* New York: Cloward-McCann.

Friedman, Lawerence M. and Stewart Macaulay. 1977. *Law and the Behavioral Sciences,* 2nd ed. New York: Bobbs-Merrill.

Fuller, Lon L. 1969. *The Morality of Law,* rev. ed. New Haven, CT: Yale University Press.

Gibbs, Jack P. 1968. "Definitions of Law and Empirical Questions." *Law and Society Review* 2:429-446.

Gibbs, Jack P. 1975. *Crime, Punishment, and Deterrence.* New York: Elsevier-North Holland.

Gibbs, Jack P. 1981. *Norms, Deviance, and Social Control: Conceptual Matters.* New York: Elsevier-North Holland.

Hagan, John. 1974. "Extra-legal Attributes and Criminal Sentencing: An Assessment of a Sociological Viewpoint." *Law and Society Review* 8:357-83.

Hagan, John. 1980. "The Legislation of Crime and Delinquency: A Review of Theory, Method, and Research." *Law and Society Review* 14: 603-28.

Hart, H.L.A. 1961. *The Concept of Law.* Oxford, England: Clarendon.

Hoebel, E. Adamson. 1968. *The Law of Primitive Man.* New York: Atheneum.

Holmes, Justice. 1897. "The Path of the Law." *Harvard Law Review* 10:457-78.

Homans, George C. 1961. *Social Behavior: Its Elementary Forms.* New York: Harcourt, Brace & World.

Jones, Harry W. 1969. *The Efficacy of Law.* Evanston, IL: Northwestern University Press.

Kelsen, Hans, 1945. *General Theory of Law and State.* Cambridge, MA: Harvard University Press.

Llewellyn, K. N. 1934. "The Constitution as an Institution." *Columbia Law Review* 34:1-40.

Llewellyn, K. N. 1951. *The Bramble Bush*. New York: Oceana.

Malinowski, Bronislaw. 1959. *Crime and Custom in Savage Society*. Paterson, NJ: Littlefield, Adams.

Marx, Karl. 1963. *The Poverty of Philosophy*. New York: International Publishers.

Olivecrona, Karl. 1971. *Law as Fact*, 2nd ed. London: Stevens & Sons.

Parsons, Talcott. 1951. *The Social System*. New York: Free Press.

Parsons, Talcott. 1980. "The Law and Social Control." Pp. 60-68 in *The Sociology of Law*, edited by William M. Evan. New York: Free Press.

Patterson, Edwin W. 1953. *Jurisprudence*. Brooklyn: Foundation Press.

Pepensky, Harold E. 1976. *Crime and Conflict: A Study of Law and Society*. London: Martin Robertson.

Rossi, Peter H. et al. 1974. "The Seriousness of Crimes: Normative Structure and Individual Differences." *American Sociological Review* 39:224-37.

Soustelle, Jacques. 1962. *The Daily Life of the Aztecs*. New York: Macmillan.

Sutherland, Edwin H. and Donald R. Cressey. 1974. *Criminology*, 9th edition. Philadelphia: Lippincott.

Turkel, Gerald. 1979. "Testing Durkheim: Some Theoretical Considerations." *Law and Society Review* 13:721-38.

Weber, Max. 1968. *Economy and Society*, Vol. 1. New York: Bedminster.

5

Behavior Modification and Social Control
Issues and Myths

LEONARD KRASNER

The model of conceptualizing and influencing human behavior subsumed under the rubric of behavior modification is intricately interwoven not only within a social, economic, and historical context, but also within a system of ethics. My concern here is largely with various controversies that touch on social control and behavior modification. Even to do this is not easy, since complexities, paradoxes, deceptions, and myths abound.

Cries of Alarm

Behavior modification and issues of social control became intermingled when psychology apparently seemed to be producing an effective technique for changing human behavior (at last). The ethical problems involved in issues of social control are not unique to or caused by behavior modification, but friends and foes alike certainly believe that the development of behavior modification engendered new issues. I once believed that and expressed it in a "hurry before it's too late" theme. "Does this mean that we, as psychologists, researchers, or even therapists, *at this point* could modify somebody's behavior in any way we wanted? The answer is no, primarily because research into the techniques of control is at the elementary stage. Science moves at a very rapid pace, however, and now is the time to concern ourselves with this problem before basic knowledge about the techniques overwhelm us" (Krasner 1962a:201). Of course, others have expressed the same belief—that at long last the complete manipulation of behavior is a possibility and that behavior modification is to receive the credit or blame.

When a generally careful and thoughtful reporter, such as Tom Wicker of the New York *Times*, criticizes "behavior modification," it is difficult to dismiss as another example of misunderstanding and misinterpretation. Wicker contends that "nothing arouses the fears of prison inmates more than so-called 'behavior modification' programs, and no wonder. Behavior modification is a catch-all term that can mean anything from brain surgery to a kind of 'Clockwork Orange' mental conditioning. It usually includes drug experimentation and in all to many cases, it is aimed more nearly at producing docile prisoners than upright citizens" (New York Times, February 8, 1974, p. 31).

In effect, Wicker accepted and enhanced a growing usage of the term "behavior modification," one that equates it with all methods of controlling and manipulating behavior, including psychosurgery and the use of drugs. For people who have been identified by their work as behavior modifiers, that uncritical usage is a disturbing development. Unfortunately, it is all too easy to dismiss it as merely a misinterpretation.

Wicker's comments appeared the day after another article in the New York *Times* described the termination of a "behavior modification" project as follows:

> In a significant victory for prison reformers, the Federal Bureau of Prisons has decided to dismantle its behavior modification project in Springfield, Mo. In the project, prison guards and doctors tried to alter the conduct of troublesome inmates by first locking them in cells for hours and depriving them of all privileges. The project known as START had become an object of fear and hatred to inmates in Federal prisons across the country. Some inmates, hearing of START in the prison grapevine, staged hunger strikes against the program. Inmates and former inmates wrote letters and articles describing START—an acronym for Special Treatment—as "Pavlovian" and "Clockwork Orange" [New York Times, February 7, 1974, p. 12].

On November 4, 1981 a cartoon appeared on the editorial page of *Newsday,* Long Island's largest newspaper, that showed a man in a white coat holding a picture of a school bus and talking to four robed judges with electrodes attached to their heads. The gentleman is saying: "I am delighted that you're all signed up for the Attorney General's behavior modification program. When you receive this image, you will receive a mild electric shock." Many other similar illustrations of contemporary popular usage of behavior modification could be cited. So it is that, by the 1980s, the term "behavior modification" became synonymous with the use of aversive procedures in the control of human behavior for social/

political purposes (Krapfl and Vargas 1977; Stolz 1978). Indeed, the term has become the symbol of evil in our society, especially at the hands of the mass media.

On the Origins of Behavior Modification

In 1965, I co-edited two volumes of collected papers on research and case studies in "behavior modification" (Krasner and Ullmann 1965; Ullmann and Krasner 1965) and placed the work of several investigators (e.g., Ferster, Staats, Bijou, Salzinger, Goldiamond, Patterson, Krasner, Sarason, Kanfer, Hastorf, Saslow, Colby, Bandura, and Sarbin) in the context of the broader field of "behavior influence" (Krasner and Ullmann 1973). The aim was to demonstrate the uniformities involved in the application of social reinforcement concepts to increasingly complex behavior. This area is germane and useful to the practicing clinical psychologist. If a single label can be given to this subject, it would be *behavior modification.* We have found it convenient to use the term *behavior influence,* as the generic term to include investigations of the ways in which human behavior is modified, changed, or influenced. It includes research on operant conditioning, psychotherapy, attitude change, hypnosis, sensory deprivation, brainwashing, drugs, modeling, and education. We conceive of a broad psychology of behavior influence that concerns itself with the basic variables determining the alteration of human behavior in both laboratory and "real life" situations. On the other hand, the term *behavior modification* refers to a very specific type of *behavior influence* (Krasner and Ullmann 1965:1-2).

We then adopted the description of behavior modification offered by Robert I. Watson (1962). In presenting a historical introduction to Bachrach's (1962) collection of research on the "experimental foundations" of clinical psychology, Watson used the term "behavior modification" to cover a multitude of approaches. "It includes behavior modification as shown in the structured interview, in verbal conditioning, in the production of experimental neuroses, and in patient-doctor relationships. In a broader sense, the topic of behavior modification is related to the whole field of learning. Studies of behavior modification are studies of learning with a particular intent—the goal of treatment" (Watson 1962:19).

Watson included among the historical forbears of behavior modification those investigators who were doing systematic research in psychotherapy. "It was a psychologist, Carl Rogers, who in 1942, through a book and an article, launched the research approach in behavioral modification through psychotherapy" (Watson 1962:20-21). Having put our presentation of behavior modification within the context of "the clinical goal of treatment," we then sought the commonalities and general principles that characterized the work of these behavior modifiers.

A first commonality is the role identification of the investigators themselves. While all of them are interested in basic research, they see socially important applications for their work. They conceive of themselves as behavioral scientists investigating the processes of changing human behavior.

Second, they investigate clinical phenomena through operationally defined and experimentally manipulated variables.

Third, all the investigators emphasize the effect of environmental stimulation in directing the individual's behavior. They virtually eliminate hypothetical concepts such as the unconscious, ego, and internal dynamics. For purposes of their present researches, even such concepts as heredity and maturation are deemphasized.

A fourth commonality is the approach to maladaptive behavior through a psychological rather than a medical model. Behavior modification deals directly with behavior rather than with "underlying" or disease factors that "cause" symptoms.

The psychological model used is that of social reinforcement. In the present volume, the term *social reinforcement* is used to emphasize the fact that other human beings are a source of meaningful stimuli that alter, direct, or maintain the individual's behavior [Krasner and Ullmann 1965:3].

Approximately fifty illustrations of "behavior modification" were included within the same Watsonian context of "clinical treatment" (Ullmann and Krasner 1965:1). The commonalities in these works were seen as "the insistence that the basis of treatment stems from learning theory, which deals with the effect of experience on behavior. . . . The basis of behavior modification is a body of experimental work dealing with the relationship between changes in the environment and changes in the subject's responses."

The terms behavior modification and behavior therapy were used interchangeably "to denote the modification of clinical or maladaptive behavior." A major element in understanding behavior modification at that point was its foucs on behavior that was observable and definable. The concern of the therapist started with this question: What do we wish to accomplish through our application of learning theory?

In the first article on "behavior therapy" in the *Annual Review of Psychology,* Krasner (1971:487-488) argued that "the unifying factor in behavior therapy is its basis in derivation from experimentally established procedures and principles. The specific experimentation varies widely but has in common all the attributes of scientific investigation including control of variables, presentation of data, replicability, and a probabilistic view of behavior. . . . behavior therapy can be broadly conceived of within the view of scientific paradigms in clash." Krasner then utilized Kuhn's (1962) concepts to describe fifteen streams of development in psychology that came together during the 1950s and 1960s in an approach to behavior change generally known as "behavior modification." These streams may be briefly summarized as follows:

(1) the concept of behaviorism in experimental psychology (e.g., Kantor 1969);

(2) the instrumental (operant) conditioning concepts of Thorndike (1931) and Skinner (1938);

(3) the technique of reciprocal inhibition, as developed by Wolpe (1956);

(4) the experimental studies of the investigators at Maudsley Hospital in London under the direction of H. J. Eysenck (1960);

(5) The investigations (1920s, 1930s, 1940s) applying conditioning concepts to human behavior problems in the United States (Watson and Rayner 1920, Mowrer and Mowrer 1938);

(6) interpretations of psychoanalysis in learning theory terms enhancing learning theory as a respectable base for clinical work;

(7) classical conditioning as the basis for explaining and changing normal and deviant behavior (Pavlov 1928);

(8) theoretical concepts and research studies of social role learning and interactionism in social psychology and sociology;

(9) research in developmental and child psychology emphasizing vicarious learning and modeling (Jones 1924; Bandura 1969);

(10) social influence studies of demand characteristics, experimenter bias, hypnosis, and placebo;

(11) an environmentally based social learning model as an alternative to the disease model of human behavior (Ullmann and Krasner 1965; Bandura 1969);

(12) dissatisfaction with traditional psychotherapy and the psychoanalytic model;

(13) the development of the clinical psychologist as scientist-practitioner;

(14) several influential psychiatrists focusing on concepts of human interaction (e.g., Adolph Meyer, Harry Stack Sullivan);

(15) a utopian stream emphasizing the planning of social environments to elicit and maintain the best of human behavior, as in Skinner's *Walden Two* (1948).

These streams were not independent and were continually changing. The elements of the belief system common to behavior modification adherents included: (1) the statement of concepts so that they can be tested experimentally; (2) the notion of the "laboratory" as ranging from animal mazes through basic human learning studies to hospitals, schoolrooms, homes, and the community; (3) research as treatment and treatment as research; and (4) an explicit strategy of therapy or change (Kazdin 1978).

One area in which even behavior modifiers have great difficulty is in language and terminology. Word usage has consequences, often aversive. When Skinner insists on utilizing the term "control," this has consequences. My own preference is to speak of behavior influence (Krasner and Ullmann 1973).

Given its history, the term "behavior modification" is likely to be abandoned by behavioral scientists because of misunderstanding and misuse by both its protagonists and its oppenents. My own preference is to develop a new concept, one denoted by the term "environmental design" (Krasner 1980). The term is not intended to be synonymous with behavior modification; rather, it represents an extention of behavior modification that is discussed later in this chapter.

As another example, Skinner's phrasing "Beyond Freedom and Dignity" as a title has had aversive impact, both among professionals and the general public. People have reacted to the title in many instances without having read the book and cite the title as illustrating the antihumanism of the behavior modifiers, particularly those influenced by Skinner (1971).

My own experience of having to live with the consequences of a title goes back to a paper presented at the "2nd Conference of Research in Psychotherapy" (Krasner 1962b). This conference took place in the ancient days of the behavior modification movement. The paper was one of the first presentations of a social learning/behavioral viewpoint at a "psychotherapy" conference. To be dramatic and to emphasize the departure from traditional psychotherapy, I entitled the paper "The Therapist as a Social Reinforcement Machine." In the paper, I very carefully qualified what was meant by the word "machine," but that did not undo the reaction to the title. In a number of subsequent critiques of behavior therapy, the title was cited as illustrating the mechanical nature and inhumanity of the behavioral position. Hence, some of the points of the paper were lost and misunderstood because of its title. In retrospect, a title such as "The Therapist as a Warm, Humane, and Loving Social Reinforcer" would have been preferable and no less inaccurate than the original. All of which points to the need for a much greater awareness and concern on the part of behavior therapists as to the social consequences of their terminology.

On Behavior Modification and Ethical/Value Issues

Krasner and Ullmann (1965:362-363) link behavior modification and concerns about social values as follows:

> The very effectiveness of behavior modification, the use of terms such as *manipulation, influence,* and *control of the environment,* and the concept that the therapist has the responsibility to determine the treatment program, all lead to concern with social values. Behavior modification, as an area of social influence, shares this problem with advertising, public relations, and education. These areas have in common individuals who have the interest and the ability to alter the behavior of other people, that is, one person determining what is desirable behavior for another. There are circumstances in which this is beneficial for the individual and society and circumstances in which this is not the case. The ethical problem is not whether behavior influence is proper and improper, but a specification of the circumstances under which behavior influence is appropriate. This view reduces the problem from a general one to a more specific operational one. While a crucial variable is the behavior to be modified, other circumstances that must be taken into account are the methods of influence used and the impact on society of the individual's changed behavior.

Many investigators are prone to hide behind a concept of science as a justification for avoiding the full consequences of their research (Krasner 1965). A large segment of those involved in behavior modification continue to see a separation between their scientific activity and value decisions. This view is eloquently expressed by Madsen (1973:598): "Who decides what values/behaviors should be taught to whom has nothing to do with behavior modification." I disagree. My argument is that behavior modification and values cannot be divorced.

Science is not a sacred cow, nor does it have an independent existence. Behavior modification is no less a social product for being a scientific discipline, and the social responsibility of behavior modifiers is to relate their work to the social context. The behavior modifier is an influencer and is continually being influenced. Specifically, behavior modifiers are being used, perhaps inadvertently, to maintain a social order. This is neither bad nor good, but we must recognize it.

Putting behavior modification into historical perspective forces recognition that the issues are *not new* or even unique to the behavioral field. Investigators in the early days of behavior modification were aware of issues and considered them focal. Currently the growing concern on the part of both professionals and the public is: "Behavior mod for what?" That question is best restated this way: What is desirable behavior on the part of human beings in a given set of circumstances and who is to decide? That question has been the central concern since the beginning of behavior modification; and it involves philosophical, social, political, and religious values as to the meaning and purpose of both scientific inquiry and life itself. It just so happens that human beings have been debating, arguing, discussing, fighting, and even killing each other over related issues throughout history.

The only thing new is a group of self-identified behaviorists who contend that they have the secret to changing, controlling, influencing, or manipulating human behavior. The magic potion lies in learning theory and the "techniques" that it has spawned. What if behaviorists are right, meaning that human behavior can be changed fairly readily? We must then face the next, more awesome, and thus far never resolved issue: What is good behavior?

The fact that behavior modification presented a challenge to "society" because of its avowed effectiveness was but one factor in arousing concern, fear, and indignation. Another and perhaps even greater factor lies in the subtle implications of the model that behaviorists espouse. Under a medical or disease model, the role of the professional person is justified by a goal: the *restoration of health*. The ethical rationale of the therapist is to restore the individual to a hypothesized state of previous health or "normality." Thus the therapist works within a clearly sanctioned societal role.

Health is defined as "The state of an organism with respect to functioning, disease, and abnormality at any given time. The state of an organism functioning normally without disease or abnormality" (Morris 1969:607). Health thus implies an absence of abnormality.

This concept of health has usefulness and meaning insofar as body function is concerned. Restoration to physical health is clearly definable in terms of physiological measurements, such as blood pressure, blood count, weight, and the like. It has no meaning in terms of human behavior. So behavior modifiers must confront this question: Who should determine the goals and purposes of behavioral change? Behavior modifiers should not continue to hide behind the myth of health restoration, but where should they seek succor?

I would like to describe some personal experiences and observations to illustrate the point that issues about values are not and cannot be removed from behavior-modification. I was involved with the planning and carrying out of one of the early "token economy programs" in a mental hospital (Atthowe and Krasner 1968). I had earlier visited Ted Ayllon and Nate

Azrin at Anna State Hospital to view their program, the first such program in a mental hospital. What impressed me about the ward I visited, a tour of which was conducted in an exciting manner by a patient, was the way in which the staff related to or interacted with the patients and the way in which patients were relating to each other. The patients were viewed as human beings and, as such, responsive to their environment. Influenced by what I had seen on this visit and by my own experiences as a participant-observer of hospital wards, I worked with Jack Atthowe in developing a program based on the same model. The goal was the development of techniques to facilitate the likelihood of staff and patients behaving toward individual patients as if they were human beings, with rights and dignity. At that point in time, the kind of token economy developed by Ayllon and Azrin seemed most promising, and we adopted it with variations.

In September 1963, a research program in behavior modification was begun which was intimately woven into the hospital's ongoing service and training programs. The objective was to create and maintain a systematic ward program within the ongoing social system of the hospital. The program reported here involves the life of the entire ward, patients, and staff, plus others who come in contact with the patients. The purpose of the program was to change the chronic patients' aberrant behavior, especially the behavior judged to be apathetic, overly dependent, detrimental, or annoying to others. The goal was to foster more responsible, active, and interested individuals who would be able to perform the routine activities associated with self-care, to make responsible decisions, and to delay immediate reinforcement in order to plan for the future [Atthowe and Krasner 1965:38].

Thus, our goals were modest, but they involved value decisions as to what we would consider "good" behavior, with an emphasis on fostering responsibility and activities. We felt that the most important way to do this was to influence the training program of the staff. The tokens served the purpose of assisting the staff in learning how to observe fellow human beings and learning how to use their own behavior to affect the patient in a positive manner.

In 1973, Wexler published a very comprehensive critique of token economies insofar as they appeared to conflict with the emerging legal notion of the "rights of patients." Wexler was particularly critical of the apparent deprivation procedures utilized by Ayllon and by myself in these early token programs. However, it must be noted that the notion of the importance of the value of "patients' rights" (e.g., to a bed, to food, to clothing, to respect from others) developed subsequent to these studies. This was due in large part to the fact that people (professional and "lay") began to look upon the mental patient as a *human being,* as a *victim,* as a *minority,* and less as a *sick* person. In effect then, it was the development of behavior modification and token economies that in itself helped foster concern with patients' rights (Kazdin 1977).

My own experience with token economies continued by developing a planned environment in a state hospital (Winkler and Krasner 1971). Without going into the details, we concluded that to the extent that we succeeded in developing a token economy program on a hospital ward, it helped maintain an undesirable social institution, the mental hospital. Hence, our own value system led us to decide not to develop further token economy programs in mental hospitals. The point is that, rightly or wrongly, our values influenced our behavior as behavior modifiers. Moreover, that is true of all behavior modifiers and, indeed, of anyone who purports to assist or care for others.

When it comes to developing an ethical or value system for behavior modifiers, Goldiamond (1974) has made a thoughtful and provocative argument. He argues (1974:2) that the Constitution of the United States should serve as a "guide for a discussion of ethical and legal issue raised by applied behavior analysis. The arguments that will be developed are that its safeguards provide an excellent guide for program development of an effective application of behavior analysis to problems of social concern and that violation of these rights can be counterproductive to the patient, to the aims of institutional agents whose incentives are therapeutic, and to the therapeutic aim of the society which sponsors the patient-therapist (programmer, teacher, etc.) relation."

Goldiamond extended his strong civil libertarian and legalistic argument to the articulation of an orientation for changing behavior that he denotes as "constructional."

> This is defined as an orientation whose solution to problems is the construction of repertoires (or their reinstatement or transfer to new situations) rather than the elimination of repertoires. Help is often sought because of the distress of suffering that certain repertoires, or their absence, entail. The prevalent approach at present focuses on the alleviation or the *elimination* of the distress through a variety of means which can include chemotherapy, psychotherapy, or behavior therapy. I shall designate these approaches as pathologically oriented. Such approaches often consider the problems in terms of a pathology which, however, it was established, or developed, or is maintained, is to be eliminated. Presented with the same problem of distress and suffering, one can orient in a different direction. The

focus here is on the production of desirables through means which *directly* increase available options or extend social repertoires, rather than *indirectly* doing so as a by-product of an eliminative procedure. Such approaches are constructionally oriented; they build repertoires [Goldiamond 1974: 4-5].

Goldiamond has thus identified the ·major value implication of the differences between the "disease" and the "behavioral" model. It follows that, in Goldiamond's terms (1974:7), "We can view the therapist not as a reinforcement machine, but as a program consultant, namely, a teacher or guide who tries to be explicit." As indicated earlier, the intent of the "social reinforcement machine" metaphor was to convey the role of the "teacher"; thus, I agree with Goldiamond's formulation.

The use of "social contract" as the basis of value decisions will combine with the concepts of learning environments (e.g., Ferster and Culbertson 1982) to provide a structure and procedures within which individuals, learn to formulate their own goals as related to their interests and to contract accordingly. The individuals's options are increased by these procedures as are their spheres of responsibility. Goldiamond (1974:10) sees these procedures also linked with "the self-control procedures being developed in clinics using the same rationale also effectively increase options and spheres of responsibility of the patient." Much of this ethical philosophy is consistent with the rationale behind the movement of behavior modification into the broader area of "environmental design."

Behaviorism and Humanism

One of the major myths that has obfuscated the ethics issues in behavior modification is that behaviorism and humanism are antithetical. Yet as Thoresen (1973:386-387) points out:

Definitions of what constitutes humanism are as diverse as the individuals offering the definitions. Interestingly, many contemporary "behaviorists," i.e., behavior therapists, behavioral counselors, and operant psychologists or social learning psychologists consider themselves humanists. ... Several reasons explain why behavior-oriented professionals see themselves this way. First of all, they focus on what the individual person *does* in the present life and not on who he *is* in terms of vague social labels or obscure descriptions. Secondly, they emphasize human problems as primarily learning situations where the person is seen as capable of changing. Thirdly, they examine how environments can be altered to reduce

and prevent human problems, and, finally they use scientific procedures to improve techniques for helping individuals.

Thorensen's criterion of a humanist is that offered by Kurtz (1969).
Clearly not all self-proclaimed humanists would accept these criteria, but it
is difficult enough to resolve definitions of behaviorism without tackling
an even more controversial concept of humanism. Unfortunately, the
distinction between behaviorists and humanists will be arbitrarily and
artificially maintained by believers in labels and by those who receive their
reinforcements for writing profound "anti-the-other-side" papers.

A final point about the artificiality of the behaviorist-humanist dichotomy is that widely diverse views and beliefs are attributed to each camp.
All reviews of the behaviorist position (Bandura 1969; Krasner 1971)
emphasize the range of diversity among behaviorists. The situation among
humanists is typified by an incident that occurred to this writer when
dining with a leading "humanist" after both of us had unwisely partici-
pated in an "behaviorist versus humanist" panel. This humanist said in
effect: "I may have some difficulty in communicating with behaviorists
like you, but that is nothing compared with the problems I have with the
kooks who are supposedly on my side!"

Behavior Modification and Behavior Control

Concerns and critiques of behavior modification are linked conceptually (in both popular and in professional views) with the broader field of
"behavior control." That term denotes a wide variety of pharmacological
and surgical procedures as well as "psychological" procedures. In an early
1950 symposium at Berkeley on the "Control of the Mind," the emphasis
was on the impact of the then developing array of new drugs, including
tranqualizers. London's (1969) book did much to associate behavior
modification procedures of the period with the coercive drug and surgical
procedures under the general rubric of "behavior control," and Skinner
has contributed to the terminological confusion by his insistence on
continuing to use "control" to describe situations that could just as easily
be given milder and less "flag-waving" terms.

As we consider the possibilities of the control of human behavior, it is
within the broader context of an increasingly bewildering control of our
external environment—greater automation, the growth of computer applications, and the general physical mechanization of society. With the
growth of mass communications, mass advertising, the growth of mass
ideas, and the overwhelming growth of numbers of people, individuality is
likely to become lost. Just as "conformity" was a provocative notion in

the late 1950s, so "control" became provocative in the 1970s and the 1980s.

A similar view of the potentialities of behavior control has been expressed by Crutchfield (1963:80):

> But the most striking new factor in the increasing threat to independent thought in a conformist world is the development of far-reaching new psychological methods of behavior control—direct electrical stimulation of the brain, high-speed computer control of man-machine systems, radical manipulation of strange and artificial environments, biochemical control, shaping of behavior through new automated techniques of programmed training—the so-called teach- .ing machines.

> All these methods have barely begun to show their remarkable potential—a potential both for destroying independent thinking and for promoting it. Just as there is a race between peaceful and destructive uses of nuclear energy and a race between medical advances which reduce death rate and those which control birth rate, so is there a race between the destructive and constructive use of these radically new techniques of behavior control. And behavior control, we shall presently see, implies thought control.

The issue of the control of behavior must also be put into a broader time perspective. Behavioral scientists can modestly and truthfully say at this point that knowledge of variables that influence behavior change is very meager. (Traditional psychotherapists are most entitled to make such modest statements.) Hence, to talk about the control of human behavior with any degree of certainty as to its eventual possibilities sounds grandiose. There are all manner of very practical difficulties in helping just one unhappy individual change his/her behavior even slightly, so that he or she may find the environment a bit more satisfying. However, relative to the age of the earth, the age of man, or even the age of psychology as a science, the scientific knowledge required for effective behavior control probably will be a reality in a short period of time, be it ten, twenty, or a hundred years.

To what extent can human behavior be controlled? Obviously, at this point, the most reasonable answer is that, given certain types of situations, certain specific behaviors can probably be strongly influenced. There is a close relation between how one perceives human nature and how much one perceives human behavior as subject to influence. Behavioristically oriented psychologists, social scientists, or philosophers grant few limitations to the potentialities of control, primarily because of the importance they attach to environmental stimuli in influencing behavior. By contrast, those who see behavior as determined primarily by inner dynamics or forces are less likely to see human behavior as controllable.

On the Future

Whereas the prediction of any human behavior is at best risky, prophecies about behavior modification are foolhardy. So the following statements pertain to what should (but may never) be happening.

- We should continue to move away from a disease-oriented model of man (with its emphasis on treatment, remediation, and adjustment) to a social learning model and an emphasis on designing environments that enable individuals to control social and economic influences on their behavior.
- We should train a greater variety and number of people (teachers, psychologists, nonprofessionals, parents, children, nurses, and the like) in environmental design principles and in the implicit value system that accompanies them.
- We should continue research involving functional analyses of social systems, such as the schoolroom, the hospital ward, the prison, the university, and the home.
- We should have closer links between work on behavior modification and works in economics, sociology, political science, education, law, and architecture. Those fields offer a gold mine of systematic observation of the impact of environmental influences on human behavior.

It is desirable that we become less concerned with conceptual models that are antithetical to the social learning model (the current growth of cognitive behavior modification illustrates a linkage of two conceptual models that are basically incompatible). Let each model be pushed to the limits of its own applications.

Some years ago I concluded a review of behavior modification with the following epitaph: "The decade of the 1960s covered the childhood and adolescence of behavior therapy (its birth was in the 1950s). The 1970s should see its development into adulthood and perhaps even maturity. Ahead will almost certainly lie old age and senility in the 1980s, but by that time it will have given birth to a newer and at this point (at least by this observer) unpredictable paradigm" (Krasner 1971:519). Now, a decade later, "traditional behavior modification" is indeed merging into a broader conceptualization of human behavior with exciting potentialities. Indeed, we are at the beginning.

A major point stemming from the social learning model is that in helping individuals, the goal is to enable them to learn how to control, influence, or design their own environment. The implied value judgement is that individual freedom is a desirable goal; and the more individuals can affect the environment, the greater is their freedom. By "environment" I mean both the people and physical objects in one's life.

In dealing with people, we are involved in a ubiquitous process, not just one of curing or helping unfortunates. Hence, *everyone* is involved in designing environments, be they individuals who seek help, therapists, researchers, schoolteachers, parents, students, wardens, or the planners of conferences on environmental designs. And the question of how to train the environmental designer could be interpreted to mean "how to train people to live in our society." The reader can and should contribute to this process by asking himself or herself this question: What kind of world do I want to live in and what can I do to help move society at least a bit in that direction?

The future is calculated guesses, because there really is great difficulty in predicting human behavior. These are things I would like to see and some I hope can be avoided:

(1) Training of people to apply general principles of behavior influence, which means questioning the status quo, thinking for themselves, avoiding reification of even behavioral concepts, rejecting fanaticism, desiring a better way of life for all people, and placing their professional activities into a broad historical perspective.

(2) Fuller exploration of the implications of social learning, behavior influence, and environmental design in both research and application. It is still in its early stages. There is a strong "urge to merge" with other models. Here Kuhn's (1970) view of the role of alternative paradigms or models in science is useful, in that it puts in perspective the possibility of living, perhaps even comfortably, with contending models. Behavior modifiers should respect other models and abandon beliefs about the superiority of their model.

(3) Greater linkage between the university and the community, between the researcher and the applier, between behavior modification and other fields concerned with environmental impact.

(4) Each behavior modifier should ask himself or herself: What am I doing professionally?

Environmental Design

In my version of "environmental design," the aspects of the environment emphasized in training procedures are very broad and complex

(Krasner 1980). The basic premise is that *all* behavior change involves value decisions on the part of the influencer or trainer. Accordingly, a research and training program in "environmental design" should link two traditions, the behavioristic and the humanistic. A growing number of graduate training programs in the various "environmental" fields reflect a concern with linking the two traditions, and that is also true of the theoretical basis of research in this "new" field (Nietzel et al. 1977).

The issues that must be faced by environmental designers are no less difficult or really different from those that have confronted behavior modifiers. Three questions are illustrative. What kind of society do we want and how do decisions take place? Who controls the designers? How can the designer best train individuals to design their own environments?

The ever meaningful issues of "justice" and "rights" still will face the merging behaviorists-humanists; but earlier controversies will fade, and former opponents increasingly will find themselves on the same side of vexing issues. Nonetheless, there will be serious opposition to the emerging humanist-behaviorist-environmental orientation because of its threat to "authority" and "elitist expertise." That opposition will promote greater agreement between the behaviorist and the humanist on the basic issues. An evaluation of their birth roots indicates that both really came from the same family and thus share the same altruistic genes (Krasner 1978).

Can we now extrapolate from current and past developments into the not very distant future of the year 2000? Two contending scenarios are suggested.

Behavior modification will become the kind of social control that its opponents have warned against. We will live in an Orwellian society, one in which psychiatrists, psychologists, sociologists, lawyers, and politicians control almost all aspects of our lives through computers, conditioning, sensory deprivation, aversive conditioning, relaxation, and a systematic token economy based on scientific principles. We will all be under some control, mostly without our awareness or consent.

Environmental design will train individuals at all levels of society to plan environments such that everyone will feel in control of his or her destiny. Productivity will be pushed to its highest level by satisfied workers in a democratic society, where everyone will be a participant-observer, not too rich and certainly not poor, with national health insurance (including, of course, mental health) for everyone.

Which scenario is the most realistic? It all depends on who is making the forecast and within what theoretical/ideological/paradigmatic framework. Freedom is Control, or did Orwell say that?

REFERENCES

Atthowe, J. M., and L. Krasner. 1968. "Preliminary Report on the Application of Contingent Reinforcement Procedures (token economy) on a 'Chronic' Psychiatric Ward." *Journal of Abnormal Psychology* 73:37-43.

Bachrach, A. J., ed. 1962. *Experimental Foundations of Clinical Psychology.* New York: Basic Books.

Bandura, A. 1969. *Principles of Behavior Modification.* New York: Holt, Rinehart & Winston.

Crutchfield, R. S. 1963. "Independent Thought in a Conformist World." Pp. 75-92 in *Control of the Mind*, Part 2, edited by S. M. Farber and R.H.L. Wilson. New York: McGraw-Hill.

Eysenck, H. J. 1960. *Behavior Therapy and the Neuroses.* London: Pergamon.

Ferster, C. B. and S. A. Culbertson. 1982. *Behavior Principles.* Englewood Cliffs, NJ: Prentice-Hall.

Goldiamond, I. 1974. "Toward a Constructional Approach to Social Problems." *Behaviorism* 2:1-80.

Jones, M. C. 1924. "The Elimination of Children's Fears." *Journal of Experimental Psychology* 7:382-90.

Kantor, J. R. 1969. *The Scientific Evolution of Psychology.* Chicago: Principia.

Kazdin, A. E. 1977. *The Token Economy: A Review and Evaluation.* New York: Plenum.

Kazdin, A. E. 1978. *History of Behavior Modification.* Baltimore: University Park Press.

Krapfl, J. E. and E. A. Vargas, eds. 1977. *Behaviorism and Ethics.* Kalamazoo, MI: Behaviordelia.

Krasner, L. 1962a. "Behavior Control and Social Responsibility." *American Psychologist* 17:199-204.

Krasner, L. 1962b. "The Therapist as a Social Reinforcement Machine." Pp. 61-94 in *Research in Psychotherapy*, edited by H. H. Strupp and L. Luborsky. Washington, DC: American Psychological Association.

Krasner, L. 1965. "The Behavioral Scientist and Social Responsibility: No Place to Hide." *Journal of Social Issues* 21:9-30.

Krasner, L. 1971. "Behavior Therapy." Pp. 483-532 in *Annual Review of Psychology*, Vol. 22. Palo Alto, CA: Annual Reviews.

Krasner, L. 1978. "The Future and the Past in the Behaviorism-Humanism Dialogue." *American Psychologist* 33:799-804.

Krasner, L., ed. 1980. *Environmental Design and Human Behavior: A Psychology of the Individual in Society.* Elmsford, NY: Pergamon.

Krasner, L. and L. P. Ullmann, eds. 1965. *Research in Behavior Modification: New Developments and Implications.* New York: Holt, Rinehart & Winston.

Krasner, L. and L. P. Ullmann. 1973. *Behavior Influence and Personality: The Social Matrix of Human Action.* New York: Holt, Rinehart & Winston.

Kuhn, T. S. 1962, 1970. *The Structure of Scientific Revolutions.* Chicago: University of Chicago Press.

Kurtz, P. 1969. "What is Humanism?" Pp. 37-53 in *Moral Problems in Contemporary Society*, edited by P. Kurtz. Englewood Cliffs, NJ: Prentice-Hall.

London, P. 1969. *Behavior Control.* New York: Harper & Row.

Madsen, C. 1973. "Values Versus Techniques: An Analysis of Behavior Modification." *Phi Delta Kappan* 54:598-610.

Morris, W. ed. 1969. *The American Heritage Dictionary of the English Language.* Boston: Houghton Mifflin.

Mowrer, O. H. and W. M. Mowrer. 1938. "Enuresis–A Method For Its Study and Treatment." *American Journal of Orthopsychiatry* 8:436-59.

Nietzel, M. T., et al. 1977. *Behavioral Approaches to Community Psychology.* Elmsford, NY: Pergamon.

Pavlov, I. P. 1928. *Lectures on Conditioned Reflexes.* New York: International Publishers.

Skinner, B. F. 1938. *The Behavior of Organisms: An Experimental Analysis.* New York: Appleton-Century-Crofts.

Skinner, B. F. 1948. *Walden Two.* New York: Macmillan.

Skinner, B. F. 1971. *Beyond Freedom and Dignity.* New York: Knopf.

Stolz, S. S. 1978. *Ethical Issues in Behavior Modification.* San Francisco: Jossey-Bass.

Thorensen, C. E. 1973. "Behavioral Humanism." Pp. 385-421 in *Behavior Modification in Education,* edited by C. E. Thorensen. Chicago: University of Chicago Press.

Thorndike, E. L. 1931. *Human Learning.* New York: Century.

Ullmann, L. P. and L. Krasner, eds. 1965. *Case Studies in Behavior Modification.* New York: Holt, Rinehart & Winston.

Watson, J. B. and R. Rayner. 1920. "Conditioned Emotional Reactions." *Journal of Experimental Psychology* 3:1-14.

Watson, R. I. 1962. "The Experimental Tradition and Clinical Psychology." Pp. 3-23 in *Experimental Foundations of Clinical Psychology,* edited by A. J. Bachrach. New York: Basic Books.

Wexler, D. R. 1973. "Token and Taboo: Behavior Modification, Token Economies, and the Law." *California Law Review* 61:81-109.

Winkler, R. C. and L. Krasner. 1971. "The Contribution of Economics to Token Economies." Paper presented at the annual meeting of the Eastern Psychological Association. New York, April 15.

Wolpe, J. 1956. *Psychotherapy by Reciprocal Inhibition.* Stanford, CA: Stanford University Press.

PART III

Physical and Fiscal Matters

Social scientists are understandably concerned with *social* control, but that concern prompts them to ignore human control over plants, animals, and inanimate things. One need not be a Marxist to appreciate the possibility that the character of control over nonhuman objects (material technology and inanimate energy sources especially) in a society at least partially determines the character of social control in that society. That is the case if only because one can imagine a human being surviving without controlling others or being controlled, but survival without any control over nonhuman things (including the use of clothing or shelter) is another matter. Yet in some societies and certainly in the United States, the division of labor and large production organizations are such as to suggest that social control determines the character of control over nonhuman things. In any case, whatever the causal direction, social control and the control of nonhuman things appear so interrelated that a treatment of one without reference to the other is grossly unrealistic.

The interrelationship is perhaps one succinct way to describe what is commonly (and vaguely) referred to as "the economy." While economists are more concerned with monetary phenomena than with technology and energy use, any description of a society's economy would be incomplete without extensive references to human control over nonhuman things in that society. For that matter, at least one constituent argument of classical economic theory pertains to human control over human behavior. Stating that argument briefly, maximum production and consumption of goods or services are realized when control by the government or monopolies over the market is at a minimum. The argument has been debated for centuries. Critics of classical economic theory maintain that the theory is the antithesis of human justice, and some have gone so far as to claim that centralized control (of one kind or another) over the market is essential for higher levels of production and consumption. There is no real prospect for resolution of the debate, but the crucial point for present purposes is that *control* always has been and always will be the central notion in the debate.

The themes pursued by Richard Adams in "The Emergence of the Regulatory Society" (Chapter 6) reflect a much broader conception of control and social control than is common in the social sciences. Whereas most social scientists seemingly think of control largely in terms of the manipulation of human behavior, Adams stresses the point that control over material and nonhuman things is virtually the defining characteristic of all manner of occupations and industries. Moreover, he does not restrict the meaning of the term social control to the counteraction of deviance. To the contrary, he describes social control as such a pervasive activity that numerous occupations and industries in highly urbanized societies can be described as "regulatory," even though most of them have little to do with reactions to deviance in the conventional sense (i.e., Adams's notion of regulation is by no means limited to law enforcement, psychiatry, or socialization).

Adams presents evidence of a trend in several countries toward the predominance of regulatory occupations and industries. His research takes on added significance because it illustrates how the notion of control can be used to analyze sociocultural phenomena at the "macro" level, in this case structural features of countries. Central to that analysis is Adams's insistence that control and energy are virtually inseparable notions. In this case the argument is that the substitution of inanimate energy (e.g., petroleum) for human energy creates conditions necessary for and perhaps requires a shift in the labor force from the transformation of nonhuman things (as in mining or manufacturing) to regulatory occupations and industries. Viewed in that light, the future of social control depends on the future of human technology. Specifically, if the long trend of substituting inanimate energy for human energy continues, the scope of social control will expand even more.

Chapter 7, by Ivar Berg, takes on special significance because of the avowed determination of President Reagan to "deregulate" the American economy. The subject is alien to treatments of social control in sociology, where for some three decades the study of social control has focused largely on the counteraction of deviance.

Berg points out that the great debate between "free marketeers" and "interventionists" on economic policy is based on a dubious dichotomy: control or no control. The dichotomy is dubious because of the presumption that the economy either is controlled by governmental actions or it is uncontrolled. Yet corporations in the United States are so large and powerful that it is pointless to deny the possibility of *corporate control* of the economy. Viewed that way, deregulation does not mean that the economy will operate without controls; rather, private controls will replace public controls. Hence, Berg's argument is that the so-called deregulation of the American economy is bound to increase private controls over the economy. It is idle to equate the notion of a free economy with private controls. The latter is conducive to monopolistic practices and price rigging, to mention only two things, that make the economy anything but "free."

6

The Emergence of
the Regulatory Society

RICHARD N. ADAMS

Attempts to picture the future of human affairs are speculative both because of the uncertainty of future individual decisions and rapid changes in values and fortunes, and the unpredictability of conjunctions of events. The problem is exacerbated by whether or not the variables themselves retain a recognizable form. An approach that deals with variables that we know will be of significance simplifies our task because we can then focus merely on the values of the variables.

Energy Analysis of Social Structure

The approach used here conceives of all human activity in terms of being an expenditure of energy—involving both the energy of the human beings themselves and other forms and sources of energy that they may bring into play. Since energy is necessary to all human action, it is a process that will operate in the future and thus provides us with a continuing variable that we may further examine in terms of its changing qualities. Another virtue of energy as a central concept is that it accounts for widely differing phenomena within a single framework, allowing, at least initially, a basis for common measurement. In the present analysis, this capacity to handle a broad variety of activity is important because all human behavior affects social control directly or indirectly. Even direct

AUTHOR'S NOTE: Work on this chapter was initiated while the author was a Fellow at the Research School of Social Science, Australian National University, Canberra. Funds were provided by the University Research Institute, University of Texas at Austin for David Knowlton to develop the data on the United States, France, Sweden, Norway, and Denmark. I am indebted to Mr. Knowlton and the aforementioned institutions for their help.

manipulation of the environment—the extraction of ores or the care of livestock—will inevitably influence other human beings.

The present method is based on three analytical distinctions. We first differentiate human energy from nonhuman energy. Human energy includes all human behavior and activities. It is the focus of our concern as social scientists and as human beings, and we want to examine it in its roles both as a dependent and independent variable. Nonhuman energy includes all the energy forms that exist in the environment that human beings draw upon in the course of living. Both forms of energy are used by human beings in the course of living out their lives. The variables that we will use in the present analysis are based on differentiating the manner in which one form of energy affects another; the different ways allow us to distinguish what will be called "energy sectors." Both human energy and nonhuman energy are based in an energy sector. The research on which this chapter rests has thus far worked primarily with human energy, and our interest in social control makes that both useful and necessary. Data on the "human energy sectors" are taken from occupational, and occasionally industrial, tables of national censuses. Data on nonhuman energy are derived from various sources, but will be used in only some of the cases.

The second distinction is between energy that changes elements in the environment through doing *substantive work* on them, and energy that affects the environment as a *trigger*, merely acting to release or inhibit potential energy already poised to act. Substantive work actually transforms the materials of the environment from one form to another by changing conditions and thus changing the nature of the things with which we deal. The things on which work is done include both human beings and all the nonhuman elements of the environment that human societies modify and reshape. Again, both human and nonhuman energy are used in both kinds of activities. In all complex societies, triggers and substantive work are inherently differentiated into hierarchical components. For reasons inherent in the dynamics of such systems, the amount of energy expended on trigger activities must always remain considerably less than that expended on substantive work (Adams 1982).

The final major distinction is that since both trigger and substantive work affect other things, both human behavior and nonhuman behavior, it is possible to differentiate whether the object of these activities is primarily (1) the behavior of biochemical or sociopsychological status of human beings as autopoietic, i.e., self-regulative, processes; or (2) the energetic status of other things in the environment. The distinction here is more subtle than the two already discussed. The autopoietic status of society and human beings refers to the regulation and direction of their social behavior on the one hand, and the care and maintenance of the human

TABLE 6.1   Four Categories of Energy Sectors, based on Kinds of Work
and Things or Energetic Processes Affected

Things, or Principle Energetic Processes, Affected by the Work	*Kinds of Work in Terms of Their Effect on Other Elements*	
	Trigger	*Substantive*
Autopoietic status of human beings and the society	Regulative (REG)	Maintenance & Reproduction (MR)
Energetic status of nonhuman things	Communication Transportation & Storage (CTS)	Transformation (TR)

organisms on the other. The energetic status of "other things" refers to the fact that all physical things exist in specific loci and specific states of equilibrium, and that energy is expended on changing these loci, and changing those states of equilibrium in accord with human plans and errors. The interrelating of the second two major variables yields four categories of energy process, the "energy sectors" that are present in every society, and for which both human and nonhuman energy are expended (see Table 6.1).

The data we have prepared are drawn from seven countries.[1] The choice of countries is *not* a systematic sample. Indeed, various questions will be left open simply because the exercise is still in the exploratory stages, and we have good reason to assume that other countries may act in very different ways from those to be examined here. The countries are Australia, Denmark, France, Great Britain, Norway, Sweden, and the United States. They were examined because data was readily available. It is obvious that they are all "Western," "Northern European," or a derivative thereof, predominently "capitalist" through most of the historical period here treated, and "industrialized." These common factors allow us to propose certain generalizations and hypotheses, but it must be remembered that this is not a systematic sample, and all such propositions are exploratory, irrespective of the language used in their expression.

The basic energy sector activity is *maintenance and reproduction,* MR, and consists of the care and reproduction of the human organisms. This includes not only the obvious tasks of procreation, infant and child care, and medical attention, but it also includes the range of professional services having to do with feeding, housekeeping, and entertaining adults as well as children. Some individuals specialize professionally in these matters, but every individual has a primary concern with his or her own care and survival. In census data, self-care is usually recognized only in the case of those individuals who do not have some stated economically remunerative occupation. This includes retirees, infants, children (including school children), the sick and the lame, as well as all individuals for whom the society (all cases here are capitalist societies) fails to identify as "economically active." Thus, people who are classified primarily as housewives are included in MR.

Ideally this counting of human activity should be done in terms of hours per day and not bodies per census year. For the moment, however, we are dependent on the census data. It should be obvious that when we deal with percentages of the population in census occupation categories in both the MR and other categories, we are not saying that, in fact, that percentage of the total human energy is so dedicated, but that that percentage of the population is differentiated as working in a given category, albeit part time or full time.

The process of maintaining and reproducing requires a wide range of environmental, nonhuman elements. The extraction, fabrication and, in general, the energetic transformation of these components from one form to another is central to human survival. It includes not only the extraction of material and energy forms from the environment (e.g., mining and agriculture), but it also includes the long chain of processes such as manufacturing, molding and reshaping the mechanical, the chemical and subnuclear transformations by which these materials are converted into forms for their ultimate destruction, consumption or discarding by human beings. This collectivity of activities we here call *transformation* (TR) because it refers to the change of the energy forms from one state to another such that there is some loss of energy by the material and an energy cost in the work of achieving the later state of the product. MR is concerned with the transformation of human beings; TR is the transformation of nonhuman forms.

Taken together, MR and TR comprise the substantive work (in an energetic sense) done by a society. If everything was nicely and naturally integrated we would not need to concern ourselves with anything more. But obviously it is not merely a question of the flow of these energy forms. We must also concern ourselves with the mechanisms that facilitate and regulate that flow. These additional activities may be divided into two major categories: *communication, transportation and storage* (CTS), and *regulation* (REG).

Communication, transportation, and storage are necessary for bringing into conjunction the human and nonhuman forms in their various states, and are collectively referred to as CTS. This category is explicitly ambiguous. All three terms refer to activities that may be used in the context of any of the other sectors. Transportation and storage, however, are concerned with inhibiting the transformation of substantive energy, with keeping things in a given energetic state. Communication is energetically different since it is an attempt to maintain continuity of a *form* only, allowing it to reappear in a variety of substantively different materials or energy flows. Thus, while MR and TR are concerned with transforming energy, CTS is concerned with continuity, specifically a continuity necessary to effect triggers that release the energy that works in all sectors. CTS activities bring together the necessary energy forms in time and space to achieve a specific kind of transformation. This suggests a special affinity between the CTS and the REG sector. CTS activities, in effect, control subsequent energy transformations in both MR and TR, as well as in REG and CTS itself.

The diverse activities that go into the planning, decision making, record keeping, and manipulating of the various triggers that inhibit and release the flows of energy that comprise the society's substantive activities are called regulation (REG) activities. This regulation or control is an energetic process of utmost importance. In simple societies, much regulatory activity is carried on as an inextricable component of the TR, MR, and CTS activities. It can be analytically differentiated, but it would be a Gordian problem to quantify such difference. The regulative work of the headman in an autonomous, horticultural or gathering community, for instance, can be identified descriptively, but at best a crude estimate of man-hours is hardly a satisfactory measure. Much regulatory activity is carried out through rituals and broadly based social activities, in the recounting of myths and their implied rules for the conduct of younger members of the society. Where the performance of the adult is the lesson and guide to the young, much behavior indistinguishably pertains to a number of processes—regulatory, maintenance and reproductive and, in some instances, also transformation and transportation. In complex societies, however, where hierarchy and specialized function are essential parts of the organization, the regulative activities can be more easily differentiated and separated out for quantitative treatment.

Our approach is initially broad. "Social control" is generally taken to apply to any activity that inhibits or facilitates the direction, quality, or amount of activity of itself or other individuals. A difference between this and the more customary approach to "social control" is that control is first seen as any process whereby a given energetic activity results in affecting the direction, quality, or amount of some energetic activity. Thus it may apply to nonhuman activities that inhibit or amplify the course of other activities, both human and nonhuman; and it equally applies to human activities acting in these ways. The underlying framework here assumes that the human individual does not live in an inert world, but rather in one replete with dynamic processes with which human beings must cope. Other human beings are merely one among various classes of such processes. The common thread that may be found in all these events, human and nonhuman, is that they are energetic; they operate within the laws of energy. Thus we approach the problem of social control as a part of the general problem of the control by human beings of the energetic world.

The study of energy in human society has, especially in the recent concern with energy availability, generally been cast in terms of the problem of human control over commercial energy. The approach taken here is that human activity itself is one form of energy transformation. The question before us, therefore, concerns the way that one kind of energetic process controls another kind of energetic process. In this sense, a dam blocking the flow of a stream may be said to control the stream. However, in dealing with human beings, it is not the simple and direct use of force that is usually the concern of studies of control, but rather indirect actions, such as the threat of the use of force, that are usually implied by "social control." These indirect actions change a simple situation of two elements—the controller and the human object of control—into a situation of three parts: the controller, the human object, and the elements or components that are used by the controller to effect the control.

Gibbs's (1981) recent innovative approach to social control restricts the term "social control" to those situations in which this third element is another human being. Other individuals are brought into the situation, either actively or passively—sometimes unknowingly—as devices the controllers use to affect the person(s) they wish to control. Since the presence of the third party often implies no conscious action by that party, I do not find any reason for insisting that it must be "human." In a number of Gibbs's illustrative cases, the third parties alluded to could readily be replaced with inanimate objects or complex processes and the outcome would be the same. Therefore, the present approach follows the three element paradigm, but without the constriction that the implement must be human. Whereas "social control" for Gibbs means the control of human behavior through the media of society or social elements, here "social control" refers to the human attempts to regulate human behavior by whatever means.

Evolving Energy Sectors

Complex society is hierarchical society, and it differs from nonhierarchical societies by splitting into two specialized components. On the one hand, a certain few individuals specialize in regulating activities of other members of the society, while on the other hand, a large proportion specializes in doing work necessary for the substantive care and provisioning of the population. Over much of the history of human hierarchical society, the proportion of the population dedicated to the specialty of regulation probably fluctuated somewhere below five percent of the total population. The rest of the population worked on the care of the individual and the provisioning of individual organic needs. This care and provisioning required time being spent in the physical care (in both organic and psychological dimensions) of persons on the one hand (MR), and in the extraction from the environment of things that were then prepared or fabricated for individuals to use (TR) on the other. While there was an important differentiation of function by sex, especially in TR tasks that required going great distances from camp, in fact every one did both TR, MR, and CTS, as well as participating in regulatory processes.

The advent of plant and animal cultivation further differentiated activities by sex, as well as the beginning of a more pronounced specialization in the regulation. The now familiar predominance of men in public activities, and of women in domestic chores, increased. This developed as a part of the process whereby nonhuman energy forms came more under human control, and became devices that differentiated activities—on the basis of various criteria.

What had been a gradual development of technologies that allowed the use of more nonhuman energy in the second millenia A.D. began to intensify in the eighteenth century with the Industrial Revolution. Unfortunately, systematic national censuses did not begin to be taken until well into the nineteenth century, so we have no consistent information on occupational changes over this early period. Beginning in 1841, in Great Britain, and in 1860 in the United States, national censuses provide some insight into changes underway. Of the countries used here, only two provide a run of data for the nineteenth century. In the following we will explore the implications of the changes in the human energy sectors, and summarize with special attention to the question of regulation.

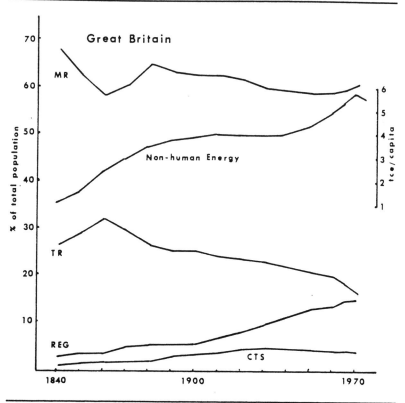

Figure 6.1:   Great Britain, 1841-1971, Human Energy Sectors as Percentage of Total Population and Nonhuman Energy in Tons of Coal Equivalent per Capita

Transformation Sector

The transformation sector comprises what is usually thought of as the productive activities of a society, and includes specifically the agricultural, mining, and manufacturing occupations. People thus occupied deal with the elements of the environment, energetic and material elements, both directly and as they are culturally molded. The course of cultural evolution has seen a gradual, if fluctuating, increase in technological capacity in dealing with the environment, and the Industrial Revolution specifically provided the basis for a rapid substitution of nonhuman fossil fuels for human energy in much substantive work. The cases of Great Britain and the United States (Figures 6.1 and 6.2) show that the increase of fossil fuels brought with it an initial increase in the proportion of the population

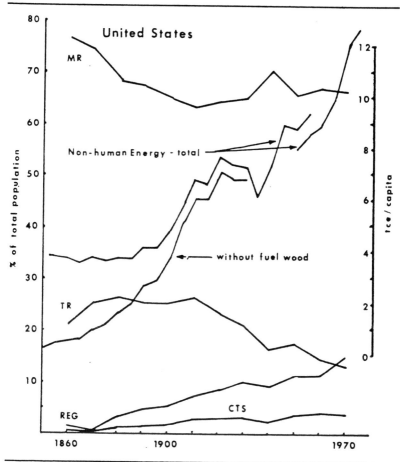

Figure 6.2:   United States, 1860-1970, Human Energy Sectors as Percentage of Total Population and Nonhuman Energy in Tons of Coal Equivalent per Capita, With and Without Fuel Wood

that was engaged in transformation activities. Unfortunately, the TR curves do not reach back far enough historically to enable us to see how they started, and at what level they started from. However, in both cases, as well as in that of Sweden and France (Figures 6.3 and 6.4), the increase turned, and a steady decline set in that continues today. The decline is obvious in the remaining cases as well (Figures 6.5, 6.6, and 6.7). In the case of Great Britain, the course of nonhuman energy and the TR curves show a remarkable mirror image, but things are not so neat in the United States and Australia. It is not possible here to explore the detailed

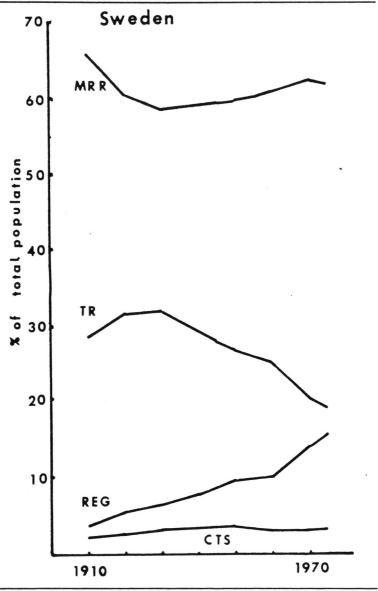

Figure 6.3:   Sweden, 1910-1975, Human Energy Sectors as Percentage of Total Population

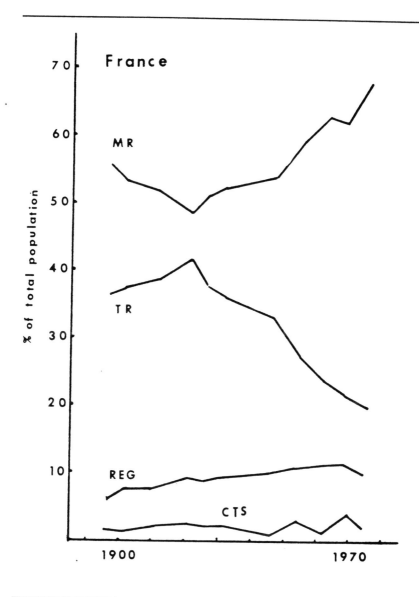

Figure 6.4: France, 1896-1975, Human Energy Sectors as Percentage of Total Population

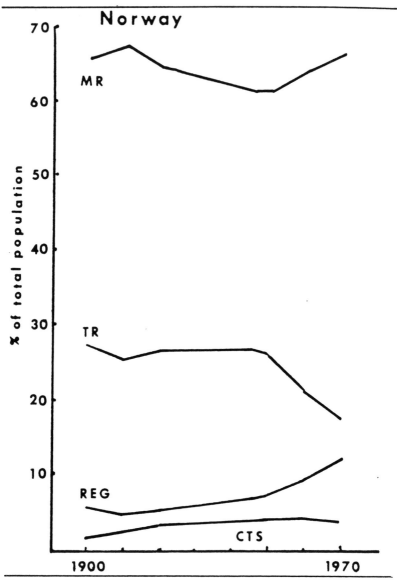

Figure 6.5:   Norway, 1900-1970, Human Energy Sectors as Percentage of Total
              Population

differences of the various cases, but there seem to be a number of factors
that need to be explored to determine precisely how the growth of
nonhuman energies actually displaced the human energy in transformation
activities. Perhaps one of the most important factors is what specific

nonhuman energy forms were being used. This is illustrated in the case of the United States where the availability of fuel wood was a windfall through much of the country's early history. The rise of the TR sector, however, seems to have been specifically influenced by the advent of fossil fuels. In a later period, there is considerable evidence that the shift to oil, natural gas, and nuclear fuels have their own distinctive effects (see Adams 1981).

The significance of the TR sector lies in the fact that it is the energy sector that is most directly affected by the introduction of nonhuman energy forms. It is precisely the work of such "energy slaves" that displaces the work of human beings. The displacement has led to the concern with "productivity," the increased production per capita laborer, a process that depended greatly on the successful displacement of human labor with nonhuman labor.

While the introduction of nonhuman energy necessarily was the result of decisions, the importance of the TR sector is that it was specifically affected by the growth of nonhuman energy. Such a direct effect presumably has been felt in a much less direct way in other sectors (as will be explored shortly). The larger effect of this displacement was to create a much larger and more complex range of problems of regulation for the society as a whole, thus requiring an increase of energy to be taken up by the REG sector. Also, in Great Britain, the United States, and Sweden, it appears as if the early growth of the TR sector drew most heavily from the maintenance and reproduction activities (MR). This phenomenon may provide a material basis for the argument that industrializing has produced an increased alienation of individuals from the ability to maintain a closer responsibility for the care of their fellows.

It is clear that the future decline of the TR sector must slow down and, at some point, level off. This suggests that the era of the Industrial Revolution might be looked upon as an *industrializing transition,* wherein nonhuman energy displaced human energy in the TR sector down to some minimum level. The question naturally arises as to what this level might be, and when it might be reached. Logically, the TR decline could be expected to continue so long as nonhuman energy is available to replace it. There are two structural circumstances that could stop the decline: (1) the nonhuman energy ceases to be available in sufficient quantities to continue the displacement; and (2) the society decides that individuals must be kept in TR activities, and the nonhuman energy is channeled so as not to replace individuals so occupied. Either of these, but more likely a combination, might occur. The first is increasingly recognized as a real threat to the more highly industrialized societies. The second is in fact in some

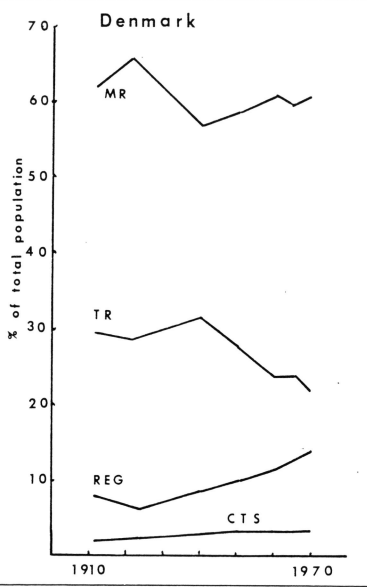

Figure 6.6:   Denmark, 1911-1970, Human Energy Sectors as Percentage of Total
Population

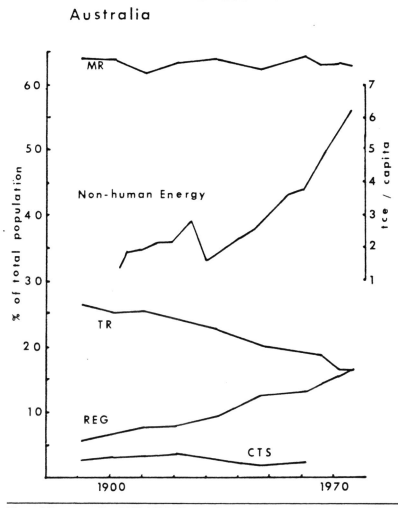

Figure 6.7:   Australia, 1891-1976, Human Energy Sectors as Percentage of Total
Population and Nonhuman Energy in Tons of Coal Equivalent per
Capita

measure an active policy today in China and some other less industrialized
nations.

The significance of the TR as a whole has been somewhat obscured by
the traditional economic labor classification of primary, secondary, and
tertiary sectors, since it is divided between the first two, a distinction that
was useful to mark more clearly the emergence of manufacturing industries. Industrialization, however, clearly has affected agriculture and
mining as much as manufacturing, and the displacement of labor in

agriculture that was so apparent in the earlier industrial phases was followed by the concomitant displacement in manufacturing.

Finally, the decline of the TR sector as a proportional part of the total society must not obscure the fact that all these societies have been demographically expanding in the course of this transition, and that absolute population expansion is as salient a factor in the total process as is the fact of the increase in nonhuman energy. It has been argued that the population expansion was made possible by the fact of displacement by nonhuman energy, and it may equally be argued that it is only the presence of that element that permits the society to continue to expand as a single society. In earlier eras of expansion, the maintenance of political hegemony over vast populations was, at best, highly vulnerable to a variety of destructive factors.

Regulatory Sector

Of more specific interest in the present context is what was happening to the other specialization of hierarchy—regulation. The data on which these figures are based include occupations that primarily have to do with government (including the military and police) and commerce. Especially in recent years, shifts in census practices have often obscured whether white-collar workers were specifically in one or the other of these sectors. But the reason for including both as phases of the REG sector is that commerce is a part of the whole market system, and the market is a primary center of decision making in these economies. Although it is often impossible to pinpoint the locus of a decision in terms of individuals or even social groups, the decision made by the market ultimately reflects, and is reflected, in decisions made by individuals engaged in the whole area of business. The reality of this is even more apparent when we deal with centralized economies where the government makes many of the decisions that are elsewhere left to the market operators.

Regulation of the society is evidently a multidimensional process. The defining issue in the present analysis is that the society regulates itself—for better or worse, and whether to its own further growth and expansion or to its own fragmentation and demise. Society is, in this respect, autopoietic, just as are living organisms. However, as is detailed elsewhere (Adams 1982), it is also neopoietic—that is, it also is concerned with decisions as to novel, potentially adaptive, behaviors to meet new problems.

Beginning again with the British and U.S. material, we see that for the earliest years for which we have data there is little apparent change in the percent of the population specializing in regulatory activities, but that a decade before the TR curve reaches its high point the REG curve begins to rise. While not perfectly smooth, the subsequent rise of the REG curve is much more constant than is the course of the TR curve, and thus suggests that it is not simply or directly responding to the effects of the increased use of nonhuman energy. While the British curve shows no reversal of the trend, the depression period in the United States does manifest a brief actual decline of perhaps two percent.

Data from other countries on this early period are similar in many respects. Denmark and Norway show the same early fluctuation, whereas Sweden and Australia manifest a fairly steady increase from the first data available. Most unusual in the entire set is the trajectory of the REG curve in France. Its course is continuingly irregular and, compared with all other cases, much higher in the earlier era, but generally very slow. Moreover, its maximum height is one of the lowest, being comparable only with that of Norway. The advent of the Labor party in Great Britain after World War II evidently is not reflected in any great change in the rate of the growth of the curve. Table 6.3 indicates that the rate of increase from before 1960 to after that date grew by only .04 percent. Only France shows a lower figure, and all other countries show increased rates of .2 to .4 percent. It is not possible to explore the various cases in detail here and, in general, will require the attention of historians of the individual countries.

There is considerably more to be said about the course of REG, but first we must review the material on the MR and CTS sectors.

Maintenance and Reproduction Sector

Since the successful reproduction of individuals is the core activity of any society, the MR sector holds a unique position with respect to the rest. Activities logically included here are not only those implicit in biological reproduction, but equally the entire course of maternal, infant and child care, socialization, and enculturation. It also includes the care of all members of the population—adults, including the elderly who are kept alive for reasons based both on utilitarian and nonutilitarian values, and indeed anyone for whom the society provides a niche. It is the society that defines who shall survive and expends energy to those ends. Also, every individual in the society spends considerable autopoietic energy in basal metabolism and doing things for his or her own benefit. The present analysis cannot adequately differentiate these activities since it would require calculations based minimally on person/hour units rather than person/year data such as we can obtain from the census. Consequently, for present purposes, we assume that everyone expends energy on the self, and we leave it out of our calculations. Equally, we cannot differentiate consistently in our data those individuals who are active in both MR activities for other people and in other categories of work (such as peasant or farm women who may be recorded in one place as housewives and in another as farm workers). Indeed, experience in the present analysis suggests that the relative amount of serious attention given to this sector of the society is appallingly slight, especially in view of its central role.

In terms of the evolving structure of society, the TR and MR categories share a concern with the substantive work of transforming energy forms from one state to another—one with nonhuman forms, the other with human forms. The influx of nonhuman energy, however, differentiated these activities and affected most specifically the TR portion. Data from Great Britain, the United States, and Sweden suggest that the first expansion in TR directly displaced people from the MR sector. As TR began to decline, however, the decline of the MR sector also slowed, and in the emergent picture they split between the MR sector and the expanding REG sector. Thus the TR decline allowed the MR sector to recuperate on the one hand, and the steady growth of REG on the other. In this, the MR and REG together comprise the economist's "tertiary" or service sector.

While the various MR curves in Figures 6.1 through 6.7 give the impression of some fluctuation, they share a most important characteristic. Unlike all the other sectors, they show no consistent tendency to wax or wane. Two observations may be made here. First is that the MR serves, in a sense, as reservoir, a "reserve army," from which the other sectors may draw and contribute to as they grow and decline. Second, it appears that, except for France, the MR sector consistently shows a tendency to seek a level around or above 60 percent. (Remember, were we to deal with person/hours of human activity devoted to these various sectors, the MR percentage level would be much higher.) However, in the context of the present data we can view the presence of an apparent minimum—here 60 percent—with some interest. It does, after all, constitute what might be considered, in terms of the old "organic" analogy, the level of social "basal metabolism" of the society. It is the process of living that is the *sine qua non* for the existence of the society. An examination of the figures gives the impression that the MR sector simply cannot be expected to go below some fundamental level without threatening the society itself. If we assume for the moment that we are dealing with a society that is not going to dissolve, then we might guess that it must maintain the MR sector above some minimum level. Staikov, in a comparison of time-budget studies, found that the portion of a 24-hour period dedicated to personal care—that is, toilet, eating, and sleeping—was 41.2 percent in Kazanlik, Bulgaria and in Jackson, Mississippi, and 45 percent in six French towns (1972:477). Obviously there is a basic amount of time that must be devoted to the care of the person. The question here is, how much of the society's time is spent in this manner?

Communication, Transportation, and Storage

It will be recalled that the CTS sector is proposed as sharing a common feature with the REG sector. Both act the role of triggers for the substantive transformation processes. Given this common feature, the shapes of the CTS curves are interesting. In general they begin very low—one to three percent—and after a slight and slow increase, they level off again at between three and five percent. If CTS activities play a regulatory role, they give no evidence of being patterned after the expanding REG curves. The reason for this is not a lack of energy increase in CTS, but that the CTS position, with respect to REG, is parallel to that between MR and TR. In both TR and CTS, nonhuman energy plays a direct role in the amount and kind of human activity that takes place. In REG and MR, it is specifically human energy that is important. As in TR, the initial period of CTS shows an increase in personnel, reflecting the addition of people to work in the expanding fossil-fuel-based transport systems. However, this seems to reflect primarily the effect of coal as the principle form of nonhuman energy. Between 1930 and 1950 it tends to level off in all countries. This very likely reflects the displacement of coal by highly capital-intensive quality of oil and natural gas as nonhuman sources of energy.

It would require further research to delineate the precise trajectory of nonhuman energy increase in the CTS sector over the periods studied here. There is, however, relevant illustrative data to indicate that there is little question that the CTS has received a very disproportionate share of this new energy source.

In nineteenth-century Great Britain, coal provided the major nonhuman energy source, and it was increasingly used for a wide variety of activities. Between 1869 and 1913 the portion of the total coal production of Great Britain that was devoted to railways, coastal steamers, and ships' bunkers rose from 6.59 percent to 12.80 percent (Adams 1982: Table 3-2). Schurr and Netschert (1960:53) estimate, for the United States in 1870, that wood still comprised a major portion of the total fuel in use, and that 96 percent of it was used in domestic heating. Of the remainder used in mechanical energy, railroads and steamboats accounted for more than half. In the decade 1899-1909, while GNP and manufacturing increased 50 to 60 percent, the railway mileage increased by 222 percent (Schurr and Netschert 1960:69-70). Between 1885 and 1905, the total coal utilized in the United States increased from 106,234 to 365,653 thousand net tons, or 340 percent, but that used by railroads increased from 31,131 to 131,655, or 420 percent (1960:73). Cook (1976:314) reports that in 1972 transportation accounted for 27.4 percent of the total energy consumption in the United States, and that between 1950 and 1970 the use of energy by automobiles increased by 171 percent (Cook 1960:328), whereas the total energy budget had increased 55 percent (see Cook 1960: Figure 2). Automobiles, in turn, accounted for 48 percent of the total energy devoted to transportation in the United States in 1941 (Cook 1960:329). The role of transportation in the growth of commercial energy is obvious, even though the United States outstrips the rest of the world in the amount dedicated to private travel.

In both storage and communication, however, it is difficult to single out data that gives a reasonable idea of the amount of nonhuman energy used, but it is reasonable to suppose that it is very little compared with that used in transportation. Calculating energy costs of communication are especially complex since that field has combined a miniaturization of processing on the one hand with costly satellite and electronic installations and air transport on the other. For the present, it is sufficient to be aware that the CTS sector as a whole is a very large user of nonhuman energy.

The relationship between the REG and CTS sectors now takes on a somewhat different aspect since, unlike the CTS, there is little reason to think that there is a vast nonhuman energy increase in the REG sector. REG and CTS contrast and complement in that one has swollen with human energy and the other with non-human energy. While the CTS is central to regulatory activities, it would be misleading to suppose that it is not also important in the activities in the transformation and maintenance and reproduction sectors as well. The making and carrying out of decisions in the increasingly complex societies of today depend upon meeting deadlines, both in terms of personal encounters and in the arrival of goods and information at appointed times.

The Emergence of the Regulatory Society

The foregoing discussion contains a number of implicit projections into the future. The tendency of the MR sector to observe a minimum in these Western capitalist societies is one. To better explore this we need data from socialist and less industrialized societies, as well as a deeper probing of the overlap of activities among the sectors. The constancy of the CTS sector seems equally impressive, but is probably more contingent on the state of the flow of nonhuman energy into the society. Of specific interest to us now is the convergence of the REG and TR curves, for this suggests a major feature of change in the forthcoming societies. Table 6.2 summarizes the particulars on the convergence of these two curves. In the United States and Australia, the intersect has already occurred; for the rest, excluding France, it is projected from the figures to occur or to have occurred between 1975 and 1987. The level of the intersect is extraordinarily consistent between the various cases, ranging between the 14 and 17 percent levels. The number of years it took to accomplish this convergence is also remarkably consistent, if one leaves aside the 115-year span of Great Britain and the uncertain projection for France. From the last high point on the TR curve it is a matter of between 32 and 68 years for the remaining countries for which there are data.

. The obvious question is, What will be the future course of these two sectors? If it is the case that the MR sector will continue to fluctuate at something around or above 60 percent, and the CTS at between 3 and 5 percent, it leaves a 35 percent range to be occupied by the REG and TR sectors. At the last reading on most of these cases, the REG trajectory had already passed 15 percent. There is one indication of the future direction of the REG.

In the nineteenth century, for the three countries with at least a decade of data, the REG increase was consistently slow—.04 to .07 percent per year (see Table 6.3). For the first six decades of the twentieth century, this rises to between .10 and .13 percent per year, and between 1960 and 1970, it jumps to between .21 and .35 percent in all countries except Great Britain. The pattern is one of not only growth, but accelerating growth. A straightforward projection of annual increases of between .2 and .3 percent would bring the REG sector of most countries to a level of between 17 and 27 percent by the year 2000. There are two contradictory conditions affecting this. On the one side, the curve is increasing exponentially, not arithmetically. This would tend to bring the future levels higher and sooner. On the other side, however, we have already noted how the MR and CTS sectors together may only allow TR and REG a maximum of 35 percent. A simple arithmetic projection of the REG under three annual rates of growth is suggested in Table 6.4. These figures, aside from France, cluster between the 20 and 26 percent level. Considerable skepticism can be given these projections for the reasons already stated. However, the degree of accord may be suggestive that there is a consistent process under way—again, excepting France.

If history dealt separately with each of these countries, or with the set of Western industrialized countries, it might be argued that the TR would have to retain a relatively high activity, and therefore the REG would soon have to level off. However, the fact of the matter is that the Western

TABLE 6.2 Transformation–Regulation Sector Intersect and Convergence

| Country | TR Sector High Points | | | | TR–REG Intersect | | Years Elapsed from TR High to Intersect | |
| | 1st TR High | | 2nd TR High | | | | | |
	Date	Level[a]	Date	Level[a]	Date	Level[a]	1st High	2nd High
Australia	1891[b]	26.24[b]	1911	25.78	1975	16–	85[b]	65
Denmark	1911[b]	29.03[b]	1940	31.13	1986[c]	17–[c]	72[b]	43
France	1921	40.15	–	–	ca 2000[c]	14[c]	94	79
Great Britain	1861	32.68	–	–	1975[c]	16+[c]	115	–
Norway	1900[b]	27.12	1946	26.83	1978[c]	15–[c]	78[b]	32
Sweden	1930	32.04	–	–	1980[c]	17+[c]	50	–
United States	1880	26.58	1900	26.57	1967–1968	14	87–88	67–68

a. In percentages.
b. Date begins series, hence it is not known whether this is historically lowest or highest.
c. Projection estimates.

TABLE 6.3 Annual Percentage Increase in the Human Energy Regulatory Sector (REG) in Various Countries

Era	Country						
	Australia	Denmark	France	Great Britain	Norway	Sweden	United States
Nineteenth century	(1891–1901) .07		(1896–1901) .38	(1851–1901) .04			(1860–1900) .05
1900–1960	(1901–1961) .11	(1921–1960) .12	(1901–1954) .06	(1901–1961) .13	(1900–1960) .07	(1910–1960) .13	(1900–1960) .10
Post-1960s	(1961–1976) .21	(1960–1970) .27	(1962–1968) .04	(1961–1971) .16	(1960–1970) .28	(1960–1975) .35	(1960–1970) .34

TABLE 6.4   Arithmetic Projections of Regulatory Curves from *circa*
1960 to 2000 A. D., based on 1960—1970 Rates

Country	Annual Rate of Increase (1960–1970)	Percentage Increase from Previous Date until 2000	Percentage Level Reached by 2000
Australia (1961–1979)	.21	8.20	21.33
Denmark	.27	10.80	21.23
France (1962–1968)	.05	1.90	13.25
Great Britain (1961–1971)	.16	6.24	20.37
Norway	.28	11.20	20.16
Sweden	.35	14.00	25.13
United States	.34	13.60	25.21

nations exist in a world energy structure, and that a great deal of the TR
activity used by industrial countries is carried out in other countries where
the TR sectors of the national populations are still very high. By the same
token, many less industrialized countries consume manufactured goods
that are produced with large amounts of nonhuman energy in industrialized countries. It is, therefore, quite conceivable that the TRs in the
industrialized nations could descend to levels that would be immediately
lethal were those countries to be thrown back for survival on their own
productive systems; and that the TRs of less industrialized countries may
remain high indefinitely.

If we look for other factors influencing the growth of the REG sector,
we need also to look at the relations that each nation holds with other
members of the world system. Regulatory activities are by no means
restricted to the control of internal processes; they also involve coping
with other nations and seeking beneficial situations for oneself. Certainly
some portion of the REG sector growth has been a response to the affairs
of other nations. Perceived military threat and the transfer of technology
has yielded regulatory expansion in many places where it would not
otherwise have been likely to grow. To take a pathological example:
During the recent war, Vietnam saw an overwhelming REG expansion,
swollen by a sizable foreign component. The current growth of the
military among Middle Eastern nations similarly reflects a response more
to the neighboring world than to a lively internal expansive tendency. The

REG expansion, then, answers not merely other internal elements that are here considered, but also the condition of other particular nations.

The important fact to remember about the regulatory sector is that it is composed of elements that are already dependent on a hierarchical system in which the substantive work is done elsewhere. Given the alternatives, many, indeed possibly most, regulatory sector members would prefer to retain their controlling positions than be melded again with the substantive sectors. Given this, they seek to expand as a part of their own self-regulating and self-reproductive processes. When the only way of expanding is to move outside a nation's own boundaries, they will do so. Hence the example of the push to international exports in capitalist countries, or the export of troops by Cuba. The argument that exporting is a capitalist necessity is well based; however, it should be seen in the larger perspective of the need of REG sectors to expand their controls. The broader need applies as much to socialist nations as to capitalist ones. Both are responding to the fact of operating in a constraining world system of other nations and societies.

Concluding Note

Allowing for the exploratory nature of the approach, the present analysis suggests a number of things about the nature of the future. The Industrial Revolution and the "industrial society" here appear to be a transition from a low-energy world to a world where a few nations may achieve rather high energy levels coupled with high human regulatory sectors and low human transformational sectors, with the likelihood that many other nations may continue to manifest relatively high TR sectors. However, these industrial nations apparently are undergoing a change from a society dominated by a population dedicated to the transformation of nonhuman materials and energy, to one dominated by people dedicated to regulation.

Put in this way, it may sound particularly ominous and strange. And to be sure, seen from 1860 it might appear strange, indeed. However, much of this regulation is already with us, and it began with the rise of the REG sector a hundred or more years ago. Decisions are made for us by people on Madison Avenue, in Washington, and in the state capital, and by government regulators, courts, labor unions, businessmen, policemen, soldiers, and so on. The difference is that more and more of us are becoming part of the sector of the population that does this.

In structural terms, the question is open as to just how much of the society can fit into this category. Where and when it levels off seems to depend, in some part, on what happens to our choices about the uses of nonhuman energy, and the subsequent effects that these have on the sectors of the population directly affected by those changes. At the same time, the nature of the REG sector is clearly increasingly internationalized so that Soviet leaders can put pressure on Polish labor union members, the Israeli prime minister can pressure American congressmen, the Coca-Cola Bottling Company can exhort Chinese to "Drink *Coke!*," and the Guatemalan military can put American professors on their hit list. World society is hierarchized on an international scale, as well as within particular societies.

Social control, in terms of the people in the society who specialize in it, is expanding, and its expansion is the result of increasing nonhuman energy. The actual process is obviously extremely complex, and the materials presented here tap only one aspect. Nevertheless, they reemphasize the importance of the visions of Huxley, Orwell, and others, who have promised the emergence of a society dominated by social controls. The emphasis in earlier years on the apparent emergence of a "service" economy, or "self-service" economy, appears in the present light to place the emphasis on the wrong syllable. People in the regulatory sector (to which economists belong) may feel that they are providing a "service" to their fellow human beings. However, as Lenin observed, to understand imperialism, one should view it from the colonies; and to understand the impact of a dominant human regulatory sector, it should also be seen from the point of view of those who continue to work in the substantive tasks of energy transformation and of the care of human beings.

Finally, there continues to be the question of the dynamics behind this entire process—the continuing increase in the relative amount of nonhuman energy pouring into the world system. Evidently, the increase in the regulatory component of industrializing societies is not sufficiently directing itself to this fundamental process.

NOTE

1. The data used here have been extracted from the occupational tables or, in a few instances, from industrial tables of the various national censuses. In some cases, such as in the Scandinavian countries and France, the basic tables for the earlier years combine the two forms of definition. In working with these materials, one is constantly aware of the lack of consistent definition from one census to another, both within and between countries, and the likelihood that the categories being classified cannot carry precisely the same meaning. There are inevitable cases, such as the French data and occasional peculiarities elsewhere, that require individual analysis, not merely in the tables themselves, but in the concurrent history of the country. This has not been possible as yet in the present research, and so the results are presented here with these cautionary observations. Details of the method are dis-

cussed in my 1981 working paper. In spite of inherent uncertainties, however, I feel that the weight of the data is indicative of the major directions that are discussed in the chapter.

REFERENCES

Adams, Richard N. 1981. "Working Paper on Relation Between Human and Non-Human Energy in Complex Society." Manuscript.

Adams, Richard N. 1982. *Paradoxical Harvest: Energy and Explanation in British History.* New York: Cambridge University Press.

Adams, Richard N. (1982) "Society as Energy Structure." Manuscript in progress.

Cook, Earl. 1976. *Man, Energy, Society.* San Francisco: W. H. Freeman.

Gibbs, Jack. 1981. *Norms, Deviance, and Social Control: Conceptual Matters.* New York: Elsevier-North Holland.

Schurr, Sam H., and Bruce C. Netschert. 1960. *Energy in the American Economy, 1850-1975.* Baltimore: The Johns Hopkins University Press.

Staikov, Zahari. 1972. "Time-budgets and Technological Progress." Pp. 460-82. In *The Use of Time,* edited by Alexander Szalai. Paris: Mouton.

7

Social Control and the Economy
In Quest of Common Denominators

IVAR BERG

Nary a reader of this volume is unfamiliar with the hoary and still very lively debate over the needs for and efficacy of controls over private economic agents. Indeed, two of the debate's oldest living antagonists were canonized in a single convocation when Gunnar Myrdal and Frederick von Hayek were named co-winners of the hallowed Nobel Medal in Economics. Myrdal has been a dedicated spokesman for the very kind of public controls that von Hayek derisively termed the paving stones on "the road to serfdom." And when leaders of Third World nations, hungry for goods and services, met with President Reagan in Cancún, Mexico, they heard a rerun of his earlier message to the 1981 IMF-World Bank meeting: Planning has failed; try free private enterprise. Almost everyone knows it and almost nobody doubts it: To control or not to control, that is the question.

On one side of this debate, self-styled free marketers emphasize the benefits that will accrue to the citizenry by shifting from "public controls" of the economy to the free play of market forces. Their protagonists emphasize the need to compensate for numerous and gross "imperfections" in markets of all types.[1] Witnesses to these debates are urged to believe that nearly all economic issues can be joined in terms of only this one pair of alternatives. The logic that informs this paradigm of the economy is significantly flawed, however, by its two-valued character. Indeed the paradigm is worse than useless to any who seek to identify the control levers in society and the controllers, because it gainsays the innumerable controls of economic processes exercised by *private* agents. The paradigm, to put it in the language of social science model builders, is misspecified. It is akin to an analysis of the American family and the American economy in which only the occupational roles of husbands are considered.[2]

To be sure, corporations have regularly been subjected to critical scrutiny, but the term "control" rarely appears in reference to the behavior of private agents. Hobbes recognized their potential powers; but he characterized corporations in the seventeenth century as worms in the entrails of the body politic, a metaphor that reduces corporations to mere parasites. And Adam Smith contended in 1776 that when two men of commerce meet, they join in a subversive conspiracy against the public interest; but he paid little attention to the more overt and thus the essentially legitimate ways and means of private agents. And in the preface to *Das Kapital*, Marx predicated his forecast that capitalism would collapse on carefully specified assumptions about the growing concentration of ownership in private hands; his focus was not capitalists' motives but the imperatives of their roles in a changing economic structure. Marx was thus essentially alone among the earliest writers to focus specifically on the *controlling* roles of private decision makers in the capitalist economy, the collapse of which he perceived to be an emergent inevitability under "capitalist conditions."

Later, near the turn of the century in the United States, the anticompetitive urges of many corporate chiefs were condemned by populist trust-busters. Still later, in the era before World War II, the monopolistic and oligopolistic inclinations of corporate leaders were documented and deplored by staffers serving the Temporary National Economic Committee. Robert A. Brady and Franz Neuman each expressed concern about corporatism; and Berle and Means, in their classic treatment, documented "the separation of the ownership from control" over corporate assets (Berg and Zald 1978). Since most of these modern critics advocated public controls over private power, their work has been basic to the formulations of public interventions. Their work accordingly figures far more in debates over the pros and cons of *public* controls in the economy than in efforts to identify and understand the controls exercised by private economic agents.

When the details of the exercise of private controls over productive resources, people, capital, government agencies, political parties, real property, and markets *are* pursued these days, it is by a comparatively small cluster of scholars in the social sciences. Their findings may become the basis for proposals by legislators and officials in regulatory agencies for *public* controls of segments of the economy.[3] Attention thus shifts away from private controls, as such, to the design and promotion of public controls; and the latter, almost by legerdemain, become the only subject on the debate over "control of the economy."[4]

Because of its two-valued logic, the debate effectively offers students of social control the sanguinary choice of being "split by a false dichotomy" or being "impaled on the horns of a dilemma," the terms of which are inadequately specified. Whether we need more or less public control in a modern industrial economy is a deserving question, but the debate is not illuminating if we seek to understand the roles of controls *per se.* A broader conception of controls in the economy is needed to bring developments in the economy into a more encompassing sociologic-theoretic schema. Attempts targeted on the design of such a schema, meantime, can well be initially informed by a review of a number of contemporary developments that are likely to shape our economy before the century's end, and all reported in the press and on the television in recent months.

Specifically, the loci of controls in the U.S. economy during the 1980s will shift from more *democratic and public-bureaucratic* controls to what we may loosely term *plutocratic* and *private-bureaucratic controls.* We are moving not from "controls" to "deregulation" but from public to *private* control of the economy. The sapient orthodoxy suggests that the issues are the same as those debated since Adam Smith, but America's new leaders are opposed, they tell us, very clearly and insistently, not to private controls in the economy but to public controls. Our new leader's rhetoric ought to be taken at face value. We should accordingly revise the terms of the agenda in the debate over controls. A clearer understanding of social controls in the context of economic developments requires that the two subsets of a single system of economic controls, one public and the other private, be juxtaposed. Such a strategy is not exactly novel; it was anticipated in the work of Thurman Arnold (1938), Joseph Schumpeter (1942), and Karl Polanyi (1944); the strategy need only be reapplied in a discussion that focuses on current developments.

Large Organizations, Industry Structure, and Performance

Free marketers have long argued that American antitrust laws and related regulations have become obsolete because of (1) the social returns that flow from the economies of scale; (2) the growing importance of nonprice issues in many markets, given the alleged significance to purchasers of suppliers' services and suppliers' dependability; (3) the interchangeability of many products; and (4) the benign postures of many foreign governments toward American corporations' large, integrated corporate competitors abroad. However, the facts of industry concentration (through horizontal and vertical integration) support criticisms of antitrust legislation far less than the free marketers would have us believe.[5] We have already witnessed very considerable increases in the numbers of firms that have merged with or acquired other firms to form conglomerate economic entities. These conglomerates are far less vulnerable to attack than vertically or horizontally integrated corporations, though the net effect of these newer forms has unquestionably been to increase further the concentration of ownership of corporate assets in the economy overall, that is, to increase "aggregate concentration."[6] To put it differently, conglomeration does not contribute to the concentration ratios within identifiable *industry* groups, but it does lead to the concentration of ownership of corporate assets in fewer hands overall. Antitrust law focuses on industry concentration and on intra-industry competition, not on "aggregate concentration."

While there is room for considerable disagreement about whether substantial "monopolistic" or "oligopolistic profits," or unique "conglomeration profits" accrue to owners (Williamson 1980; Mueller 1980), there can be no doubt that with increases in the aggregate concentration of corporate wealth there accrues, at the very least, something like a proportionate increase in the potential socioeconomic power of fewer and fewer economic leaders. When we add the potential power of interlocked directorates (Pennings 1980; Berg and Zald 1980; Sonquist and Koenig 1975) and the "restructuring" of the finance sector,[7] it suggests Franz Neumann's *Behemoth*. This "large strong animal's" power may not be fully mobilized or used systematically in self-serving ways, but its capacities to act self-interestedly cannot be gainsaid (Berg and Zald 1980; Sonquist and Koenig 1975). Moreover, this concentration and the economic controls it affords to private agents will increase for several reasons.

Consider that a subcommittee of the House Judiciary Committee is preparing for early 1982 hearings on conglomerates' effects and, inevitably, the possible needs for regulation. The Senate Judiciary Committee held hearings on the subject in 1978 and a subcommittee of the House Committee on Small Business held hearings on conglomerates in 1980. One main issue in these hearings relates to the question of whether costly money becomes costlier and less productive (thus fueling inflation) when borrowed dollars are used to make acquisitions rather than investments in new plants and equipment. If so, the owners and managers of merged companies thus exercise important controls over the degree of inflation both directly (vis-à-vis credit) and indirectly (to the extent that new, efficient physical capital is not produced). At some point these hearings may very well generate proposals to develop new regulatory arrangements. If so, the development will be entirely in keeping with the terms of the familiar debate; but note that the concerns of political leaders and critics will have been sparked by the *de facto* regulatory roles of large corporate aggregates.

It is not in the least bit likely that the conglomeration waves will be rolled back. Consider, first, that there has not been, even prior to Mr. Reagan's tenure in the White House, a successful legal suit by third-party plaintiffs against would-be conglomerators in the post-World War II era, a fact reflecting the lack of clear guidelines for the courts in that matter (Ewing 1979).

Second, as the New York *Times* reported on October 16, 1981, the Reagan administration intends to reduce enforcement budgets. The Securities and Exchange Commission (SEC) reported, on that date, that "a proposed 12% cut in its budget would severely handicap its operations . . . it would have to drop 20% of its employees and close as many as six offices and sharply reduce its enforcement capacity."

Third, Mr. Reagan's SEC chief, John S. R. Shad, believes that there is "a net economic gain" in large mergers and in "reducing excessive registration, reporting and other regulatory burdens," and that "the SEC [under his leadership is] moving toward more self-regulation by the securities industry." After a news conference on July 13, according to the New York *Times,* Mr. Shad "gave his blessing to the recent waves of corporate mergers and takeovers."

In tandem with Mr. Shad, Mr. William F. Baxter, head of the Justice Department's antitrust division, has announced that "he will ignore . . . 'clear judicial precedent' from the Supreme Court that manufacturers cannot set the retailer's price." Describing such precedents as "rubbish," Mr. Baxter has also said that he will ignore equally clear Supreme Court rulings against mergers and other arrangements in the chain of production or distribution of a product.[8] Note how misleading the control/no control distinction is in this context: A *public* agent, charged with *publicly* given mandates and putatively constrained by legal precedents, simply determines to transfer social control functions from his bureaucracy to a relatively few large bureaucracies in the private realm. The term "private sector" thus becomes a euphemism for what quite evidently is or is becoming a political-jurisdictional realm. Thus, a vice president of AT&T and an assistant attorney general in the Department of Justice reached a consent decree in the landmark suit involving that corporation; the resolution was not reached by a judge within the framework of antitrust law. Indeed, the dismissal violated the standards set down in antitrust case law!

The transmutation of control functions, moreover, is not affected through a "legal-rational" process but by *ukase,* by fiat. Mr. Baxter's language usuage is revealing: A would-be antiregulator, the SEC chief really spoke to the New York *Times* on July 13 not of *eliminating* regulations, but of *"moving toward more self regulation . . . by industry."* There is no denial here of regulatory need; the dispute is openly acknowledged to be over the division of labor between duly constituted public authority holders and those over whom they have legal suzerainity. Mr. Baxter, by the way, identifies the mandate for his position in the results of the 1980 presidential elections. He made nothing in his press conference of the fact that Mr. Reagan's intentions to reassign social control machinery from public to private agents was positively endorsed by a scant 27 percent of the nation's eligible voters.

The New York *Times* noted that Mr. Shad announced on August 31, 1981, that "corporations hurt their image by disclosing too much unfavorable information" and that he "intends to limit the amount of such information required in SEC public reports." Mr. Shad, "according to some former and present SEC officials, could mark a fundamental shift in the agency's direction. They say he places less emphasis on its original legislative mandate as an independent regulatory agency intended to help protect investors and more emphasis on helping the Reagan administration's economic policies and on promoting the securities industry." Mr. Shad intends, the *Times* reported, to "facilitate the accumulation of capital by public [i.e., privately owned] corporations by removing regulations. . . . In addition to reducing corporate disclosure about outside accounting relationships [with accounting firms that provide their clients with consulting services at the same time that they audit them!] Mr. Shad wants to limit negative information that corporations disclose in the annual (10-K) report." Mr. Shad "said that some lawyers 'over comply' with SEC disclosure requirements and that what is needed is more 'balanced disclosures.' . . . One type of overcompliance mentioned by Mr. Shad was the listing of pending litigation against a company." What with a Republican majority in the U.S. Senate, it is unlikely that Senators Kennedy or Metzenbaum, two leading Senate Judiciary Committee critics of Mr. Shad's version of deregulation, will be able to reverse the course of coming events.

We note also that the chief of the Federal Trade Commission (FTC) is marching quite in step with the others to the "new federalism" drummer. Mr. Miller outlined a number of policy shifts for the FTC on October 26, 1981 in his first press conference since taking office. He informed reporters that he has "strong reservations about longstanding claims." Mr. Miller added that his agency should suspend "its controversial program seeking information from companies on profitability of various lines of business." The reports of the press conference were recorded in both the *Wall Street Journal* and the New York *Times* on October 27. Some readers may not know that for lack of precisely such information, the role of the market in the investment sphere is significantly reduced. Investors may better choose whether to diversify their equity holdings *or* to invest in a diversified conglomerate if they know how well conglomerates' subsidiaries are doing. Such knowledge is obscured in a conglomerate's consolidated financial reports, as it is in cases of vertical and horizontal integration. The issue is a most important one. Smaller firms can be severely hurt by inefficient competitors who survive because they benefit from subsidies allocated to them from profitable kin by a corporate parent's leaders.[9] These developments leave little room for the all too convenient idea, espoused by deregulators, that the market is the *opposite* of controls.

Finally, as the New York *Times* reported on October 10, 1981, the Reagan administration has developed a national indicators system "to be assured that it has the best and latest social, economic and demographic data at hand before it makes a move and the best data for monitoring the effects of its actions." The *Times* reporter pointed out, not a little sardonically, that "the agencies that provide these data are [now] busily eliminating or reducing the many censuses and surveys they collect in necessary response to budget cuts." According to the *Times,* Edmund J. Spar, president of Market Statistics Co., said he was "absolutely terrified" by the cutbacks. "These censuses are vital," Mr. Spar said, "to executives [who plot] sales and advertising strategies." Among threatened data, of interest to almost all groups: the FTC's quarterly financial reports, the source of data on corporate profits for the all-important national income accounts. The New York *Times'* caption for the story sums it up: "Data on Cuts Imperiled by Cuts in Data." The implications of this development for the effectiveness or onerousness of myriad mechanisms and instruments of social control are mind-boggling.

The Power to Tax is the Power to Deploy [10]

When we move on to evolving fiscal policies, we see additional signs of the shift from public controls to those of "plutocratic bureaucrats."

Consider, first, that "the overall tax system had drifted from progressive to proportional or perhaps even to slightly regressive [in the period 1950-1970]." That conclusion stems from what Reynolds and Smolensky (1977:92) allow is an imperfect but nonetheless well-designed, well-executed, and imaginative empirical study. The authors reached the conclusion only after taking account of "transfer payments" to lower-income citizens. The belief of many free marketers—that these payments have excessively democratizing effects on income distribution—received no support.

Changes in the tax regulations since the 1980 presidential election increased tax regressiveness, even if Mr. Reagan's economic plans for a resurgent economy succeed in all the particulars he has enumerated. This is so because the particular transfer payments that have slowed the regressive tendencies noted by Reynolds and Smolensky (1977) are among those direct outlays and tax expenditures (like federal student loan guarantee programs) that will be significantly reduced by the administration. The size of the openings in the much discussed "safety net" cannot be gauged at this writing.[11]

We need not wait very long, however, to identify the short-run beneficiaries of tax changes, nor to recognize that the demonstrably significant control functions of taxes cannot be concealed by calling them "incentives." And it is not at all unlikely, if more than just slightly ironic, that the short-run beneficiaries will be well represented in the ranks of self-styled deregulators. "Your taxes," they are telling their liberal critics, "are penalty-like controls, while our taxes are incentives. You offer work disincentives to low-income citizens, while we propose simply to encourage them to work. You control while we inspire. You accord welfare, while we stimulate private enterprise."

Right off, we know that there will be continuing advantages to those well-heeled economic units who traffic in existing physical capital, rental apartment buildings, and business enterprises. Tax reductions without commensurate declinations in federal outlays will force public borrowing in competition with private borrowing, thus driving up interest rates to levels that can be tolerated far more readily by larger, well-situated entities than by smaller operators in the economy. At the same time, the threat of needs for public borrowing, generated by deficits in the public accounts, can be used to justify selective cuts in public outlays, cuts in the form of savings from "decontrols." The uncut residuals, once again, are incentives, not controls, as in the case of tobacco acreage allocations.

Unless bipartisan opposition can be mounted against an entirely new tax expenditure, we will likely see an expansion in the ghost ownership of leasible plant and equipment. The regulations allow the actual user of a particular type of physical capital, if his business is unprofitable, to "sell" what amounts to the depreciation allowances (recently liberalized) on the equipment to profit-making corporations. Those corporations because of their profitability, are in need of these tax deductions.

In all these cases—mergers and acquisitions (both very much encouraged by new tax regulations; interest on loans is tax deductible and stock transfers are not taxed at all), high interest rates, and depreciation allowances—the free marketers do not assure us of job and income-producing investments in new plants and equipment. They are thus not planning for economic growth; rather, they are using the tax system's components as mechanisms for the redistribution of income, which, in plain language, is to say as mechanisms of control over opportunities, accesses, and benefits. Taxes and especially tax expenditures are to be used as mechanisms of control over income distribution. Even as older federal programs targeted on lower-income Americans have been terminated or their budgets reduced, corporate managers, through ghost ownership of depreciable capital, will be able to avoid tax payments costing the treasury department between $27 and $50 billion in the period 1982-1986. That amount is equal to one-third of the federal deficit projected by Republican leaders for 1983! Meanwhile, it is not unlikely that welfare mothers will be held responsible for mounting federal deficits and for driving up interest rates by their wanton ways.

The private returns to a relatively few in all this may or may not be matched by proportionate increases in the welfare of those larger numbers, who would assertedly be the recipients of benefits that "trickle down" from those with fresh incentives. The term "free enterprise," when used to conceal subsidy-like effects of tax schemes and tax expenditures (like depreciation allowances, and "off budget" loan guarantees to corporations), is at best a snare and, at worst, an exercise in delusion.

More pointedly, it is a question-begging exercise to say that uncollected taxes do not, after all, belong to the government or to the larger population of citizens. Investors, for example, have at least as great an interest in the machinery of military defense as those who have fears of would-be foreign conquerors. Perhaps they have an even greater interest in stopping the would-be conquerors who seek to take over nations in which American investors have well-developed economic structures and arrangements.

The point here is most assuredly not to finger a Marxist rosary, in Schumpeter's fine phrase, but to underscore the proposition that social control is as social control does, neither more nor less. Social control is not what self-styled libertarians do not like, and incentives are not less instruments of social control simply because they wear a different label. The wonderful exchanges among Alice, the March Hare, and the Mad Hatter come to mind. Alice is not the only victim of Mad Hatter's clever tergiversations:

"Then you should say what you mean," the March Hare went on.

"I do," Alice hastily replied; "at least I mean what I say—that's the same thing, you know."

"Not the same thing a bit!" said the Hatter.

"Why you might just as well say that 'I see what I eat' is the same thing as 'I eat what I see!' "

Corporate Controls and the Rights of Citizens

It is a well-established legal principle that employers have the unilateral right to discharge employees, subject only to contractual restrictions that have been stipulated in agreements between corporate employers and individual employees or between corporations and their employees' bargaining agents. Given that less than a quarter of employed Americans are direct parties to collective bargaining agreements, the principle can readily be translated into the proposition that the other three-quarters of employees are ultimately at the mercy of managers. It follows that the greater the employing firm's size and market position, and the looser the labor market, the greater is the unilateral capacity of the employer to deprive employees of civil rights and civil liberties.[12]

From my own current field research on the effects of conglomeration on collective bargaining, I can report that "industrial common law," a system of implicit and explicit bargaining at the local plant level and one praised in 1960 by the Supreme Court,[13] is giving way to what Weber called "legal-rational bureaucratic forms." Labor-management agreements in that expiring system were agreements more than contracts in the best legal sense of the latter term. They are now becoming contracts in every detailed legal sense. Both the bargaining over the documents and the relationships in the grievance processes set up therein have become extremely "legalistic"; and as lawyers from a subsidiary's parent firm deal with their peers from the national or international union, the scope of local managers', workers', and union leaders' initiatives has been significantly reduced. In consequence, shop-level conditions in the mainly large manufacturing firms are far less the constructions of the immediately affected parties and far more the "legal-rational" constructions of lawyers, *sine ira et studio.* Given the great likelihood that Mr. Reagan's National Labor Relations Board and his Department of Labor will follow the FTC's, the SEC's, and the Justice Department's leads, we will see more "public controls" give way to "private control" by corporate attorneys, who play union locals off against each other, especially in large corporations and in conglomerate firms.

Beyond the few American workers who are more or less protected by contractual guarantees and in labor-management agreements, 75 percent of all workers are without any assured ways of bending management's will. It is true that even some of our largest enterprises have heard the shrill sounds of "whistleblowers"—employees who have "gone public" against corporations for allegedly violating the law, for offending, abusing, or violating their clients, their employees, or both. But the most detailed analysis available of prototypic cases does not leave one sanguine about a lone employee's capacities to tame corporate power (Westin 1981). Indeed, even if one approves of allowing corporations wide margins of controls over their employees, one must confront the emerging literature on employee abuse. There we hear the lonely voices of heroic, mortified, and injured employees who tried unsuccessfully to caution their employers against miscreant, abusive, sickening, hazardous, and even horrendously dangerous practices or policies, before going public with their charges.

In Westin's recent volume (1981) on whistleblowers, ten victims of their whistleblowing virtues report instances in which they suffered persecution, humiliation, vilification, and discharges after peaceably and constructively trying to persuade their employers of highly problematic workplace practices, accounting methods, or product imperfections. One case involved an Eastern Airlines pilot who discovered a flaw in a new "automatic pilot" device during simulation exercises. It was subsequently installed and contributed directly to a crash in which 102 persons died. In each of the cases, the "whistleblowers" were vilified, ordered to obtain psychiatric care, frozen in their jobs, or fired. Even allowing for the somewhat one-sided reportage—a good deal of the reported evidence was given by aggrieved employees—the stories have considerable "face validity."

In a second publication, Rashke (1981) presents a detailed history of Karen Silkwood's mysterious death after she tried to stop the dangerously sloppy management of "hot," carcinogenic materials at the Kerr-McGee Company's plutonium plant, near Oklahoma City. She died in an auto crash on her way to a meeting with a New York *Times* reporter, under conditions and after a long series of frightening events that leave the reader persuaded that her "auto accident" was better managed than the company's legal obligations. Recent well-publicized announcements about the restricted future of such agencies as the Occupational Safety and Health Administration make future Karen Silkwoods unlikely. She at least had the force of laws behind her charges. The prospects of successful ventures of the type she mounted, after failing to persuade supervisors and middle managers (as in the ten cases reported by Westin), will diminish as the regulation of safety and health matters is left to private parties.

Conclusion

This brief excursion into the state of what Adolf Berle (1963) most helpfully called the "American Economic Republic" does not prove that we will be governed by plutocrats, an elite of wealthy people in operative control of the "Fortune 500." I have offered "for instances" that are suggestive; but a "for instance" is, nortoriously, not proof. The die does appear to be cast, however. And the issues identified here are most assuredly not new ones, a fact that points to the depth of the commitment of free marketers to renew an older social order. The self-styled deregulators, after all, assure us that they mean to repeal more than three-quarters of America's economic history.

Space permitting, it would have been possible to tack many more pages to the foregoing discussion. Those pages would provide a review of the drift toward public controls since the Pujo committee's investigation of the financial industry in 1912; the trustbuster's heydays; the old post-World War I investigations of the armaments industry; the TNEC explorations mentioned earlier; the New, the Fair, and other Deals; and the logic behind interventions by New Frontiersmen and Great Society Builders. It would also have been possible to explore the evidence concerning whether "the regulated" had come, gradually, by the 1970s, to "coopt" the public agencies that regulated them (Noll 1971).

A review of only contemporary developments must suffice for the present purpose. It is, after all, the president's intent to encourage the trends here adumbrated; it has not been the present author's intent to limn subtleties or to palpate, with the sensitive fingers of a trained surgeon, what some may conceive to be the lumps in the entrails of Hobbes's body politic. We are, after all, regularly encouraged by the president and his executive branch leaders to take them at their word. But they are now speaking less and less about the need to deregulate. More and more, they talk about self-regulation. More and more, they act in ways that will leave ever wider margins for initiatives by institutional investors and large corporations' leaders. These claims are made in forceful ways, with a good deal of rhetorical skill. But whether the economy and its control in 1984 and beyond will resemble the picture now painted by free marketers depends on unpredictable circumstances. At this writing, the president.is beginning to face opposition from both sides of the aisle. But whether or not our new leaders succeed in every initiative, those now in essential public control have made their intentions very clear, indeed. Readers will inevitably speculate, according to their own lights, about the character of the road these intentions pave. But we have our leaders' assurances and a good deal of manifest evidence that the show is on the road.

In place of the tripartite countervailing powers—big business, big labor, and big government—celebrated by John Kenneth Galbraith and other admirers of "pluralism" in the 1950s, we can discern a second stage in the development of Galbraith's "new industrial state." Given the long-range planning Galbraith sees as a necessity for effective, modern industrial growth, it is ironic that the most significant brake on his implied version of *1984* is the decidedly short-run targeting of the "incentives" embodied in new tax laws. Managers, meanwhile, stand to gain far more job security by sensibly managed mergers than by risky long-term investments in new physical plant, the amortizations of which (and thus the returns for which) are much longer-term in character (Amihud and Lev 1981).

Whether some of the leading beneficiaries of the New Federalism will be chary of supporting their White House benefactor, as in the case of the financial community, remains to be seen. The temptation on Wall Street to blame wasteful expenditures on welfare mothers for high federal expenditures and to seek still more incentives by further welfare cuts appears to know no bounds, even as the elements of a new system of controls are set in place.

A review of the science of economics conducted along the lines suggested here will persuade one that this science has never really focused on market and nonmarket systems for dealing with scarcity and distribution. The subject before the house of Adam Smith has *always* been that of controls, private versus public, however effectively the free marketers have managed to write the agenda for debates on public economic policy and to define the terms describing the agenda's items. To factor the controls to private economic agents out by a nominalist's wave of the hand is to limit discourse in ways that are not productive of clear thinking. Alice's discussion of the matter with Humpty Dumpty comes to mind:

> "When I use a word," Humpty Dumpty said, in a rather scornful tone, "it means just what I chose it to mean—neither more or less."
>
> "The question is," said Alice, "whether you *can* make words mean so many different things."
>
> "The question is," said Humpty Dumpty, "which is to be master—that's all."

That oft-quoted passage is apt in many contexts, but it is rarely mentioned, further, that Humpty Dumpty did back off, at least a little. He allowed that when he used words dispositively, "he always paid them extra." By Humpty Dumpty's logic, the partisans in debates over controls and deregulation owe these words a colossal sum. The debt began when self-annointed disciples of Adam Smith first misused the great moral professor's *Wealth of Nations* (Ginzberg 1934), and the rate of interest should be compounded annually.

Describing the issues in the conventional debate about economic well-being as involving public *and* private controls has an implication for the study of social control. That study would be better informed by focusing on the general case of controls in the economy than on the special case of the "public sector" as *the* control apparatus in an economy. To that end, a conceptualization of social control should not be limited to the "counteraction of deviance," which is really what the planners and regulators have in mind.

Consider, for example, that though their members may be more politically liberal than most of Mr. Reagan's business backers, the local unions of the United Automobile Workers Union are as much concerned with their local prerogatives vis-à-vis their union's international office as the president's corporate supporters are vis-à-vis our central government. A theory focused on businessmen's desires to be free of central direction will be more valuable if it extends to the demiurges of local unionists as well. Intramural arrangements in unions are part and parcel of control mechanisms in the economy. Hence, those arrangements ought not be treated in connection only with the pros and cons of "autocracy and union democracy," while treating the corporation/government complex as an entirely different case involving the pros and cons of "controls versus free enterprise."

The union-company comparison suggests that we consider controls in the economy—its parts and pieces—generically rather than those exclusively in the public sector. The distinction between public and private sectors of the economy is a progressively less illuminating one. Thus, federal auditors are literally resident in private corporations—from airframes manufacturers and shipyards to universities—that receive large grants and contracts from Uncle Sam. Privately owned corporations collect the bulk of our income taxes and report on our incomes; and corporations (and unions), acting as "fronts," have federal agents on their payrolls.

A number of public controls are thus shared with, delegated to, and otherwise effectuated by private agents. Private controls by industrial relations personnel and financial offices are jointly exercised with monitors from federal agencies. Questions included in our decennial censuses are prepared with help from social scientists, including those in the marketing departments of large corporations and trade associations. Scarcely an economist of stature in America's universities is not a consultant to one or another federal agency or congressional committee. And presidential commissions—on youth, aging, the family, and crime—are well populated by corporate leaders, full-time academics, and representatives of a wide array of private, nonprofit organizations.

The blurred quality of the lines between our main economic sectors helps remind us of the diminished utility of limiting our attention in discussions of the prerequisites for growth to the *relative* efficacy of public controls and private enterprise. Private airlines operate out of public airports to serve passengers who arrive in public buses or private taxis (the latter with publicly controlled medallions), that use public parkways. Steelmakers' sales are often facilitated by publicly accorded "trigger prices"; these are set by public leaders in response to competition from private overseas firms whose managers, in turn, enjoy public support from their home governments. Private banks have interim control over taxes deposited in them by private employers and are free to use them, in roll-over fashion, as part of their required reserve margins. Scientists in universities—some state, some private—collect royalties from licenses to patents on discoveries that emanate from publicly supported research. Federal granting and contracting agencies use peer reviewers from public and private universities to make controlling judgments about researchers' proposals. New York City's government is currently "selling" the depreciation allowances on its buses to a private profit-making syndicate in need of tax offsets. It was President Dwight Eisenhower, finally, who cautioned Americans about the most visible of the public/private partnerships, the so-called military-industrial complex.

Questions about efficacy might better be addressed in thoughtful studies of such "partnerships" of public and private controllers than in studies of "control/no control" differences. If we formulate questions about controls in the more comprehensive fashion, we can save ourselves the drains on our intellectual capital, incurred in accord with Humpty Dumpty's strictures, when we must "pay extra" to the word control.

NOTES

1. For a lucid statement on behalf of antiplanners about the strategic roles in economic growth of the balance between private and social returns in private investment decisions, see North (1974:19-20; 96-104). Planners, meanwhile, worry about private returns being too far above social returns, due to oligopolistic profits, to justify their antagonists' preferences for laissez-faire policies. If, in the meantime, this chapter is reasonably lucid, it is because of the considerable editorial advice accorded me by this book's editor!

2. We do, of course, often make decisions as if paid work is real work and as if a partner's homemaking activities belong in a different universe of discourse. School

teachers thus contribute to "human capital formation," while the mothers are, in current usage, only "parenting." By a different but not a bit less arbitrary logic, a college professor is a kind of social worker, who attends to smaller or larger groups of unemployed youths.

3. There are some exceptions, such as efforts to calculate the "external costs" of pollution incident to production in industries, where large corporation's coffers afford funds sufficient to check would-be "environmentalists."

4. We need not detain ourselves with the charge, often targeted on neo-Marxists, that an emphasis on private controls ends all too quickly in a "conspiracy theory." The question of whether a few large corporations have total, significant, or marginal powers through collaboration is one that deserves careful discussion; but space limitations precluded a treatment of the question. Conspiratorial or not, the degree of corporate power is not easily gauged. For a brief review see Berg and Zald (1978).

5. For necessarily complicated but revealing analyses, see Scherer (1980), Williamson (1980), and the chapters by contributors to Blair and Lanzillotti (1981). Note that the problematic data do not prove the pro-regulators right. I leave aside, in the present context, the matter of whether the social gains of integration (economies of scale, for example) are offset by social-political costs.

6. See Mueller (1980).

7. I refer here to the growing importance of large institutional investors, mergers of brokerage houses, the acquisitions of financial organizations by manufacturers and retailers, the growth of bank holding companies, and the entrance of banks into the brokerage business.

8. Senator Howard M. Metzenbaum, "Is William Baxter Anti-antitrust?" New York *Times,* October 18, 1981, p. 2F.

9. The "divorce" of investors in security markets from corporate controls is further assured by new tax regulations that permit the Ford Motor Company to collect $100 million from IBM by having IBM pay $1 billion for equipment purchased by Ford in 1981. In return, IBM, a profitable firm, can depreciate the equipment for tax purposes because it has earned profits that it seeks to offset. Ford's owners, whose company cannot use the depreciation allowances because of having been a profit loser in 1981, are thus subsidized, and the stringency of a test in the financial market is avoided. The details were described in the New York *Times,* 1981e.

10. With apologies to Justice John Marshall, who held that "the power to tax is the power to destroy," and to Justice Oliver Wendell Holmes who later held that "the power to tax is not the power to destroy while this Court sits." Many merger-bound managers, meantime, refer to conglomeration as "asset redeployment."

11. Mr. Reagan's supporters would quickly add that the allegedly positive effects of a program aimed at putting the unemployed back to work and at discouraging sloth will, perforce, take many years to achieve. With the apparent exception of Mr. Stockman, Mr. Reagan's team argues that all will be better off when the president's policies have done their work. Mr. Stockman's statements on the subject before Congressional Committees and to magazine reporters are not readily parsed.

12. There is, of course, a relatively smaller number of essentially service workers—key scientists, some successfully self-employed persons, "tenured" professors, and those in special labor markets—for whom demand is high even when the larger labor market is very loose. Managers are, themselves, increasingly vulnerable to

discharge and are among the service workers whose unemployment rates are rising faster than those for blue-collar workers. For details see J. Kuhn (1979: 105).

13. *United Steelworkers of America* v. *American Manufacturing et al.* (1960).

REFERENCES

Ahmihud, Yakov and Baruch Lev. 1981. "Risk Reduction as a Managerial Motive for Conglomerate Mergers." *Bell Journal of Economics* 12:605-17.

Arnold, Thurman W. 1938. *The Folklore of Capitalism.* New Haven, CT: Yale University Press.

Berg, Ivar and Mayer Zald. 1978. "Business and Society." *Annual Review of Sociology* 4:115-43.

Berle, Adolf A. 1963. *The American Economic Republic.* New York: Harcourt, Brace.

Blair, Roger D. and Robert F. Lanzillotti, eds. 1981. *The Conglomerate Corporation.* Cambridge, MA: Oelgeschlager, Gunn & Hain.

Ewing Ky P., Jr. 1979. "Merger Law: Whence it Came and Where it is Going." Remarks before the Westchester-Fairfield Corporate Counsel Association, Stanford, CT.

Galbraith, John Kenneth. 1956. *American Capitalism.* Boston: Houghton Mifflin.

Galbraith, John Kenneth. 1967. *The New Industrial State.* New York: New American Library.

Ginzberg, Eli. 1934. *The House of Adam Smith.* New York: Columbia University Press.

Kuhn, James W. 1979. "The Labor Force." P. 105 in *Inflation and National Survival,* edited by Clarence C. Walton. New York: Academy of Political Science and The American Council of Life Insurance.

Metzenbaum, Howard M. 1981. "Is William Baxter Anti-antitrust?" New York *Times,* October 18, 1981, p. 2F.

Mueller, D. C., ed. 1980. *The Determinants and Effects of Mergers.* Cambridge, MA: Oelgeschlager, Gunn & Hain.

Noll, Roger G. 1971. *Reforming Regulation: Studies in the Regulation of Economic Activity.* Washington, DC: Brookings.

North, Douglas C. 1974. *Growth & Welfare in the American Past.* Englewood Cliffs, NJ: Prentice-Hall.

Pennings, J. M. 1980. *Interlocking Directorates.* San Francisco: Jossey-Bass.

Polanyi, Karl. 1944. *The Great Transformation: The Political and Economic Origins of Our Time.* New York: Rinehart.

Rashke, Richard. 1981. *The Killing of Karen Silkwood.* Boston: Houghton-Mifflin.

Reynolds, Morgan and Eugene Smolensky. 1977. *Public Expenditures, Taxes and the Distribution of Income.* New York: Academic.

Scherer, F. M. 1980. *Industrial Market Structure and Economic Performance.* New York: Rand-McNally.

Schumpeter, Joseph A. 1942. *Capitalism, Socialism and Democracy.* New York: Harper.

Sonquist, John A. and Thomas Koenig. 1975. "Interlocking Directorates in the Top U.S. Corporations." Pp. 185-195 in *New Directions in Power Structure Research* (Special Issue of *The Insurgent Sociologist*, Vol. 5, Issue 3), edited by William Domhoff.

United Steelworkers v. American Manufacturing Co., 363 U.S. 564 (1960).

United Steelworkers of America v. Warrior and Gulf Naviation Co., 363 U.S. 574 (1960).

United Steelworkers of America v. Enterprise Wheel and Car Corp., 363 U.S. 593 (1960).

Westin, Alan F. 1981. *Whistleblowing, Loyalty and Dissent in the Corporation.* New York: McGraw-Hill.

Williamson, Oliver E. 1980. "Commentary." Pp. 78-88 in *The Economics of Firm Size, Market Structure and Social Performance*, edited by John Siegfried. Proceedings of a Conference sponsored by the Bureau of Economics, Federal Trade Commission, July, 1980.

PART IV

Control and Other Major Institutions

As suggested in the Introduction to Part II, one alternative to the counteraction-of-deviance conception of social control is the earlier "institutional" focus of E. A. Ross, in which particular institutions are treated as the primary loci of social control. That focus does little to clarify the notion of social control, but it can be construed as implying that certain institutions are more strategic in social control than others. Such identification is also implied by the designation in Part II of government, law, and behavior modification as special subjects.

The identification of government and law as strategic institutions in social control may appear obvious, but there is an extensive literature in which sociologists question the efficacy of government and law as means of social control. For the disciples of W. G. Sumner (*Folkways*), laws are effective only if consistent with the *mores,* which is tantamount to dismissing the institution of law as superfluous. For still other sociologists, effective social control is found only at the "micro" level of social life, as in Richard T. LaPiere's claim (*Social Control*) that individuals are susceptible to control primarily because of their regard for status in small, intimate groups. LaPiere's position and Sumner's position are similar in that both imply this argument—government and law are too far removed from everyday social life to be effective means of social control. That argument would extend even to the experimental work by psychologists on behavior modification.

While the Sumners and LaPieres of sociology can be interpreted as asserting the primacy of *informal* social control, that term is all but meaningless, especially if taken as connoting something more than "extralegal." Thus, is television formal or informal social control? Granting that the distinction between legal and extralegal control is not clear-cut, it is far more defensible than the formal-informal distinction. Moreover, with few exceptions (e.g., B. Malinowski in *Crime and Custom in Savage Society* and E. Ehrlich in *Principles of the Sociology of Law*), social scientists assume a distinction between law or government and such institutions as the family, education, religion, science, art, and mass media. The suggestion is not that "extralegal" institutions are more important than law or government in social control. It is doubtful whether a defensible judgment about such relative importance can be made for even one particular society, let alone generalized. Nonetheless, whatever one's conception of social control may be, it is inconceivable that extralegal institutions are irrelevant. That is all the more the case since (contrary to the Ross tradition) the question is not just whether institutions contribute to social control but also how social control is exercised within and over institutions.

Considering all societies—past or present, nonliterate or literate—no institution rivals the family as a locus of social control, and that is the case whether or not socialization is construed as the counteraction of deviance. Hence, in speculating about the future of social control, one of the central questions is this: What does the future hold for the family as an institution? That question is pursued in Chapter 8 by Rose Laub Coser.

While granting that the long run trend points to further diminution of "patriarchal" control in the family context and a shift in control from the family to other institutions (e.g., formal education), Coser argues that the family continues to play a major role in social control. Moreover, despite a rising rate of marital disruption, there is no basis for anticipating the disappearance of the family or marriage.

Orwell's arming Big Brother (*1984*) with an awsome communication technology is one reason why critics of television depict it as a dangerous instrument of social control. Yet the effectiveness of television in the manipulation of behavior and concomitant dangers are subjects of intense debate among behavioral scientists and social critics. The immediate question is the size of the audience and the relative dominance of television among mass media, for television cannot be an effective or particularly dangerous instrument of social control if it has a small audience and does not dominate the mass media. That question is treated at length by George Comstock in Chapter 9. A lengthy treatment is necessary because the question is more complex than it appears. For one thing, there are several facets of audience size, such as the number of viewers and amount of viewing time. "Who views what" is no less relevant, as it is one thing for, say, children to watch cartoon shows but another for adults to watch a debate between political opponents.

Comstock is rightly cautious in his conclusions about the *present* effectiveness and dangers of television as an instrument of social control.

Nonetheless, his survey clearly suggests a real *potential* for effective and dangerous manipulations of behavior through television. In several countries the number of viewers and the average amount of viewing time are truly staggering, and other forms of mass media simply do not compete effectively with television. So it is not surprising that television has altered all manner of human activities (e.g., reduced attendance at social gatherings outside the home). But the impact of television on several types of behaviors, such as aggression and voting, remains debatable; and the assessment of its impact is very difficult. Most importantly, research on the impact of contemporary television rarely confronts some questions that would be crucial in the study of television as an instrument of social control. Consider two examples. First, to what extent can the use of television to control behavior be concealed? And, second, to what extent is television's effectiveness contingent on ignorance of the audience that they are objects of attempted control?

As long as social scientists are preoccupied with explaining social order, they will not be attracted to a conceptualization of social control as the intentional manipulation of human behavior. The implicit argument is that such a complex and inclusive phenomenon as social order cannot be created and maintained by conscious and deliberate actions alone. Tacit acceptance of that argument prompts social scientists (sociologists and anthropologists in particular) to view institutions and perhaps even "culture" as the sources of social control. Such a view is advanced by Diana Crane in Chapter 10.

Although Crane is primarily concerned with religion, science, art, and the mass media as institutions and as loci of social control, she treats cultural differentiation and cultural integration as the larger concerns. The immediate question in that connection is this: How can cultural integration coexist with cultural differentiation? The question has implications for social control if it is assumed that normative consensus (or shared values) is the primary basis of "regulation" in human society. Since increases in cultural differentiation scarcely promote normative consensus, it appears that social control is bound to decline. Stating the matter in another way, once institutions no longer support the same set of *societal* norms and values, their social control function at that level is altered. However, increasing cultural differentiation does not make control through mass media more inevitable or feasible. As Crane points out, the proliferation of tastes and interests (concomitant with increasing cultural differentiation) may make it more difficult for television or any mass medium to attract a truly large audience.

8

The American Family
Changing Patterns of Social Control

ROSE LAUB COSER

In 1978, one Greta Rideout sued her husband John for first-degree rape. John Rideout was the first man prosecuted on such a charge while living with wife. He could have gotten twenty years. He was lucky: He was acquitted by jury trial on December 27 that year; the couple reconciled, and then divorced. Around the same time, there were several suits brought by adolescent children against their parents for failure to send them to college, some of which ended with a court order to the parents to make such education available to their offspring.

Are such events indicators of the demise of the American family, or loss of control over its members? Where husbands lose their traditional conjugal rights over their wives, where children challenge their parents' authority in public, the sanctity of the family seems to be seriously threatened. While the sanctity—the notion that nothing can be changed—may be threatened, I believe that the family as an institution will continue to exist even though individual families may break up and reconstitute themselves in different forms, or family living may be redefined.

Agents of Social Control

The authority of the husband over the wife and the authority of parents over the children for the sake of their socialization would seem to be the main issues involved in what is perceived to be the threat to the American family. I shall argue that relations between spouses and the socialization of children have been under some degree of government or community control in the past; and that what is being threatened today is the patriarchal family, not the family as such, if by family we understand a group that includes at least one adult and children where adults are responsible for the well-being of the children and of each other, as well as for the children's growth and development.

One can easily be carried away to exaggerate the magnitude of the above events by recalling nostalgically that in the seventeénth century in the Puritan family, which "is considered by social scientists to provide a basic model from which the modern American family developed" (Farber 1972:1), male dominance was unquestioned. What is not being remembered is that in Puritan law a husband could not strike his wife, nor "could he command her to do anything contrary to the laws of God," laws that were explicitly defined in the civil code (Morgan 1966:45; Farber 1972:4).

As to the children's right to expect their parents to provide for their education, this also was established as early as 1648 in Massachusetts, when selectmen ordered to enforce the law for training children and servants within the family. Bremner et al. (1970:40) quote from Laws and Liberties of Massachusetts (Farrand 1929:11):

> Forasmuch as the good education of children is of Singular behoof and benefit to any commonwealth, and whereas many parents and masters are too indulgent and negligent of their duty in that kind: It is therefore ordered that the selectmen of every town, in the several precincts and quarters where they dwell, shall have a vigilant eye over their brethren and neighbors to see, first, that none of them shall suffer so much barbarism in any of their families as not to endeavor to teach by themselves, or others, their children and apprentices so much learning as may enable them perfectly to read the English tongue and knowledge of the capital laws, upon penalty of twenty shillings for each neglect therein.

In no society and at no time is the upbringing of children left to the parents alone. To be sure, parents are usually entrusted with training and disciplining their children, but these remain matters of concern for the community at large. Our own history abounds in examples. Massachusetts in 1660 held men proved to be fathers of bastards liable for the children's support, and in 1675, the Suffolk County Court (also in Massachusetts) removed children from unsuitable homes. Virginia, between 1661 and 1662, preserved orphans' estates for their education; and in 1682 Pennsylvania ruled that parents, masters and guardians, must see that their children are educated and trained—although the Crown disallowed the law (Bremner et al. 1970:817-818).

There has always been public interference in the families of the poor. It is assumed that their children are not well off—not such a wrong assumption since they are poor! In 1646, Massachusetts courts assumed responsibility for poor and idle children, and in 1672 Boston ordered poor families to bind out their children as servants. In 1699 North Carolina binded out poor orphans; and so on and so forth (Bremner, et al. 1970:818).

It will be objected that even though the community interferes through its governments and courts in the socialization of children, such socialization takes place within families, under the supervision of as well as protection by the parents. But in fact, patriarchal authority in the Puritan family is clearly delegated authority. "The major task of civil government was to oversee family heads in the performance of their duty." The Puritan leaders knew that "without the assistance of household heads, they would be unsuccessful in accomplishing their task of establishing a saintly community" (Farber, 1972:29). "Families [were recognized] as 'the root whence church and Commonwealth commeth' (Boston Sermons, January 14, 1671-1672); the 'foundation of all societies' (Samuel Hooker, *Righteousness Rained from Heaven*, 1677:25); and 'the Nurseries of All Societies' (Cotton Mather, *A Family Well-Ordered*, 1699:3). 'Well-Ordered Families,' Cotton Mather explained, 'naturally produce a good Order in other Societies' " (Morgan 1966:143-144).

With some modifications, modern America still holds to this principle, namely, that the family is responsible for the way the young grow up to assume their responsibilities as citizens, workers, and family members in turn. This is one of the main reasons why the family is being glorified. This is why there is malaise about events and facts such as the ones I mentioned, that would seem to indicate or predict the family's demise, which is seen as synonymous with the vanishing of paternal authority. We must add, however, that while among the Puritans, responsibility for all family government seemed to rest with the heads of the family, namely men, the culture of the nineteenth century saw the glorification of the mother as the guardian of the family and the home, and as its moral leader.

My first question is whether the training of children, that is, the teaching of skills such as it was understood by the Puritans and still is today, as well as the absorption of moral values, as understood in the seventeenth or the nineteenth century, or today, takes place mainly through the family. We know that the learning of skills and the internalization of values starts at about age six or seven. This is the age at which children start going to school, that is, leave the parental home for four to six hours a day. This is soon followed by Cub Scout/Brownie, YMCA/YWCA, and sports activities, and by four to five hours, on the average, in front of television. (Today children from preschool through sixth grade spend between 31 and 33 hours a week in front of television.) In other Western societies where television is, perhaps, not so popular, children are bogged down by much more homework than are children in this country. My point is that there are not many waking hours left in the day for parents to teach their children.

Lest it be objected that this is indeed part of the trouble, that television and youth activities are part of the culture that destroys the family, let me recall that children usually did not spend much time with their parents, regardless of public education. The poor, we have already seen, have always been subject to public scrutiny, and their children can be removed from home if authorities so decide. But how about the rich? In England, in our own time or rather at the height of the British Empire, children of the upper class were sent away to boarding school at the age of seven; the practice exists still today (and if not at seven, they are sent away at the age of twelve). In our own society, in the past children were sent into apprenticeship at an early age for the duration of six to twelve years. That is, they lived away from home, away from father *and* mother. In eighteenth-century Salem, "Voluntary apprentices normally served for seven years. Boys were apprenticed between ten and fourteen years of age and served until they were twenty-one. Girls served to age eighteen or until marriage. Compulsory apprentices served until they were twenty-one, regardless of their age at the time of indenture. Since some were placed in infancy, their term of service often far exceeded seven years" (Bremner et al. 1970:104).

If, as I am trying to show however briefly, socialization is hardly ever accomplished by the family mainly, then what is? Perhaps, indeed, the family has no exclusive function, and this alone gives rise to terror in those who want the family to be sacred. Although I hold nothing sacred, I believe that the family has some important functions and that, if these could not be served, there would be a serious threat to the fabric of society.

The Claim Structure

The one most important function of the family is, I submit, the mutual support, material but especially emotional, of its members, adults and children, a support of which children get the biggest share in their younger years at least. For this to be possible there has to be a network that is tied together through institutionalized rights and obligations. This network consists of the two families of orientation who are in reciprocal relation with the family of procreation in what I call a *claim structure*.[1] By this I mean that members of a family and kin have legitimate claims on one another. The institutionalization of claims, with its implicit obligation to live up to them, establishes a mutual system of social control not in the specific, restricted sense of policing behavior but in the broader sense of establishing on a firm basis a hierarchy of mutual services and allegiances.

There is, indeed, a hierarchy in the priority of who has a claim on whom. If a man or woman gets stuck at 2 a.m. with a flat tire, he/she calls the spouse. If the spouse is ill or absent, the father, or mother (if living) will be called; if they are not living or are absent for some reason, it will be a brother or sister or a brother-in-law or a sister-in-law. Should some married person whose spouse is present call a father or brother in an emergency, eyebrows will be raised: "What's the matter with John? or Mary?" That is, obligation to help is less determined by individual feelings, than by the knowledge that individual feelings ought to be mobilized into action under some, but not other, social conditions. Such mutual claims are part of a social structure of reciprocity, and reciprocity is the essential rationale for the foundation of families through marriage. Families are universal not because there always have been families in all societies—an empirical generalization—but because their existence, through marriage outside the family, firmly establishes a network of reciprocal rights and obligations, of services, and of alliances between the families that become joined through the marital selection of the young. This is easy to demonstrate in the case of primitive societies. Lévi-Strauss has done this in masterly fashion, establishing that exchange—of people, of services, and of goods—is the essence of all human society (Lévi-Strauss 1974).[2]

In the South Sea Islands, Margaret Mead's (1935:80-81) informer explained that he would not marry his own sister because then he would not have a brother-in-law to go hunting with. Our eighteenth-century Salem merchant could have given a similar reply: He needed a brother-in-law as a partner to go seafaring with. Alliances and exchanges were, of course, not limited to one's brother-in-law, but the economy of Salem at that time depended on the alliance of families and on reciprocal services with lateral kin on both sides for commerce, or for exchange of children as apprentices for having one's own children trained and socialized by a brother in return for services received from nieces and nephews (Farber 1972).

But what about our own society? Could it be that indeed the modern family has lost its *raison d'être*? Our economic and educational systems are independent from families. What is important is not only that the family has lost much of its functions of producing goods for sale or for consumption. More important from the sociological perspective is the fact that the family seems to have lost the need for entering into social relations with other families as families. Our individualism is not only an ethos; it is based on a way of life in which interdependence between family units becomes obsolescent *or so it would seem.*

Not so. True, in our differentiated society economic exchange takes place primarily in the market, only incidentally between some families. But exchange of services is still an essential part of the conditions for individual survival, and it takes place within an ordered claim structure. If there is one universal function of the family as an institution, namely of a group that becomes constituted through marriage between two unrelated individuals who will have offspring, it is the fact that the families of orientation previously unrelated now constitute a supportive network for the next generation of the newly wed and their forthcoming children. Together these families become part of a two-to-three-generational network of people who have claims on each other.

One important reason for worrying about the rising divorce rate is that divorce threatens the stability of the claim structure, that is, the institutionalization of rights and obligations among well-defined kin. In other respects it could be argued that the hue and cry about our ever-rising divorce rate is vastly exaggerated.

To be sure, children suffer from the break-up, though usually only temporarily (Wallerstein and Kelly 1980). But if we consider marital disruptions generally, it turns out that the "proportion of children affected by parental disruption during their childhood actually went down over the century and began to rise only in the last few years. Not until 1965 did divorce surpass death as a cause for the loss of a parent. . . . Until the last few years divorce rates did not rise fast enough to balance falling death rates, and thus the total number of marital disruptions affecting children did not increase" (Bane 1976:29-30).

Mary Jo Bane presents a remarkable table. She shows that at all ages the percentage of women living with their husband is the same in 1970 as it was in 1910. Today's higher divorce rate seems to be compensated for by a fall in the death rate (see Table 8.1).

As far as children are concerned, the lower fertility rate contributes its share to the decline in orphanhood, since in large families the latter-born, having older parents, are more likely to be orphaned. Moreover, children are no longer sent to orphanages or other institutions, and are rarely sent to relatives in the case of a deceased or departed spouse (although foster parents have become important socializers for many poor children). As Mary Jo Bane (1976) also argues, it seems to be better for children to live with at least one parent than to live in an orphanage. We do not know— there is no research I am aware of—whether children raised by one parent are better off than children raised by grandparents or aunts and uncles, but my guess is they are.

If we are interested in the ties between parents and children, the fact is that these are stronger than in the past: More children live with at least

TABLE 8.1   Ever-Married Women Living With Their Husbands
(in percentages)

Census Year	Age of women		
	45–49	*50–54*	*55–64*
1910	70.2	64.7	55.0
1940	68.4	64.0	54.9
1970	69.9	65.7	56.6

SOURCES: 1940 Census, *Differential Fertility 1940 and 1910,* Tables 13-16; 1970
Census, *Marital Status,* Table 1, in Bane (1976).

one parent; children are rarely sent away to boarding schools and they are
certainly not being bound to masters in apprenticeship, even though foster
parenting has become an important institution. Yet we must ask what
marriages that are disrupted through divorce do to the claim structure,
compared with marriages that are disrupted through the death of a spouse.

Death pulls kith and kin together; divorce pulls them apart. When a
spouse dies, and especially when children of preschool or school age are
left, grandparents or aunts or uncles—in that order of priority—will come
to help take care of small matters and large. When a spouse leaves, in
contrast, such support cannot be expected. On the contrary, it has been
observed that when a couple is about to split up, friends and relatives who
previously called regularly on the couple would now stay away (Wallerstein and Kelly 1980:35-54). It is felt to be a matter of tact not to bother
a family that seems to be in trouble. Children who would need more
attention than usual in these times of stress get less attention. Nor can
they easily turn to other relatives with a distress that is caused by in-family
troubles. Separation and divorce are considered private matters, and pri-
vacy should not be invaded. Death, in contrast, though recognized as a
private source of grief, is considered a public matter, as ceremonies and
patterned group behavior at such occasions testifies. Not only during and
immediately after the disruption is there a difference in the tone of
interaction. The difference continues, for the claims are not clear. Can the
divorced or deserted woman go to her mother to ask for help? Perhaps,
perhaps not. Suppose the mother says: "When you got married to that jerk
you claimed it's nobody's business but yours. So now don't come to
bother me." Will this mother be subject to sanctions by friends, neighbors,
and kin? Perhaps by some, not by others; it will all be a matter of personal

opinion, but surely the daughter has little claim. While in our culture we do not advocate the type of marriage in Thomas Mann's Buddenbrooks family, which was negotiated by the consul for his daughter Tony, as sociologists we must recognize that while Tony had to submit to her father's authority for her marriage, she could count on her father's support when the marriage went foul, when Grunlich absconded. The father had a claim on his daughter's obedience, and she in turn had a claim on his support (as well as, typically, on support from her oldest brother Thomas) when times went bad (Thomas Mann, 1901).

Let us get back to the modern family after divorce. The children have a claim on the father to be sure (of all divorced fathers who have children only one-third contribute to their support) usually for specified times in the week and the year (Chambers, 1979). But what about the paternal grandparents? We do not know. What about the father's sisters and brothers—will they still behave like aunts and uncles are expected to behave? Can mother call on them when in need? This probably depends on the personal relationships that developed before the divorce, but there is no socially recognized claim. Only recently has some research been begun to ascertain what happens to what Furstenberg calls "reconstituted families."[3] His early data indicate that there is mutual support by ex-kin, but that this is unpredictable. My question is not whether some friendships exist with an ex-spouse's relative, or whether some of them have a good or a bad character. In the case of widowhood or orphanhood also there is no guarantee against indecency or bad manners. My point is that there are no institutionalized patterned expectations according to which judgment can be made about people's behavior, and in the name of which pressure can be exercised, because only under such circumstances can there be social control to live up to obligations. Where there is no claim structure, there is little opportunity for informal social control.

It is noteworthy that we do not even have a nomenclature for naming people in the ex-kinship structure. Is an ex-husband's brother still a brother-in-law? And for reconstituted families the question arises: Who is the social father? The child has two social fathers (unless adopted by the stepfather), one who has legal authority, the other who has authority over the reconstituted household (Furstenberg 1981). This raises some questions about the second principle of universality of the family: the principle of legitimacy.

Social Placement, Emotional Capital, and Divorce

The principle of legitimacy states that every child shall have a father, that is, a social father (Malinowski 1930). This assures the social placement of the child. Some societies are, in their structure, more dependent than others on social placement through families (Coser and Coser 1972). The more ascriptive the society, the more important the principle of legitimacy. The more oriented toward rewarding people for individual achievement, the more flexible the injunction against illegitimacy. Our own society tends in this direction with the stigma against illegitimacy having lost much of its severity. Does this mean that the family will be obsolete if we indeed should achieve the perfect achievement-oriented, i.e., meritocratic society that our commitment to equality might indeed lead us to? If children make it "on their own" through their individual achievements in school and on the job, they do not need parents, or a social father, to supply them with the necessary capital for their social and economic successes. *Again, not so.* Although, or precisely because inheritance of land and capital is not as salient for an achievement-oriented society as for an ascription-oriented one, what is important is the passing on of what the French sociologist Pierre Bourdieu (1977:187 and *passim*) has called *cultural capital*—i.e., the connections, the familiarity with a world "that counts"—i.e., with universities, professions, museums, and theater, to mention just a few. This type of capital is acquired from parents and from the family's social position as defined by network, residence, and schooling patterns.

In addition to the cultural capital the family provides, there is, perhaps even more important, *the emotional capital* that is passed on in the secure environment of protecting and loving parents. In order to induce in their children the qualities necessary for individual achievement, parents must supply the children (at the same time as they supply each other) the emotional security and affective gratification necessary for character building. I want to argue that, far from not needing a family, the modern individual needs a family more than ever. The demands on modern individuals for dealing with people and events that are unfamiliar or only vaguely familiar are so rigorous that without a thorough psychological preparation in a collectivity such as the family, whose members are committed to mutual emotional support, they cannot make it. It is in mutual support that the claim structure asserts itself. If our families—as did families at all times—often lack what it takes for such accomplishment, this is precisely the point I am making: It accounts in no small measure for the psychological inadequacies that have been written about so much in regard to the modern individual.

The need for mutual support accounts, I believe, for the fact that Americans live in families more than any other people. While the divorce rate is the highest in the world, so is the marriage rate: 90 to 95 percent of all Americans marry. And the remarriage rate is high as well. Degler

(1980:458) reports that by 1970 only 3.6 percent of divorced men aged 35-44 and only 5.5 percent of divorced women of those ages had not remarried. Most divorced persons remarry within five years, and most stay married: Few Americans have more than two marriages. Table 8.2 shows that marriage is good for everybody but it is better for men than for women (Gove 1973).

Both men and women seem to suffer more from divorce than from widowhood, but women suffer less from divorce than men if mortality is an indicator of lack of well-being.

Divorce does not indicate that people do not want or cannot live in families; it may indicate that they have high demands. Indeed, with the function of the family reduced to that of a reciprocal support system within and between nuclear units, there is little reason to keep a family together if this function, which is not so easy to serve anyway, is not properly filled. Intolerable marriages are more intolerable if there are no compensatory functions for the family to serve. Where interdependence of marital partners is not based primarily on material support either in the form of financial provision or of maintaining the household, men have lost their utility (Goode 1980) if love and affection do not bind the partners together. This is a lot to ask, at the same time as it becomes an essential ingredient of family life. Nothing much is needed in life together other than love and affection if a partner is not needed for status or money. And this will, I believe, more and more be the pattern in American society with women working, able to support themselves and, for the middle class at least, to derive their own occupational status through their own individual achievement. This brings me to an important point, namely that of women's independent work and achievement.

Women's Independence and the Family

A specter is haunting the country: Women work! It seems that women's work is responsible for everything: high delinquency and crime rates, high divorce rates, change in sex mores, radical rebellions, and a new psychology, to believe Christopher Lasch (1979): narcissism. Women's work has stricken terror into the hearts of many American men *and* women. I submit that what is feared is not the fact that women work; it is the fact that women work for their own rewards and their own satisfaction, that they become independent of their husbands whose status and authority has traditionally been based on their occupational achievement and on being their families' providers. The status and authority of men have not only depended on what they did, but on the fact that, as Talcott Parsons

TABLE 8.2   Mortality Coefficients for All Causes* for Never Married,
___Widowed, and Divorced Whites, United States, 1960

| | Single Status | | |
Sex	Never Married	Widowed	Divorced
Male	1.81	2.33	2.96
Female	1.55	1.64	1.77

NOTE: Ratios produced by dividing the mortality rate of the unmarried by the
    mortality rate of the married.
SOURCE: Gove (1973).
*These include the following: suicide, homicide, major accident, pedestrian accident,
other accidents, cirhosis of the liver, tuberculosis, diabetes, leukemia, and aleukemia.

has pointed out, they had at home one person who did *not* achieve and
who was dependent on *them* (Parsons 1949; Parsons and Bales 1955). I
submit that the issue is not that of women working; the issue is that of
their independence and individual status.

Women always worked. Carl Degler (1980:363) gives a dramatic description of women's work in the seventeenth and eighteenth centuries:

Their tasks were not only diverse but almost endless. . . . One trav-
eler in 18th-century Carolina reported that "the ordinary women
take care of Cows, Hogs, and other small Cattle, make Butter and
Cheese, spin cotton and flax, help to sow and reap corn, wind silk
from the worms, gather Fruit and look after the House" [Spruill
1977:82]. Looking after the house . . . included not only cleaning
the physical interior but the washing and mending of the family's
clothes, preparing meals, under the handicaps of an open fireplace
and no running water, preserving various kinds of foods, making all
the soap, candles, and most of the medicines used by the family, as
well as the clothes for the family. . . . On top of all this, of course,
was the bearing and rearing of children. . . . Unlike the work of the
husband-farmer, women's work went on after dark and at an undi-
minished pace throughout the year.

There was, of course, a segregated division of labor and a clear-cut
authority structure in which women were subordinate to men. As long as
this remained the case, the authority and status structure was on a firm
basis. In our own days as well, as long as women do not threaten male
superiority it is all right for them to work in the home, or to make money
in ancillary fashion, to supplement family income. What has come to be

called the 59 percent solution—the fact that women make 59 cents for every dollar men make—is ingenious because it makes it possible for employers to obtain cheap labor with little danger of class conflict at the same time as it keeps women subordinate in the home, not only because women make less, but because their jobs are not worth keeping on a regular basis since they offer small monetary reward and little opportunity. So most women continue to be committed mainly to the family, making little money part of the time and part of the year. Thus, women can live up to their cultural mandate of caring for the family (Coser and Rokoff 1971).

For women to demand equal pay for equal work, to demand that they not be segregated in what is now a dual labor market (Giele 1978:104ff.; Coser 1980) conjures up an image of neglected children and broken families. What is at stake, I believe, is not the children[4] and not the family as a collective of adults and children, but the *patriarchal* family. Women's independent work, equally rewarded as the work of men, is seen as one of the last straws in the already dwindling haystack of male authority.

As to the children, the importance of child care is not to be sneered at although many "new women" (who usually do not yet have any children) try to ignore this in their defensiveness against what they perceive as coercive mothering. In reality, working mothers in general make satisfactory arrangements for their children. If they do not, it is likely to be the result of poverty, so that the fault lies with other difficulties. On the average, working mothers spend less time on child care than nonworking mothers, but the difference is small (Bane 1976:16). Nonworking mothers do not spend a great deal of time with their children either. A national study done in 1965 found that the average nonworking mother spends less than an hour-and-a-half on child care. Bane (1976:16-17) quotes a study of 1300 Syracuse families in 1967-1968 that showed that the average nonworking mother spent 66 minutes a day in physical care of *all* family members, and 48 minutes in other sorts of care on a typical weekday during the school year. This study also found that the correlations between the amount of time women spent on physical care of family members and whether or not they were employed were very small (Walker and Woods 1976). There is evidence that working mothers, especially in the middle class, try to make up for their working by setting aside time for exclusive attention to their children. They probably read more to their children and spend more time in planned activities with them than do nonworking mothers (Bane 1976:16-17). Lois Hoffman (1980) reports that studies have thus far not demonstrated adverse effects of quality day care for infants and young children. She quotes the studies of Hock (1979) and Cohen (1978) on the quality of mother-child interaction during the first year that showed no difference between working and nonworking mothers. Further, Hoffman (1980) quotes studies by Gold et al., of 4-year-olds whose mothers had worked since birth compared with 4-year-olds whose mothers had not worked. In two samples, both middle-class but one of English-speaking and one of French-speaking (Canadian) children, the working mothers' children showed better social adjustment (Gold and Andres 1978; Gold et al. 1979). Another study reported by Hoffman found that the mother's employment status was not related to the child's competence, but the most competent children had mothers who worked (Owen and Chase-Lansdale 1978).

As to the divorce rate, it is indeed at an all-time high. Today, 40 percent, and by the year 2000 this may increase to one out of two marriages, will end in divorce. In the eighties two out of five children will spend an average of five to six years with only one parent (Hetherington 1979). This increase can indeed be interpreted, I believe, to be a result of women's gains in independence. The historian Carl Degler (1980) believes that already in the nineteenth century the various reasons for divorce indicated that women were not willing to be the subordinates of old. He bolsters his argument by showing that two other issues that arose in the nineteenth century indicated a push toward women's independence: the reaction to abortions, and the reaction to women's demand for the vote.

Toward the latter part of the century, divorce became defined as a "problem," at about the same time as the crusade against abortions took place. Prior to the Civil war, there was no strong opposition to abortion, and when the opposition mounted, it was not the Catholic Church, or churches in general, that had the power to enforce antiabortion laws. The opposition came from physicians (Conrad and Schneider 1981:158-162), from women, from the public at large. According to Carl Degler (1980) it was an opposition against individualistic decision making by women. Of all the means for reducing fertility, abortion is the one that can be decided on and carried out by a woman alone. It does not need a husband's consent or even knowledge. Such independence was judged to "threaten woman-hood," i.e., the family. Still today, apart from religious opposition there is a strong element of anti-individualism as far as women are concerned, that informs the fight against the right to abortion.

Typical of the unwillingness to grant women their individuality was the opposition to giving women the right to vote. The fight for the vote lasted a good 70 years, at a time when women had much less trouble gaining legal rights and property rights. Just as in the case of abortion, many women opposed the vote for women, which was advocated in the name of the American ethos of individualism. The demands of the suffragists remained unheeded as long as they were made in terms of individual rights. It is only when the suffragists changed their tactics and pointed to their expertise and interests as mothers and wives on issues such as housing and welfare that the vote was finally granted to women. As long as they claimed that they wanted to make individual decisions their demands were considered subversive of the family (Degler 1980).

Similarly, today much of the outcry about the rising divorce rate, and about women's work, is due to what the public at large sees as indicators of women's individualism and independence.

Divorce, especially its rising incidence in the middle class, may well be related to the willingness of and opportunities for women to work outside the home. Not only does divorce become more frequent at a time when women are less willing to stay in an intolerable marriage if they are not dependent on their husbands' income; or when women expect from their husbands mainly love and affection and attention, since they do not depend much on the husband's money and status. Not only could divorce be related to the fact that women, being in the outside world where they can make contacts and enlarge their network, meet other men who remind them that alternatives are available. There is a deeper issue buried here: the issue of patriarchy. Women's financial and status independence threatens the status of their husbands, if the latter are made to feel "inferior." That such a threat is real is corroborated by the fact that divorce and especially separation rates have always been higher in the lower than in the upper classes. With few exceptions, poverty usually is associated with a high proportion of father-absent households, because if the husband cannot provide he loses status. This is true for blacks, for the nineteenth-century Irish, for the nineteenth-century Italians both in this country and in Italy, and for other poor immigrants. It seems that the American middle-class family up to now frequently has been held together by the dependence of wives. Our whole notion of masculinity rests on the image of the man who is a leader in his family. In Mirra Komarovsky's study *The Unemployed Man and His Family* (1971), it turned out that the authority of the father suffered in families where being the provider was his most important role.[5]

So far I have argued as if a woman's gainful employment is a spur to her independence, and a threat to a husband's traditional role. This may well be so in many cases. However, through gainful employment a woman contributes to the husband's independence as well. A man who wants to divorce his wife can make this decision more easily if he does not have to anticipate paying alimony for her. In addition, if he wants to divorce his wife because he is in love with another woman, he will make his decision more easily if the other woman has a well-paying job, for whether or not he pays alimony, he may have to pay for his children from his first marriage. In other words, divorce is not only easier for women when they are financially independent, but it is easier for men as well if the women in their lives make their own livelihood. *Mutis mutandum,* a divorcee who has a well-paying job will find it easier to remarry because she makes life easier for a prospective husband, especially if he also is divorced. For him, having to support two households is no small matter. It might be argued that in general a well-paying occupation for a woman today seems to become the functional equivalent of the old-time dowry. A woman with a good income raises the well-being and status of the family and contributes to the accumulation of cultural capital.

In summary, I do not think that the American family will go under. It will change, as it has changed before, perhaps more than it has changed before. What will be waning is the patriarchal family, which has already been weakened over the years. The transition may be difficult, new norms and values will probably develop not only in regard to the division of labor in childrearing and home management, but in regard to the claim structure before and after divorce, and in reconstituted families.

NOTES

1. The concept of "claim structure" was coined by Kathy Bartholomew-Dahlman of the State University of New York at Stony Brook.

2. A brilliant contribution to the theory of feminism is to be found in Gayle Rubin's reformulation of Lévi-Strauss's theory of social exchange (Rubin 1975).

3. Amazingly little research has been done on the social structure of families that have one or two divorced parents, the research being done now by Furstenberg (1981) on "reconstituted families" being a laudable exception. He and his associate find that the claim structure is "up for grabs," so to speak, i.e., that the distribution of rights and obligations has to be negotiated individually (Furstenberg and Spanier 1980).

4. There is a myth about a child-oriented American culture. Indeed, the well-being of children is used as an argument for claiming that mothers should not go out to work. However, a look at our suburban communities with their lack of bicycle paths, absence of playgrounds, and the ever-dwindling number of recreation halls such as the YMCA/YWCA should make us question our so-called child orientation.

5. Erik Grønseth (1970) has done extensive work analyzing the man's role as provider of the family, and showing that this role is an important source of family inequality.

REFERENCES

Bane, Mary Jo. 1976. *Here to Stay: American Families in the Twentieth Century.* New York: Basic Books.

Bourdieu, Pierre. 1977. *Outline of a Theory of Practice.* Cambridge, England: Cambridge University Press.

Bremner, Robert H., et al. 1970. *Children and Youth in America: A Documentary History,* Vol. 1:1600-1865. Cambridge, MA: Harvard University Press.

Chambers, David C. 1979. *Making Fathers Pay: The Enforcement of Child Support.* Chicago: University of Chicago Press.

Cohen, S. E. 1978. "Maternal Employment and Mother-Child Interaction." *Merrill-Palmer Quarterly* 24:189-97.

Conrad, Peter and Rochelle Kern. 1981. *The Sociology of Health and Illness: Critical Perspectives.* New York: St. Martin's.

Conrad, Peter and Joseph W. Schneider. 1981. "Professionalization, Monopoly, and the Structure of Medical Practice." Pp. 155-65 in Conrad and Kern (1981).

Coser, Rose Laub, ed. 1974. *The Family, Its Structures and Functions.* New York: St. Martin's.

Coser, Rose Laub. 1980. "Women and Work." *Dissent* 27:51-55.

Coser, Rose Laub and Gerald Rokoff. 1971. "Women in the Occupational World: Social Disruption and Conflict." *Social Problems* 18:535-54.

Coser, Rose Laub and Lewis A. Coser. 1972. "The Principle of Legitimacy and Its Patterned Infringement in Social Revolutions." Pp. 119-30 in Sussman and Cogswell (1972).

Degler, Carl N. 1980. *At Odds: Women and the Family in America From the Revolution to the Present.* New York: Oxford University Press.

Farber, Bernard. 1972. *Guardians of Virtue: Salem Families in 1800.* New York: Basic Books.

Farrand, Max, ed. 1929. *Laws and Liberties of Massachusetts.* Reprinted from the copy of the 1648 edition. Cambridge, Massachusetts.

Fogel, Robert, et al., eds. Forthcoming. *Aging, Stability and Change in the Family.* New York: Academic Press.

Furstenberg, Frank and Graham Spanier. 1980. "Marital Dissolution and Generational Ties." Paper read at the 33rd Annual Meeting of the Gerontological Society, San Diego.

Furstenberg, Frank. (Forthcoming). "Remarriage and Intergenerational Relations." In press in Fogel et al.

Giele, Janet Zollinger. 1978. *Women and the Future.* New York: Free Press.

Gold, D. and D. Andres. 1978. "Relations Between Maternal Employment and Development of Nursery School Children." *Canadian Journal of Behavioral Sciences* 10:116-29.

Gold, D. et al. 1979. "The Development of Francophone Nursery-School Children with Employed and Nonemployed Mothers." *Canadian Journal of Behavioral Sciences* 11:169-73.

Goode, William J. 1980. "Why Men Resist." *Dissent* 27:181-93.

Gove, Walter R. 1973. "Sex, Marital Status, and Mortality." *American Journal of Sociology* 79:45-67.

Grønseth, Erik. 1970. "The Dysfunctionality of the Husband Provider Role in Industrialized Societies." Paper for the VIIth World Congress of Sociology, mimeo.

Hetherington, E. Mavis. 1979. "Divorce: A Child's Perspective." *American Psychologist* 34:851-58.

Hock, E. 1979. "Working and Nonworking Mothers and Their Infants: A Comparative Study of Maternal Caregiving Characteristics and Infant Social Behavior." *Merrill-Palmer Quarterly* 26:79-101.

Hoffman, Lois Wladis. 1980. "Maternal Employment: 1979." *American Psychologist* 34:859-64.

Komarovsky, Mirra. 1971. *The Unemployed Man and His Family.* New York: Arno Press.

Lasch, Christopher. 1979. *The Culture of Narcissism*. New York: Norton.

Lévi-Strauss, Claude. 1974. "Reciprocity, the Essence of Social Life." Pp. 3-12 in R. L. Coser (1974).

Malinowski, Bronislaw. 1930. "Parenthood, the Basis of Social Structure." Pp. 113-68 in R. L. Coser (1974).

Mann, Thomas. 1901. *Buddenbrooks*. New York: Vintage.

Mead, Margaret. 1935. *Sex and Temperament in Three Different Societies*. New York: Morrow.

Morgan, Edmund S. 1966. *The Puritan Family*. New York: Harper.

Owen, M. T. and L. Chase-Lansdale. 1978. "Maternal Employment and Its Relationship to Peer Competence of Pre-schoolers." Unpublished manuscript, University of Michigan.

Parsons, Talcott. 1949. *Essays in Sociological Theory: Pure and Applied*. New York: Free Press.

Parsons, Talcott and Robert F. Bales. 1955. *Family, Socialization, and Interaction Process*. New York: Free Press.

Rubin, Gayle. 1975. "The Traffic in Women: Notes on the 'Political Economy' of Sex." In *Toward an Anthropology of Women*, edited by Rayna Rapp Reiter. New York: Monthly Review Press.

Spruill, Julia Cherry. 1977. *Women's Life and Work in the Southern Colonies*. New York: Norton.

Sussman, Marvin B. and Betty E. Cogswell. eds. 1972. *Cross-National Family Research*. Leiden, Netherlands: E. J. Brill.

Walker, Kathryn E. and Margaret E. Woods. 1976. *Time Use: A Measure of Household Production of Family Goods and Services*. Washington, DC: American Home Economics Association.

Wallerstein, Judith S. and Joan B. Kelly. 1980. *Surviving the Breakup: How Children and Parents Cope with Divorce*. New York: Basic Books.

9

Information Management and Mass Media
Menace or Myth?

GEORGE A. COMSTOCK

There has been no topic more central in the scholarly and empirical examination of the mass media than their role in social control. Every literature review, laboratory experiment, survey pertinent to the mass media, and all the theories from which they derive, bear witness to the questions raised by the media in the context of social control. It is hard to think of an exception. Yet, in regard to the media, "social control" is also a topic that has been treated far more often implicitly than explicitly, and the search for a "classic" or comprehensive statement is without reward. This is so despite the fact that every concept that has become prominent in the empirical study of the media—two-step flow, disinhibition, crystallization, arousal, selective perception, observational learning, agenda setting, and the like—qualifies or confirms their efficacy as instruments of influence.

The paradox exemplifies the constraint placed on the substance of knowledge by the manner in which its production is organized. The mass media are the recurrent (but neither consistent nor primary) focus of many disciplines and fields; and the resulting provincialism that gives an inquiry strength within its intended domain typically leaves its implications, elsewhere or in a larger framework, unexplored. Political scientists focus on voting and opinion; psychologists, on the processes that manifest themselves in behavior and attitude change; specialists in child development, on attention and comprehension; professors of marketing, on the division of tastes and preferences among audience segments; and sociologists, on the social factors necessary for explaining effects or noneffects of the media. In the departments and schools of communication and journalism, the emphasis on the techniques and practices of the media, and the implicit acceptance of their modes of operation, do not encourage the profound skepticism connoted by the term "social control." Not that American society has been deprived of criticism of the media, much of which is given sustenance by these empirical inquiries. Almost every datum has been open to enlistment in some assault on violence, on children's television viewing, on the advertisement and glamorization of alcohol and cigarettes, on bias and sensationalism in news, on one or another "irresponsibility"; so much so that practitioners in the media are ever ready to embrace Oliver Goldsmith's 1764 remark: "Every absurdity has now a champion."

Social control as a focus of research thus has a covert quality, despite the ubiquitous relevance of the research to the concept. This relevance becomes more discernible when the research is construed as having three dimensions:

(1) Quantitative or qualitative analyses of text and content, as exemplified by the interpretation of television news content as celebrating American norms (Gans 1979), either polarizing or trivializing with respect to radical social change (Gitlin 1980), or conveying the theme of individual powerlessness (Dahlgren 1981).

(2) Investigations into the psychological and social mechanisms by which the media might affect thought and behavior, exemplified by the extensive experimental documentation that television portrayals vary in their ability to influence viewers as a function of the rewards, social approval, and pertinence attributed to the portrayed behavior (Bandura 1973; Comstock et al., 1978); the role of local "opinion leaders" in interpreting the information disseminated by the mass media for others (Lazarsfeld et al. 1944; Katz and Lazarsfeld 1955); and the contribution of selective exposure and selective perception in minimizing the quantity of discomforting information reaching people (Klapper 1960; Sears 1967).

(3) Attempts to associate exposure to the mass media with thought and behavior, as exemplified by the many inquiries into the influence of the media during elections (Kraus and Davis 1976) and into the possible contribution of violent television entertainment to aggression and delinquency (Belson 1978; Chaffee 1972; Comstock et al. 1978; Lefkowitz et al. 1977).

Between these dimensions, theory shuttles as an agent of exchange. We remain interested in media content in spite of the inability of content alone to inform us of effects, not as a curiosity or a specialty in itself, but because theories of one kind or another support the belief that one rather than another of the possible outcomes is more likely with respect to a given audience. The same occurs for the frequent dilemmas posed by the inability of experiments to certify their relevance to events outside the laboratory and of surveys to bestow confidence that causation lurks behind one or another recorded association between variables. These theories command allegiance because some of the propositions that derive from them have survived empirical test. Ultimately, however, a topic such as the mass media and social control cannot escape a speculative cast, for so much of what can plausibly be ascribed to the media on the basis of theory is beyond empirical test.

Past into Present

. In order to understand the future of the mass media in social control, two aspects of their history require attention. They are the progressive increase in the mass media's place in everyday social life and their character as social innovation.

Since the emergence of the mass media in the seventeenth century, the place of the media in people's lives has grown larger. Each newly developed medium has increased the ability of the media to reach a larger audience, and at each step the amount of time and attention devoted to the media has increased.

Television exemplifies the historical evolution of the media. First, there is the matter of time use. Television significantly increased the amount of time that the average adult daily devotes to the mass media—a phenomenon observable not only in the United States but worldwide (Robinson 1972; Robinson and Converse 1972; Robinson et al. 1972; Szalai 1972). Television also exemplifies the tendency for media to increase their audience as people become accustomed to them, at least until a newer medium encroaches on the time and money expended on the old. The "novelty hypothesis" held that television viewing would decrease once the medium became familiar. It has been thoroughly discredited. Audience measurement in the United States has documented that the average hours of set use per day has increased steadily since the 1950s (Comstock et al. 1978). Second, there are the superior means of attracting and communicating to an audience possessed by successive media. Radio overcame the limitations imposed by the literacy required by print, and motion pictures combined the visual and aural in a simulation of real life. Television brought the communicatory prowess of motion pictures into the home and eliminated the financial and geographical constraints on attendance, transforming a recurrent departure from everyday tasks into daily activity. Third, there is the continual effort by the mass media to increase their audience, which in the case of television has become an ancillary technology in itself in the use of random sampling, automatic recording of viewer program selection, and computer analysis to calculate "ratings" and "shares." What has occurred in the case of television is simply the most recent, although arguably the longest, stride in a process that has been underway for centuries.

Yet, the mass media should not be thought of as principally technologies for disseminating information. They are not simply techniques appended to society, but a social innovation distinctive in the same sense as is the corporation and organized religion.

Gutenberg's publication of his 14-line bible in 1456 initiated a series of technological developments that would progressively enhance the efficiency by which a single source could reach a large number of persons. The functions sociologists designate as served by the mass media (Lasswell 1971; Lazarsfeld and Merton 1971; Mendelsohn 1966; Wright 1975) are basic to society and antedate the media. These functions include: surveillance, or newsgathering; interpretation and prescription, as in editorializing; transfer of culture; reinforcement of norms and continual assertion of widely shared values; conferral of status through attention and praise; and diversion and entertainment. The mass media, however, represent more than new ways of fulfilling old needs.

Sociologists come somewhat closer to identifying what is distinct about the mass media in specifying the attributes that set the media apart from other modes of communication: the large size, diverse composition, and anonymity of the audience; the rapidity with which messages are transmitted; the transitory exposure to the message; the public availability of that message; and the fact that the communicator is an organization. Even so, these characteristics are the appearance rather than the substance of the matter. The distinctiveness of the media lies in their social role. This social role is the calculated manufacture of messages and symbols for transmission to an audience as large at the time of transmission as the communicator can achieve within the limits of purpose, genre, and medium.

The social innovation that is the mass media resides in the ends to which communications technology has been put. These ends have three aspects. One is the *task* assumed by the media—to devise something to which a large number of persons will wish to attend. Another is the *criterion* by which success is judged—the garnering of the largest possible audience within the inevitable limits of the specific means of dissemination. The third is the *historic inevitability* of the enlargement of the role of the media in social life—the stepwise regularity by which the media's evolving technology has increased their capability to attract and hold the attention of the public.

Media and Social Institutions

Some of the many ways in which the media can play a role in social control become apparent when we examine the relationship between them and selected social institutions, with primary attention to the most attended to of the media, television. The institutions are socialization, religion, social relations, leisure, public security, and citizenship (Comstock 1978).

Socialization

The television set is in operation for more than seven hours a day during the fall and winter in the average American household, and it is inevitably part of the framework within which family members interact. More than half of American households have two or more television sets, with the result that a certain amount of viewing is done individually or with the family split into groups. The medium thus appears to reduce common experience and exchange within the family; for example, the amount of conversation that would otherwise occur (Robinson 1972; Szalai 1972).

Data collected in England indicate that television has also altered the kinds of activities in which family members engage (Belson 1959, 1960). Somewhat more time was spent at home in the evenings, but all of that additional time was spent viewing television. Acquisition of a television set initially reduced time spent on both frequently and infrequently pursued hobbies and interests. After six years, only the activities classified as engaged in frequently remained depressed. Time spent on child care was reduced, as were differences among socioeconomic strata in the pattern of home activity. Thus, television has altered family life beyond the exposure of family members to its programming.

Television is also construed by many as a source of vicarious socialization that competes with parents, teachers, and other acknowledged agents. The evidence in behalf of such a view is convincing, but the degree of influence is a matter of conjecture.

Most of what children view is adult programming. The average child two years of age and older views about thirty hours a week until he or she enters high school, when viewing declines somewhat. Television becomes a source of information when other sources are absent. Children learn about celebrities (Schramm et al. 1961), unfamiliar occupations (DeFleur and DeFleur 1967), major news events (Tolley 1973), and dating behavior (Gerson 1966). The effect has been to remove control over information entering the home from parents. In fact, television may run counter to parental intent.

There are also several dozen laboratory experiments demonstrating that the observation of an act performed in a television or film portrayal increases the likelihood that a child subsequently will behave similarly (Bandura 1973; Bandura et al. 1963). Observing television, like the observation of others in real life, adds to the child's behavioral repertoire. Additionally, there are several dozen laboratory experiments demonstrating that the level or intensity at which behavior is engaged in can be altered by exposure to television and film portrayals (Berkowitz 1962, 1973). The vicarious experience heightens or reduces inhibitions, or changes the response considered appropriate to a given cue.

The two experimental strands have focused largely on the influence of violent portrayals on subsequent aggressiveness. In support of the hypothesis that "television violence" encourages aggressiveness, their findings converge with positive correlations between everyday violence viewing and aggression against peers reported in several surveys. (Andison 1977; Belson 1978; Chaffee 1972; Comstock et al. 1978; Eysenck and Nias 1978; Liebert et al. 1973; Surgeon General's Scientific Advisory Committee on Television and Social Behavior 1972). There are also enough laboratory experiments demonstrating some influence of television and film portrayals on behavior other than aggressiveness to indicate that such vicarious experience can influence a wide range of behavior (Comstock et al. 1978). These effects are achieved through the instruction given by television in how to behave in a particular way, in the likelihood of reward or punishment for such behavior, in the degree to which the behavior will enjoy social approval, and in the suitability of that behavior in a given set of circumstances.

Religion

Gerbner (1967, 1972) has proposed that television in the United States be looked upon as analogous to a religious institution. Although such a likening may appear to be little more than rhetorical flourish, there are several parallels. Religion, education, and mass media are all systems by which the public is acculturated—introduced to the norms, conventions, and taboos of society. What sets religion and mass media apart is their reiterative presence throughout life. Television also resembles a religion in that the basis of its economic power is the acceptance of its communications by the intended audience. Where television and religion differ is that values are urged implicitly by the former and explicitly by the latter. Nevertheless, the two inevitably place objects for emulation before the public.

The talk show host may not sermonize, but his guests are there to be envied and admired. The news shows dispatch information on the good and bad news in society. The actors and actresses of television drama embody the essence of the right stuff for many. Gerbner and Gross (1976) would also argue that there is a moral cast to the prominence of violence in television drama, with violent tales not only continually aligning good against evil, but conveying, like religion, the lesson that the world is filled with perils.

There is evidence that television infringes on the prominence of religion. Data from a number of countries indicate that the introduction of television reduced the amount of time devoted to conventional religious practices by the average person (Robinson 1972). The power of the medium to enter spheres once reserved for the sacred is exemplified by the acceptance of television broadcasting on religious holidays from which it was initially barred in Israel (Katz and Gurevitch 1976).

A more obvious relationship between television and religion in the United States is the use of the medium to broadcast services. The adult audience on Sunday morning, when many of these programs are scheduled, is about thirteen million (persons eighteen and older per average minute between 7 a.m. and 1 p.m.—the cumulative audience would be larger, but nonreligious programs also account for some viewing).

To date, religious television infrequently has been an extension of the standard denominations. It has largely presented preachers who consciously and calculatedly attempt to attract viewers and financial contributions. What meaning is to be attached to this phenomenon? Surely, some viewers turn to television because it is difficult or impossible for them to attend a local service. Others may find something in religious television more satisfying than anything they have encountered in a church. Thus, the degree to which the audience for religious television is a congregation displaced or a congregation created is moot.

Social Relations

Does violent television entertainment encourage delinquency, crime, and serious antisocial acts? It is more respectful of the evidence from American surveys and laboratory experiments to say that television *certainly may* than to assert that it undoubtedly does so. While violent portrayals repeatedly have been demonstrated to increase subsequent aggressiveness in laboratory experiments, and positive correlations between everyday aggressiveness and violence viewing in several surveys give those findings a claim to external generalizability, "aggressiveness" in these instances is far from synonymous with "delinquency, crime, and serious antisocial acts."

A conservative position would be that the evidence clearly establishes some of the mechanisms through which such an effect could occur, but not more. At the extreme, such a view would attribute the behavior in question entirely to situational and personal factors.

That is certainly too extreme. Television instructs not only in the how of behavior but also in its social valuation and appropriateness, all of which will have their role in determining what emerges from those situational and personal factors. The occasional instances when television and film portrayals are followed by destructive emulation in real life—the most carefully documented being the increase in airline bomb threats following the broadcasts of the Rod Serling play, *Doomsday Flight* (Bandura 1973)—would appear to illustrate precisely such a contribution. Further, there are Belson's (1978) data on media use and delinquency among 1500 London male adolescents, which extend the positive correlations between violence viewing and aggressiveness to a correlation between such viewing and acts of crime and brutality.

Milgram and Shotland's (1973) field experiment found no association between viewing a charity box theft in a *Medical Center* episode and committing the same act when the viewers were given an opportunity to do so a few days later. However, an association would have required media influence of magnum force. Thus, the American experiments and surveys suggest that violence viewing encourages aggressiveness that may be translated into antisocial behavior. Real life events and recent data from England support the view that such a translation occurs.

Television entertainment displays worldly goods beyond the means of many in its audience, and this fact may join with the frequency of violent portrayals in contributing to social disruption. Nevertheless, television also functions to ameliorate the stresses and conflicts of the social order. Although viewing varies by social strata and ethnicity, it is sufficiently frequent and similar across groups to be considered a national experience (Bower 1973; Comstock et al. 1978). The emphasis is strongly on white, middle-class mores. Thus outlying groups are assimilated to such a perspective (Bogart 1962, 1965). At the same time, the normative and conventional character of television drama and advertising tends to reinforce the social hierarchy as white males are predominant by number and by the authority they display (Gerbner and Gross 1976; Long and Simon 1974; McArthur and Resko 1975; Seggar and Wheeler 1973).

Television to date has been largely a national medium that attempts to please a highly heterogeneous audience. Inevitably, it has trafficked primarily in those symbols that people have in common and not those that facilitate individual or group identities.

Leisure

Data on media behavior and time use in the United States and elsewhere document that television has increased the time Americans spend on the mass media by about an hour a day (Bogart 1972; Coffin 1955; Parker 1960, 1963; Robinson and Converse 1972; Szalai 1972). Three-fourths of all mass media time is devoted to television, and television viewing accounts for a third of all leisure time.

These figures represent an unprecedented increase in the centrality of mass media in modern society. American leisure has been changed by television. Time allocation has been altered, and the options available have been revised.

Television apparently has reduced the time that in its absence would be spent at social gatherings away from home, on household tasks and child care, listening to radio, reading magazines and books, moviegoing, sleeping, and in miscellaneous leisure activities. By affecting time allocation, television has altered the economic viability of other media and activities. Some have been stifled, others reshaped.

Movie theater attendance has declined, and movies themselves have become more violent and sexually explicit in the competition to attract audiences. Mass audience periodicals, such as the *Saturday Evening Post, Collier's, Life,* and *Look,* died as advertisers turned to television; but special interest magazines prospered, television having ignored such interests in its pursuit of mass appeal. Comic book sales decreased from about 600 million to 300 million annually between the early 1950s and 1970 as children found a more convenient source of fantasy. In book publishing, retail sale of fiction, poetry, and drama declined from 22 to 13 percent of all titles, although the total number of such titles increased over the same period. Similarly, there was a decline in the library circulation of fiction titles several times the magnitude of the slight decline for nonfiction titles subsequent to television's introduction.

Adults too were turning to television for their fantasies. Before television, radio was a network medium with a varied schedule designed to appeal to a heterogeneous national audience. It has become thoroughly local, largely a conveyor of music, with each station aiming at a narrow target audience.

Until the 1970s, per capita daily newspaper circulation kept pace with population growth and at worst appeared to be denied only the growth that might have followed from the rising educational level after World War II by television. However, circulation began to lag behind population growth. Afternoon newspapers have been particularly hurt because they face competition not only from evening television viewing but also from television news, the impediments of midday or earlier deadlines, and increasingly difficult distribution problems as suburbs expand and traffic congestion grows. Most of the cities where afternoon papers are dominant are those with huge numbers of assembly line workers, many of whom go to work too early to read a morning paper.

Television has also reshaped other media by the additional profitability it offers their products. Large portions of the costs of theater movies are now amortized by sales to television. Novels sell not only to "the movies," but also to television for miniseries and made-for-TV movies. Publishers avidly seek titles suitable for promotion on talk shows.

Leisure options beyond the media have similarly been revised by television. Minor league baseball is now a dwarf, with attendance falling from 42 to 10 million annually over the two decades ending in 1970. Boxing, now in resurgence as a television sports feature, was in decline for years as fans turned to whatever "action" was offered by television. Professional football, on the other hand, has gained prominence, and it is via television that the Super Bowl has become an unofficial national holiday. Television, while on the whole suppressing the amount of time that would be spent reading, regularly directs public attention to one or another serious literary work, and there is a rapids where sales were once a trickle.

Here is the heart of the matter. When television substitutes for another medium or activity, they suffocate and must change or die. When television primarily directs attention, the object flourishes.

Public Security

"The whole world is watching!" Chicago, 1968. The demonstrators' chant has become the slogan for television's power to focus the attention of the public on one or another extraordinary event. Also, the implication exists that television makes it impossible for officials to shroud their behavior. The camera records while words are already a step along in the editorial process.

Television news expresses journalistic values as a whole, although with its own emphases on stories suitable for film and brief acounts of conflict—jeopardy and transgression that at their best are baby tales resolved in ninety seconds. Nevertheless, certain characteristics of television in some instances fit it for a somewhat stronger role than the other media.

Television coverage has become the most prominent symbol of wide public attention. Media coverage of acts of crime, violence, and terrorism may encourage replication, and television coverage may give concreteness, realism, and actuality to an event that will encourage emulation (i.e., the *Doomsday Flight* phenomenon).

Because "the whole world" is watching, television may become an unwilling participant in events. While exposure to public view may restrain officials in negotiating over hostages or responding to public disorder, it may also exacerbate dreadful events by giving all the participants a heightened sense of being part of high drama. Similarly, coverage itself may become the goal. Disaffected groups consistently seek publicity, and often attempt to contrive the humiliation of those in power. The attention of "the whole world" makes television the ideal medium for such purposes.

After the American withdrawal from Vietnam, General Westmoreland offered the opinion that television had made war unacceptable to the American people. The camera embraced the ugliness that the conventions of print journalism shielded. Certainly the four-minute NBC color film of the assassination of an unarmed prisoner by a South Vietnamese general symbolized the contradictions of that war for many (Bailey and Lichty 1972). The point again is that the media sometimes influence the events they cover, and while television is not unique in this respect it does have its own aptitude for such influence.

Citizenship

Television has reshaped American politics through its effects on the behavior of politicians (Lang and Lang 1968; Mendelsohn and Crespi 1970). Campaigns are managed to maximize favorable television coverage, communications gurus are preeminent on campaign staffs, and television advertising expenditures are prominent in campaign budgets.

These effects of the medium are observable from local to presidential politics. The presidential nominating conventions have been reshaped by television. No longer is there much suspense in the voting, for the enormous journalistic forces deployed by the networks have tallied everyone in advance. That vision of "the whole world" watching enters again, as the parties increasingly orchestrate conventions to give voters a favorable impression. No longer are they the deliberative bodies they once were, with "dark horses," sizable blocks of delegates committed to several different candidates, and a substantial number of uncommitted delegates. The increase in the number of primaries, and the attention given both them and other contests for delegates by the media, have resulted in an electoral process where the viability of a candidacy is decided early, near-winners become labeled as losers, and the front-runner arrives at the convention to be certified rather than chosen. Television has been a major factor in this conversion of local and state delegate selection to a national story.

Contemporary presidential debates are also the creature of television. The evidence indicates that the enormous size of their audiences must be discounted in terms of exposure to the exchange because of inattention; that they are nevertheless more likely to be viewed by those with some uncertainty than those with firm convictions about whom they are going to vote for; that they produce measurable shifts in voter enthusiasm and support but not any measurable independent influence on election day; that their efficacy in delineating differences between the candidates is impeded by the emphasis that the media give to style, setting, slips and flubs, and the public's perception of who "won"; and that these confrontations typically facilitate the reduction of political animosity (Comstock et al. 1978; Dennis and Chaffee 1978; Dennis et al. 1979; Katz and Feldman 1962; Kraus 1962, 1979; Sears and Chaffee 1979).

Television is named by a large majority of Americans as their principal source of news (Roper 1980), but a closer look at the available data makes it clear that to date newspapers remain a more prominent factor in elections (Clarke and Fredin 1978; Comstock et al. 1978; Patterson 1980). Newspapers reach more people than does evening network news, the people reached by newspapers are somewhat more likely to vote, newspaper accounts are better recalled, newspaper readership is associated with greater knowledge about political issues while television news viewing is not, and newspaper readership figures more consistently in the use of rational criteria for choosing among candidates. The conventions of television news, which emphasize the visual and the dramatic, simply do not favor the explication of issues. Thus, it is not surprising to find paradoxes such as a positive association between exposure to paid-for political spots and knowledge of the issues, and no association between exposure to evening network news and such knowledge (Patterson and McClure 1973).

Media coverage of a presidential election campaign does not seem to make much difference in shifting voter allegiance from one candidate to another, but it does heighten interest in the campaign and support for the chosen candidate (Comstock et al. 1978). One reason is that in the typical campaign of the past more than three-fourths of all voters had made up their minds by the end of the conventions. Another is the ability of people to assimilate, reject, or ignore information contrary to their viewpoint. Nevertheless, it would be rash to conclude that the media are part of the process without affecting its direction. The emphases of news coverage help establish the issues that the public perceives as important, and it is around these issues that partisan conflicts develop and are resolved. In this respect, the media are particularly influential with issues that do not touch intimately on people's daily lives, such as foreign affairs, energy when there is no gas shortage, and education when there are no neighborhood protests over busing.

There are historical trends that forecast increasing influence of the mass media on voter decision making (DeVries and Tarrance 1972; Dreyer 1971; Kraus and Davis 1976; Nie et al. 1976). The proportion of voters unaligned with any party has been increasing; faith in the party system and in politicians generally has been declining; and issues and ideology are becoming increasingly the basis of voter choice. These trends diverge from the pattern so apparent after World War II when strong party allegiance was much more common. Then, that allegiance predicted a substantial proportion of the eventual vote, and once prior voting history, socioeconomic status, region, rural or urban residence, race, and religion were taken into account, there was very little left that conceivably could be explained by exposure to the mass media. Furthermore, within each party there are increasing numbers who consider themselves liberal or conservative rather than at the center, so that often the party's candidate has difficulty gaining the support of all members. As party loyalties decline and ideological allegiances increase, politics becomes more volatile and the electorate less predictable.

The consequence of these varied trends is that the influence of what voters learn from the media is enhanced and the role of the media in "crystallization and reinforcement" (in effect the cultivation of party loyalty) is reduced. The irony is that the evolution of the media has placed a medium at the forefront whose power to focus attention on singular events (i.e., assassinations, moon shots) is unparalleled, but whose norms have rendered it ineffective in the education of voters.

Limits on Management

These examples depict some of the ways in which the mass media participate in social control, but they do not address the question of information management (i.e., the manipulation of the public through the media). The values that dictate the conduct of the media, the efficacy of the techniques they employ, and the prowess they typically demonstrate impose definite limits on the feasibility of effective information management.

Values

The media in the United States are not agents of government. The posture of the media toward government is often described and acknowledged by both sides as adversarial. The activities of the United States

Government Printing Office, the various films and television programs financed by federal funds under the rubric of public betterment, federal support for public television, and subsidies for print media made up of special postage rates in no way comprise the consistent voice of official purpose that is found in totalitarian societies.

Independence of media and government was established as a principle by the First Amendment. Even radio and television broadcasting, subject by the Communications Act of 1934 to regulation for the "public interest, convenience, and necessity," has been held to few standards for program content beyond balanced news coverage of major issues, equal access for contending political candidates outside of news coverage, and some demonstration of willingness to assess and serve community needs. For the past half century of broadcasting, the concept of independence of communications content from government control has prevailed. Newspapers and magazines have always been beyond the shadow of regulation.

Economically, the media depend on market success. They pay their way by producing profits for their owners. This makes audience acceptance preeminent among their goals. The larger the circulation, the greater the revenue from sales. The larger the audience, the greater the rate that can be charged for advertising space or time. Thus, the media seek to entertain and inform the public on their terms.

The mass media in the United States have assumed the role of providing news that is objective, fair, nonpartisan, and that includes differing and often contradictory opinions. Schramm (1957) characterized this ethic as an unwritten contract with the public. Unbiased coverage enhanced public respect, with the result that government interference increasingly became unacceptable to the public. The media cannot surrrender any of their independence to anyone without risking its full surrender to the government. This perspective, in which the media remain their own masters as long as they are fair and broad-minded, has become accepted implicitly not only in news but in entertainment. The consequence is that in both news and entertainment the media have come to evade and resist their enlistment in behalf of any cause except those they come to embrace voluntarily. Information management on a pervasive and widespread basis is antithetical to their character, although the media are undeniably its servant from time to time in the coverage of major issues. Propagandizing is in conflict with both their ethics and economic goals. Controversy, contention, and conflict are attractions. When views within our society differ, the media will carry messages that are essentially self-canceling.

Techniques and Prowess

Assessing the effectiveness of techniques that can be employed in using the mass media to influence their audiences is problematic. This is not to deny that there have been demonstrable effects of exposure to messages in the media contrived to influence the public, such as information campaigns, or that the media do not have broad and profound effects on the way people think and behave. The media simply remain unreliable agents for changing thought and behavior.

The media may or may not disseminate the information in question. For some, the message may encourage the very behavior it is intended to discourage simply by drawing it to public attention; thus campaigns to reduce racial prejudice may make antagonisms more salient. Many may fail to comprehend the message. Repetition is highly desirable, but it may be accompanied by ever-lessening impact. The portrayal of risk for noncompliance may further conformity to the advocated course of action, but it may also encourage denial to avoid anxiety-producing thoughts.

There is a large body of empirical evidence encouraging deep skepticism over media prowess (Bauer 1971; Hovland 1954; Katz 1971; Klapper 1960; McGuire 1969; Weiss 1969, 1971). The broad conclusions that emerge from an examination of the numerous empirical examinations of media effectiveness in changing attitudes and behavior is that (Comstock, in press):

(1) Based on the attributes of the audience member, typically, behavior following media exposure is consistent with what would have been expected in the absence of exposure.
(2) These attributes include age, sex, ethnicity, socioeconomic status (which subsumes education, income, and occupation), region and place of residence, political affiliation, prior behavioral history, group norms, and individual interests and motives.
(3) Typically, decisions to which mass media messages are relevant are reached before the messages are received, and not substantially changed thereafter.

The factors responsible constitute a social psychology constraining media influence:

(1) selective exposure, by which people filter out much information marginal in interest or in conflict with their opinions and behavior;
(2) selective perception, by which people interpret messages in accord with their opinions and behavior, altering the meaning so as to minimize conflict;
(3) rationalization, by which arguments justifying the status quo are invoked to counter information advocating a change in opinions or behavior;
(4) avoidance, by which some and often many of those to whom a particular message applies evade not only this message but any

content that might heighten the salience of or direct attention to the topic; and

(5) inoculation and counterinculcation, by which messages received prior or subsequent to the current message render it ineffectual.

The theories that predict media influence must be taken as either largely explaining a net effect of content not directed toward a particular outcome, or the means by which the likelihood of media influence can be heightened without any assurance of success. They convert to theories of sure manipulation only when control is complete over exposure, interpretation, and the background of competing messages.

The two most comprehensive and empirically supported formulations are social learning theory (Bandura 1969, 1973, 1978; Rushton 1980) and the health belief model (Becker et al. 1977, 1978; Becker and Maiman 1975). Although they differ in many particulars, essentially they complement one another and converge in the factors on which media influence is contingent. Once the sometimes difficult hurdles of exposure and comprehension are crossed, influence depends on the manipulation of expectations. Social learning theory emphasizes the portrayal of behavior as rewarded or effective in attaining desired ends, as enjoying social approval or being the norm for the circumstances, and as pertinent to one or another situation that will be encountered by an audience member. Each has been demonstrated to facilitate emulatory behavior. Social learning theory also posits that television and film are particularly powerful because they involve behavioral observation, a very common way by which people learn new ways of behaving or acquire impressions that result in the revision of current behavior. The health belief model emphasizes the portrayal of benefits to be derived from pursuing a course of action. It posits that behavior can be changed by nurturing the motive to achieve well-being, heightening the perceived risk for certain kinds of behavior, and offering alternatives that will be perceived as efficacious in achieving enhanced well-being.

Although there are many instances in which information campaigns have disappointed their sponsors, there also has been documented success (Hyman and Sheatsley 1947; Mendelsohn 1973). Three campaigns readily confute the view that the limitations on employing the media to shape public behavior render them invariably impotent (Comstock, in press). No behavior is more difficult to influence than pleasurable substance use; yet cigarette smoking by both men and women in the United States is at its lowest point in 45 years. The proportion of people who believe cigarette smoking is a health risk has risen sharply over the past thirty years, and a majority of the public reports that they have *never* been warned about smoking by a physician (Gallup 1981; United States Surgeon General

1981). The implication is that the public information campaign against smoking is slowly succeeding, even though it faces the counterpropaganda of an advertising campaign costing millions annually. The "Take a Bite Out of Crime" campaign, featuring a dog in a trenchcoat analogous to "Smokey the Bear," reached about one-third of the public in its first six months in 1979-1980. Among those exposed, there were modest shifts in attitudes and behavior related to crime prevention in the direction urged by the television and radio spots, newspaper and magazine ads, posters, and brochures (Mendelsohn et al 1981). In the Stanford three-community coronary risk field experiment, a media campaign extending over two years and featuring fifty television spots, three hours of television programming, over one hundred radio spots, several hours of radio programming, weekly newspaper columns, newspaper advertisements and stories, billboards, posters, and mailings reduced behavior associated with risk of coronary disease. Persons receiving face-to-face instruction and counseling in addition to the media campaign reduced their risk-related behavior more sharply by the end of the first year, and, by the end of the second year the mass media campaign had proven almost equally effective (Farquar et al. 1977). In the first of the two latter campaigns, the helter-skelter dissemination indigenous to public service advertising was to some degree overcome in the very short term. In the second, the community inculcation by the media guaranteed substantial exposure, and coronary risk was measurably reduced.

The Future of Information Management

There is no question that the mass media participate in the social control process in many ways. There should also be no question that there is a latent potential for control through information management that stands quite apart from the short-term manipulation of news of which government officials are so often accused. The two principal necessary conditions for exerting control through the media are attention and consistency of messages. Technological and economic developments appear to guarantee that the former will continue to increase and that the capability for bringing about the latter will grow.

By the end of 1981, of the 81.5 million American households with television sets, the proportion connected to cable was approaching one-third, and the added programming and diversity ensures that the media will continue to increase the share of leisure time they consume. The narrow-casting aspects of cable make it possible to design programs to achieve specific ends with comparatively homogeneous audiences—the same kind of homogeneity that radio cultivates with its specialized age-graded formats. The two-way capabilities of cable additionally bestow the power to elicit opinions on public issues, to disseminate books and pamphlets upon request, to sell products, and to record and maintain archives on the programming viewed, views expressed, and items ordered. Thus, involvement in issues becomes more open to manipulation, and interests and opinions more susceptible to scrutiny.

Economic trends appear to increase the similarity of outlook likely to find expression in the media (Compaigne 1979; Whiteside 1981). The media have always been marked by a sizable degree of concentration of ownership that today is not particularly greater than in the past and that is modest in comparison with other industries. Quality, price, and product improvement—the goals presumably served by competition—take on a distinctive character when information and entertainment are produced; and the degree and kind of concentration that exists merits implacable examination.

Metropolitan newspapers are growing ever fewer in number, fewer readers have a choice of competing newspapers, and chain ownership is increasing. Communication groups encompass newspapers, television and radio stations, magazines, and book publishing firms. Communication is sometimes only a small part of a group's economic activities. Conglomerates increasingly have incorporated communication groups within their giant umbrellas of ownership. Newspapers, magazines, and publishing firms that were once held by a family or partnership have sold their stock publicly to evade dissolution by inheritance tax. The media increasingly are being held to purely corporate standards of performance, which means profitability, undiluted by the vigorous personal visions of their former owners. The media are also more frequently being employed jointly to promote a product that has been created largely for exploitation.

Does it need to be said that money has always mattered? It is not that market success was once unimportant, but that it has come to matter so much and so often to the exclusion of anything else. It is incomplete but accurate to say that broadcast television is the ultimate mass medium, and so it has become a key component in the marriage of the media. Books are conceived and written principally because of their suitability for promotion on television talk shows and by celebrities. Novels and movies are manufactured in tandem so that each will promote the other. The novel ends up in display racks in supermarkets and chain stores, and both are advertised on television. Books are published because they fit the expectations of the chain stores with respect to popularity. In many ways, then, the media have fallen under a pervasive outlook, and many of the outlets of the media—newspapers, magazines, radio and television stations, cable companies, and book publishers—are controlled by a single organization.

Thus, in regard to information management, the flirtation with the notion of myth must be abandoned, and the concept of menace entertained with misgiving.   ——

REFERENCES

Andison, F. S. 1977. "Television Violence and Viewer Aggression: A Cumulation of Study Results, 1956-1976." *Public Opinion Quarterly* 41:314-31.

Bailey, G. A. and L. W. Lichty. 1972. "Rough Justice on a Saigon Street: A Gatekeeper Study of NBC's Tet Execution Film." *Journalism Quarterly* ·49:221-29.

Bandura, A. 1969. *Principles of Behavior Modification.* New York: Holt, Rinehart & Winston.

Bandura, A. 1973. *Aggression: A Social Learning Analysis.* Englewood Cliffs, NJ: Prentice-Hall.

Bandura, A. 1978. "Social Learning Theory of Aggression." *Journal of Communication* 28:12-29.

Bandura, A., et al. 1963. "Imitation of Film-mediated Aggressive Models." *Journal of Abnormal and Social Psychology* 66:3-11.

Bauer, R. A. 1971. "The Obstinate Audience: Influence Process from the Point of View of Social Communication." Pp. 326-426 in *The Process and Effects of Mass Communication,* rev. ed., edited by W. Schramm and D. F. Roberts. Urbana: University of Illinois Press.

Becker, M. H. and L. A. Maiman. 1975. "Sociobehavioral Determinants of Compliance with Health and Medical Care Recommendations." *Medical Care* 13:10-24.

Becker, M. H., et al. 1977. "The Health Belief Model and Prediction of Dietary Compliance: A Field Experiment." *Journal of Health and Social Behavior* 18:348-66.

Becker, M. H., et al. 1978. "Compliance with a Medical Regimen for Asthma: A Test of the Health Belief Model." *Public Health Reports* 93:268-77.

Belson, W. A. 1959. "Effects of Television on Interests and Initiative of Adult Viewers in Greater London." *British Journal of Psychology* 50:145-58.

Belson, W. A. 1960. "The Effects of Television upon Family Life." *Discovery* 21:1-5.

Belson, W. A. 1978. *Television Violence and the Adolescent Boy.* London: Saxon House.

Berkowitz, L. 1962. *Aggression: A Social Psychological Analysis.* New York: McGraw-Hill.

Berkowitz, L. 1973. "Words and Symbols as Stimuli to Aggressive Responses." Pp. 113-43 in *Control of Aggression: Implications from Basic Research,* edited by J. F. Knutson. Chicago: Aldine-Atherton.

Bogart, L. 1962. "American Television: A Brief Survey of Research Findings." *Journal of Social Issues* 18:36-42.

Bogart, L. 1965. "The Mass Media and the Blue-collar Worker." Pp. 416-28 in *Blue-collar World: Studies of the American Worker,* edited by A. Shostak and W. Gomberg. Englewood Cliffs, NJ: Prentice-Hall.

Bogart, L. 1972. *The Age of Television,* 3rd ed. New York: Frederick Unger.

Bower, R. T. 1973. *Television and the Public.* New York: Holt, Rinehart & Winston.

Chaffee, S. H. 1972. "Television and Adolescent Aggressiveness (Overview)." Pp. 1-34 in *Television and Adolescent Aggressiveness,* Vol. 3, of *Television and Social Behavior,* edited by G. A. Comstock and E. A. Rubinstein. Washington, DC: U.S. Government Printing Office.

Clarke, P. and E. Fredin. 1978. "Newspapers, Television and Political Reasoning." *Public Opinion Quarterly* 42:143-60.

Coffin, T. E. 1955. "Television's Impact on Society." *American Psychologist* 10:630-41.

Compaigne, B. M., ed. 1979. *Who Owns the Media?* New York: Harmony Books.

Comstock, G. 1978. "The Impact of Television on American Institutions." *Journal of Communication* 28:12-28.

Comstock, G. In press. "Mass Media and Social Change." In *Handbook of Community Intervention,* edited by E. Seidman. Beverly Hills, CA: Sage.

Comstock, G. A. and E. A. Rubinstein, eds. 1972. *Media Content and Control,* Vol. 1 of *Television and Social Behavior.* Washington, DC: U.S. Government Printing Office.

Comstock, G. A. and E. A. Rubinstein, eds. 1972. *Television and Adolescent Aggressiveness,* Vol. 3, of *Television and Social Behavior.* Washington, DC: U.S. Government Printing Office.

Comstock, G., et al. 1978. *Television and Human Behavior.* New York: Columbia University Press.

Dahlgren, P. 1981. "TV News and Suppression of Reflexivity." Pp. 101-14 in *Mass Media and Social Change,* edited by E. Katz and T. Szecsko. Beverly Hills, CA: Sage.

DeFleur, M. L. and L. B. DeFleur. 1967. "The Relative Contribution of Television as a Learning Source for Children's Occupational Knowledge." *American Sociological Review* 32:777-89.

Dennis, J. and S. H. Chaffee. 1978. "Legitimation in the 1976 U.S. Election Campaign." *Communication Research* 5:371-94.

Dennis, J., et al. 1979. "Impact of the Debates upon Partisan Image and Issue Voting." Pp. 314-330 in *The Great Debates: Carter vs. Ford, 1976,* edited by S. Kraus. Bloomington: Indiana University Press.

DeVries, W. and L. Tarrance, Jr. 1972. *The Ticket-splitter: A New Force in American Politics.* Grand Rapids, MI: Eerdsman.

Dreyer, E. C. 1971. "Media Use and Electoral Choices: Some Political Consequences of Information Exposure." *Public Opinion Quarterly* 35:544-53.

Eysenck, H. J. and D.K.B. Nias. 1978. *Sex, Violence, and the Media.* London: Maurice Temple Smith.

Farquhar, J. W., et al. 1977. "Community Education for Cardiovascular Health." *The Lancet* 1:1192-5.

The Gallup Report. 1981. "Gallup Smoking Audit." July, No. 190, pp. 2-17.

Gans, H. J. 1979. *Deciding What's News.* New York: Pantheon.

Gerbner, G. 1967. "Mass Media and Human Communication Theory." Pp. 40-60 in *Human Communication Theory: Original Essays,* edited by F. E. Dance. New York: Holt, Rinehart & Winston.

Gerbner, G. 1972. "Violence in Television Drama: Trends and Symbolic Functions." Pp. 28-187 in *Media Content and Control,* Vol. 1, of *Television and Social Behavior,* edited by G. A. Comstock and E. A. Rubinstein. Washington, DC: U.S. Government Printing Office.

Gerbner, G. and L. Gross. 1976. "Living with Television: The Violence Profile." *Journal of Communication* 26:173-99.

Gerbner, G. and L. Gross. 1980. "The Violent Face of Television and Its Lessons." Pp. 149-62 in *Children and the Faces of Television: Teaching, Violence, Selling*, edited by E. Palmer and A. Dorr. New York: Academic Press.

Gerbner, G., et al. 1979. *Violence Profile No. 10: Trends in Network Television Drama and Viewer Conceptions of Social Reality*. Philadelphia: University of Pennsylvania.

Gerbner, G., et al. 1980. "The 'Mainstreaming' of America: Violence Profile No. 11." *Journal of Communication* 30:10-29.

Gerson, W. M. 1966. "Mass Media Socialization Behavior: Negro-White Differences." *Social Forces* 45:40-50.

Gitlin, T. 1980. *The Whole World Watching*. Berkeley: University of California Press.

Hovland, C. I. 1954. "Effects of the Mass Media of Communication." Pp. 1062-1103 in *Handbook of Social Psychology*, Vol. 2, edited by G. Lindzey. Cambridge, MA: Addison-Wesley.

Hyman, H. H. and P. B. Sheatsley. 1947. "Some Reasons Why Information Campaigns Fail." *Public Opinion Quarterly* 11:412-23.

Katz, E. 1971. "Platforms and Windows: Broadcasting's Role in Election Campaigns." *Journalism Quarterly* 48:304-14.

Katz, E. and J. J. Feldman. 1962. "The Debates in Light of Research: A Survey of Surveys." Pp. 173-223 in *The Great Debates: Kennedy vs. Nixon, 1960*, edited by S. Kraus. Bloomington: Indiana University Press.

Katz, E. and M. Gurevitch. 1976. *The Secularization of Leisure: Culture and Communication in Israel*. Cambridge, MA: Harvard University Press.

Katz, E. and P. Lazarsfeld. 1955. *Personal Influence*. New York: Free Press.

Katz, E. and T. Szecsko, eds. 1981. *Mass Media and Social Change*. Beverly Hills, CA: Sage.

Klapper, J. T. 1960. *The Effects of Mass Communication*. New York: Free Press.

Kraus, S., ed. 1962. *The Great Debates: Kennedy vs. Nixon, 1960*. Bloomington: Indiana University Press.

Kraus, S., ed. 1979. *The Great Debates: Carter vs. Ford, 1976*. Bloomington: Indiana University Press.

Kraus, S. and D. Davis. 1976. *The Effect of Mass Communication on Political Behavior*. University Park: Pennsylvania State University Press.

Lang, K. and G. E. Lang. 1968. *Politics and Television*. Chicago: Quadrangle Books.

Lasswell, H. D. 1971. "The Structure and Function of Communication in Society." Pp. 84-99 in *The Process and Effects of Mass Communication*, rev. ed., edited by W. Schramm and D. F. Roberts. Urbana: University of Illinois Press.

Lazarsfeld, P. F., and R. K. Merton. 1971. "Mass Communication, Popular Taste, and Organized Social Action." Pp. 554-78 in *The Process and Effects of Mass Communication*, rev. ed., edited by W. Schramm and D. F. Roberts. Urbana: University of Illinois Press.

Lazarsfeld, P. F., et al. 1944. *The People's Choice: How the Voter Makes Up His Mind in a Presidential Campaign*. New York: Duell, Sloan & Pearce.

Lefkowitz, M. M., et al. 1977. *Growing Up to be Violent*. Elmsford, NY: Pergamon.

Liebert, R. M., et al. 1973. *The Early Window: Effects of Television on Children and Youth*. Elmsford, NY: Pergamon.

Lindzey, G., ed. 1954. *Handbook of Social Psychology*, Vol. 2. Cambridge, MA: Addison-Wesley.

Lindzey, G. and E. Aronson, eds. 1969. *Applied Social Psychology*, Vol. 5, of *The Handbook of Social Psychology*. Reading, MA: Addison-Wesley.

Long, M. L. and R. J. Simon. 1974. "The Roles and Statuses of Women on Children and Family TV Programs." *Journalism Quarterly* 51:107-10.

McArthur, L. Z. and B. G. Resko. 1975. "The Portrayal of Men and Women in American Television Commercials." *Journal of Social Psychology* 97:209-20.

McGuire, W. J. 1969. "The Nature of Attitudes and Attitude Change." Pp. 136-314 in *Applied Social Psychology*, Vol. 5, of *The Handbook of Social Psychology*, edited by G. Lindzey and E. Aronson. Reading, MA: Addison-Wesley.

Mendelsohn, H. A. 1966. *Mass Entertainment*. New Haven, CT: College and University Press.

Mendelsohn, H. A. and I. Crespi. 1970. *Polls, Television, and the New Politics*. San Francisco: Chandler.

Mendelsohn, H. A., et al. 1981. *Public Communications and the Prevention of Crime: Evaluations and Strategies*. A report to the National Institute for Justice, Law Enforcement Administration, Washington, D.C. Denver, CO: University of Denver Center for Mass Communications Research and Policy.

Milgram, S. and R. L. Shotland. 1973. *Television and Antisocial Behavior: Field Experiments*. New York: Academic.

Nie, N. H., et al. 1976. *The Changing American Voter*. Cambridge, MA: Harvard University Press.

Parker, E. B. 1960. "The Functions of Television for Children." Ph.D. Dissertation, Stanford University.

Parker, E. B. 1963. "The Effects of Television on Library Circulation." *Public Opinion Quarterly* 27:578-89.

Patterson, T. E. 1980. *The Mass Media Election*. New York: Praeger.

Patterson, T. E. and R. D. McClure. 1973. "Political Advertising: Voter Reaction." Paper presented at the meeting of the American Association for Public Opinion Research, Ashville, North Carolina.

Robinson, J. P. 1972. "Television's Impact on Everyday Life: Some Cross-national Evidence." Pp. 410-31 in *Television in Day-to-day Life: Patterns of Use*, Vol. 4, of *Television and Social Behavior*, edited by E. A. Rubinstein, et al. Washington, DC: U.S. Government Printing Office.

Robinson, J. P. and P. E. Converse. 1972. "The Impact of Television on Mass Media Usages: A Cross-national Comparison." Pp. 197-212 in *The Use of Time: Daily Activities of Urban and Suburban Populations in Twelve Countries*, edited by A. Szalai. The Hague: Mouton.

Robinson, J. P., et al. 1972. "Everyday Life in Twelve Countries." Pp. 113-44 in *The Use of Time: Daily Activities of Urban and Suburban Populations in Twelve Countries*, edited by A. Szalai. The Hague: Mouton.

The Roper Organization. 1980. *Evolving Public Opinion Toward Television and Other Mass Media: 1959-1980*. New York: Television Information Office.

Rubinstein, E. A., et al., eds. 1972. *Television in Day-to-day Life: Patterns of Use*, Vol. 4, of *Television and Social Behavior*. Washington, DC: Government Printing Office.

Rushton, J. P. 1980. *Altruism, Socialization, and Society*. Englewood Cliffs, NJ: Prentice-Hall.

Schramm, W. 1957. *Responsibility in Mass Communications*. New York: Harper.

Schramm, W. and D. F. Roberts, eds. 1971. *The Process and Effects of Mass Communication*, rev. ed. Urbana: University of Illinois Press.

Schramm, W., et al. 1961. *Television in the Lives of Our Children.* Stanford, CA: Stanford University Press.

Sears, D. O. 1967. "Selective Exposure to Information: A Critical Review." *Public Opinion Quarterly* 31:194-213.

Sears, D. O. and S. H. Chaffee. 1979. "Uses and Effects of the 1976 Debates: An Overview of Empirical Studies." Pp. 223-61 in *The Great Debates: Carter vs. Ford, 1976,* edited by S. Kraus. Bloomington: Indiana University Press.

Seggar, J. F. and P. Wheeler. 1973. "World of Work on TV: Ethnic and Sex Representation in TV Drama." *Journal of Broadcasting* 17:201-14.

Seidman, E., ed. In press. *Handbook of Community Intervention.* Beverly Hills, CA: Sage.

Surgeon General's Scientific Advisory Committee on Television and Social Behavior. 1972. *Television and Growing Up: The Impact of Televised Violence.* Report to the Surgeon General, United States Public Health Service. Washington, DC: U.S. Government Printing Office.

Szalai, A., ed. 1972. *The Use of Time: Daily Activities of Urban and Suburban Populations in Twelve Countries.* The Hague: Mouton.

Tolley, H., Jr. 1973. *Children and War: Political Socialization to International Conflict.* New York: Teachers College Press, Columbia University.

United States Surgeon General. 1981. *The Health Consequences of Smoking for Women.* Rockville, MD: U.S. Department of Health and Human Services.

Weiss, W. 1969. "Effects of the Mass Media of Communication." Pp. 77-195 in *Applied Social Psychology,* Vol. 5, of *The Handbook of Social Psychology,* edited by G. Lindzey and E. Aronson. Reading, MA: Addison-Wesley.

Weiss, W. 1971. "Mass Communication." Pp. 309-336 in *Annual Review of Psychology,* Vol. 22. Palo Alto, CA: Annual Review Press.

Whiteside, T. 1981. *The Blockbuster Complex.* Middletown, CT: Wesleyan University Press.

Wright, C. R. 1975. *Mass Communication: A Sociological Perspective,* rev. ed. New York: Random House.

10

Cultural Differentiation, Cultural Integration, and Social Control

DIANA CRANE

The concept of social control refers both to social order—the regulation of social behavior—and to consensus—widely shared values and perceptions. However, sociologists have been more concerned with institutions that maintain social order (such as police, government, and the law) than with institutions that create and maintain consensus. The latter are primarily cultural institutions, especially those pertaining to education, religion, popular culture, the arts, and the sciences. Although some attention has been paid to the role of religion in furthering consensus, the role of other cultural institutions in that regard is poorly understood.

In what sense is it meaningful to speak of consensus in a society, such as the United States, where cultural differentiation is pronounced? In fact, one has to consider the number and variety of popular cultures, subcultures, and countercultures. Whereas a popular culture generates widely shared values, the opposite is true of subcultures and countercultures. Accordingly, a major problem for sociological theory is to understand how cultural integration and cultural diversity may coexist.

Functionalists have postulated a dominant culture that comprises the core values of a society. The following statement about art by Albrecht (1968:390) is illustrative:

Directly or indirectly, art may bolster the morale of groups and help create a sense of unity, of social solidarity. As used by dissident groups, it may create awareness of social issues and provide rallying cries for action and social change. In our society, it may thus be used to criticize as well as to support the social order while performing essentially the same function: that of heightening awareness of the context in which it appears and constituting an objective form symbolizing essential values of that context.

By contrast, conflict theorists view culture as reflecting the values of elites and as reinforcing social inequality. In their view, ideas and values, including the content of cultural forms, are manipulated to create or undermine the legitimacy of a social group's position. In other words, cultural products disseminate ideologies designed to maintain the status quo or, alternatively, to oppose it (Collins 1975).

Other sociologists, in the symbolic interactionist tradition, have concentrated on cultural symbols themselves and their meanings for different social groups rather than interrelations among subcultures (one exception is Fine and Kleinman 1979; and for a thorough review of different approaches to cultural institutions, see Peterson 1979). A few sociologists (e.g., Bell 1976) see the social structure and cultural institutions as developing independently of one another.

Four attributes of cultural products[1] are central to any discussion of their role in contemporary society: (1) their publics, (2) the social organization of their creation, (3) their dissemination process, and (4) their content. In many analyses of so-called popular culture, these attributes are not clearly delineated. For example, until recently (see Peterson 1979) sociologists tended to speak of two types of cultural products: (1) mass culture, which was seen as being disseminated to large audiences by mass media, and (2) high culture, including the fine arts and intellectual life, which was portrayed as being superior in terms of aesthetic criteria but in danger of being stifled by mass culture.

By contrast, Gans (1974:10) clarified the subject to some extent by distinguishing between (1) taste publics—the audiences that make similar choices of cultural content according to similar aesthetic standards; (2) taste cultures, which include values and related aesthetic standards, the cultural forms that express the values, and the media through which they are disseminated; and (3) the creators of various types of culture, popular or otherwise. According to Gans, taste publics differ in terms of social class, which he defines largely in terms of education. Some cultural forms do draw their audiences from a particular social class. For example, certain art forms, such as opera, classical music, and fine art, are consumed largely by the upper middle class (DiMaggio and Useem 1978); but other cultural forms, such as jazz, popular music, and comics, draw audiences from all social classes. Still other cultural forms draw selectively from various social classes to form a subgroup. Such a subgroup is socially mixed, but its members share certain attitudes and values, and in that sense they constitute a culture class (Peterson and DiMaggio 1975).

The foregoing suggests that it is useful to distinguish between (1) a mass audience, which is undifferentiated in terms of demographic or attitudinal variables; (2) a taste culture audience, which is differentiated in terms of demographic variables such as age or social class; (3) a culture class audience, which is differentiated in terms of attitudes and values or a "world view"; and (4) an audience whose members are linked to one another both by a world view and social relationships, such that it constitutes a particular kind of social group known as a social circle (Kadushin 1968). The last audience is the smallest and the most homogenous.

Cultural products are created in various types of organizational settings, and those settings can be conceptualized as different types of reward systems (Crane 1976). Some cultural products are produced in large corporations, where management makes major decisions about cultural content. The extent of management control over cultural content depends upon the economics of the particular cultural industry, especially the extent to which it is dominated by an oligopoly. The more oligopolistic the industry, the less control producers of cultural materials have over the content of their materials (DiMaggio 1977). By contrast, other forms of culture, including basic science, avant-garde arts, and theology, are produced (often in academic settings) by professionals or specialists, who have considerable autonomy and who share distinctive subcultures of their own. There are also numerous cultlike movements in the arts, the sciences, and religion that include relatively transient and loosely structured organizations in which leaders promulgate their ideas to followers. Those followers in turn tend to shift their allegiance from one organization to another in such a way that the entire set of groups is linked by social relationships and is sometimes called "the cultic milieu" (Campbell 1972).

Apart from the audiences for a cultural product, and the organizational contexts in which it is created, it is necessary to illustrate how the dissemination of different forms of culture varies and to indicate some major differences in the nature of the content that is disseminated. Channels for the dissemination of cultural products vary in terms of whether or not members of the audience can interact with and thereby influence the producers of culture, and whether the channels are used to disseminate only a particular type of content (specialized) or a broad range of content (unspecialized). The content of a cultural form can be described in terms of its diversity or homogeneity and the extent to which its values and symbols are comprehensible without specialized training or knowledge (i.e., esoteric/nonesoteric). One way of conceptualizing these differences is in terms of the extent to which formulas or paradigms are used in the creation of cultural products.

A formula is a system of conventions and rules for producing a particular type of cultural product (Cawelti 1976). Since the typical formula combines elements that have universal appeal, cultural products that employ formulas tend to be highly standardized. "Innovation" consists of minor variations within the limits of the formula.

By contrast, paradigms are ways of looking at the world and techniques for creating new combinations of elements (Masterman 1970). The goal is to exhaust the possibilities inherent in the paradigm and to replace it with a new one. Paradigms can be exceedingly complex and esoteric. There are thousands of paradigms but only a handful of basic formulas (Cawelti 1976). Paradigms evolve rapidly; formulas change only slightly over many decades.[2]

In contrast to the cultural differentiation that is implied in this framework for analyzing cultural forms, both functionalist and conflict theories assume the existence of a dominant culture, meaning a set of norms, values, and symbols that is either widely accepted throughout society or imposed by the mass media. In either case, cultural institutions serve several functions. According to one interpretation of the functionalist perspective (Goodlad 1971:27), the content of cultural forms serves four functions:

> (a) they perform a cognitive function in informing members about social structure and about the behavior expected from individual members of the community if that social structure is to be preserved; (b) they are likely to be vehicles for the expression of emotion at matters of tension in social structure; (c) the themes . . . are likely to be those most frequently felt in real life; . . . (d) as an instrumental element . . . (they) have as their manifest or latent functions the task of exercising social control.

Conceivably, in contemporary society, the major religious denominations, science, or the mass media could serve these or similar functions. I will discuss each of these possibilities in turn. I will then turn to an analysis of the implications of increasing cultural differentiation for understanding social control and consensus.

Religious Denominations and Consensus

Some religious denominations attract large numbers of followers and appear to offer a coherent value system (Herberg 1955; Heirich 1974). For example, there are four denominations with over five million members and five with over two-and-a-half million members.[3] However, recent statistics show that these organizations have been experiencing declines in membership, church attendance, and financial contributions (Roof 1976; Hartman 1976). As a case in point, the membership of the United Methodist Church declined by one million between 1964 and 1974. Studies of these organizations suggest that their members are not representative of the population as a whole. The members tend to come from small communities, and there is some evidence that people over 35 are more likely to report a religious affiliation (Newport 1979). If those under 35 do join a religious organization, it is likely to be a cult or a sect. Finally, there has been a dramatic increase in recent years in the proportion of the population reporting to Gallup polls that religion is losing its influence in American society.[4]

In the 1950s, Herberg (1955:88) argued that the major religious denominations expressed a coherent set of values, the "American Way of Life ... the operating faith of the American people." There are analogies between his interpretation of the dominant themes in these religions and Bellah's observations (1967) on civil religion. Bellah postulated a general consensus as to the values of American society, a blend of religious nationalism, faith in democratic ideals, and a reprimand for Americans who do not live up to these ideals. However, in 1975 Bellah wrote that "American civil religion is an empty and broken shell." He described "the collective identity" of the American people as waning with a correlative increase in political cynicism and apathy.

Other writers have challenged the view that value consensus in American society is based on religion. Luckman (1967) argues that the dominant institutions in American society are the polity and the economy, with a focus on specific goals and norms rather than a coherent value system. He claims that organized religion has become less relevant to everyday concerns. Individuals construct their own personal belief systems, explore a wide range of religious alternatives, and choose from an assortment of "ultimate" meanings, as they see fit.

Fenn (1972) also argues that traditional religious values are no longer relevant when it comes to what people actually do in work and politics. For example, the Protestant ethic is inappropriate in a period of automation, when full employment is an unattainable ideal. Bell (1976) emphasizes the incongruities between the values that predominate in economic and political institutions compared to cultural institutions. According to Bell (1976:37), religion and the arts are "dominated by an anti-rational, anti-intellectual temper in which the self is taken as the touchstone of cultural judgments and the effect on the self is the measure of the aesthetic worth of experience."

Approximately 1200 different religious groups are now present in American society (Melton 1977), and more religious groups emerged in the

1960s than at any other period in American history. The values and perspectives of the new religious groups are diverse, but they differ from those of American civil religion and traditional religion. The 1960s witnessed new religious movements in the Asian tradition, such as Hare Krishna and the Unification Church; new occult movements, focusing on contact with extraterrestrial beings; new quasi-religious movements belonging to the so-called Human Potential Movement (Stone 1976); and new versions of Pentecostalism and charismatic cults. These new religions are parts of a major shift in the nature of personal belief systems in American culture, one that has been underway since the mid-nineteenth century. The change is away from an emphasis on religious salvation and an afterlife attained through spiritual perfection to an emphasis on belief systems that enable individuals to (1) gain greater control over their minds and bodies or (2) answer questions about the meaning and significance of life.

Science and Consensus

Some authors have argued that contemporary society is a knowledge-based society whose chief resource is its highly educated, specialized, technical, scientific, and professional personnel (Bell 1976; Holzner and Marx 1979). Since World War II, there has been a marked increase in (1) government expenditures for research and development, (2) scientific and technical personnel, and (3) the production of scientific information. Holzner and Marx (1979:180) comment:

> Whether one considers the frequency of scientific discoveries or counts the number of employed scientists, or reviews the expansion of specialized educational structures designed to produce and disseminate knowledge, the picture of rapidly expanding organizational frameworks constructed specifically for the production of specialized, technical bodies of knowledge remains the same.

Yet it seems unlikely that basic science or so-called "high" technology can promote cultural integration in contemporary society. While the proliferation of science centers suggests an increasing popular interest in scientific discoveries (Kimche 1978), scientific methods and approaches are difficult for the average person to comprehend. Many individuals are more attracted by marginal cultures, either pseudoscientific movements (sciences asking inappropriate questions or using inappropriate methods) or antiscience movements. In the latter case, there is an effort to develop "alternative" sciences or technologies that are intended to be more appropriate for the needs of individuals than business organizations.[5]

On the other hand, a rudimentary level of technical knowledge (e.g., how to tinker with an automobile engine) is widespread in American society; and if the home computer becomes as commonplace as the automobile, the technical expertise of the population as a whole will increase. However, the ability to operate a computer does not imply an understanding of scientific method.

Popular Culture and Consensus

It is possible that the mass media rather than religion or science provide a basis for individuals to identify with the larger community or society. Allen (1977:236) says:

> Normative integration in complex societies is a special problem. For normative integration to occur, there must be a series of social links—groups, associations, communities, and other intermediate organizations—between the individual and society . . . functional and normative integration in both large and small social systems are at least facilitated by, and to some degree dependent upon, mass communication, even if not primarily a result of media effects on social systems.

Similarly, Nelson (1976) argues that television, popular magazines, detective fiction, and films are the equivalent of worship services in the American cultural religion, in that these media affirm and support the dominant American cultural belief system. The breadth of the television audience appears to lend credence to such arguments. Sets are turned on for an average of seven hours a day (Steinberg 1980:150), and the average adult watches about three hours of television per day (Hirsch 1980:411). However, examination of the content of television drama suggests that the common symbols and shared experiences provided by television are too narrow and unreal to generate a meaningful cultural consensus.

Downing (1980) found that both daytime and prime-time television shows are very selective interpretations of American society with respect to thematic content, the typical behaviors of males and females, and the demographic backgrounds of the characters. The dominant theme of the soap opera is romantic love, and Downing (1980:304) says that:

> so important is the motif of romantic love to the American daytime television serial that the dramas would have little substance without it. . . . The principal business of the daytime serial is conversation and the major topic is love.

Television images of men and women are highly selective. Men are presented as unidimensional—"all-true, all-powerful, all-good, always at the disposal of women and children" (Downing 1980:310). As Berman (1981) found in his study of the style of life portrayed in American advertising, soap opera's presentation of American life is dated; it does not reflect the concerns of contemporary women.

Demographically, the characters are not representative of American society, nor of the typical soap opera audience. Middle-class professionals and their wives are overrepresented. Nonwhite persons, children, the aged, and blue-collar workers are underrepresented. By contrast, the typical viewer is "a southern or midwestern woman from a large household with relatively low educational and income levels" (Downing 1980:309).

Prime-time television presents an even more selective view of American society. Downing describes it as a society of powerful, unmarried white males, leading a constituency of provocative women, subordinate black men, and ineffective aging persons. It is a society where "sex has replaced violence as a dramatic vehicle for demonstrating the exercise of power," but crime and violence remain major motifs.

Downing argues that prime-time television drama is actually projecting two symbolic worlds. The first is an adult world in which there is an attempt to deal with real problems in a mature way and to present characters that have some depth and multidimensionality. The second and more common is an adolescent world where the major themes are escapist: fantasies, adventure stories, comedies, and morality tales.

By contrast, Goodlad (1971) found that television dramas and popular plays presented in England from 1955-1965 tended to deal with relations between individuals and society. He says (1971:174, 188):

> the most popular forms of play were found to be those with morality themes in which social deviance is censured. . . . The evidence adduced in this study is that popular drama is not only a monitor of a community's morality but that it or its functional equivalents . . . is the very mechanism by which a society maintains its moral integrity and coherence.

The predominant theme in the British plays was morality, especially transgressions against society. The second most popular theme was love, but its treatment was very different from that in American television. British plays dealt with problems raised by monogamy or in finding a spouse.

It appears that a functionalist interpretation of culture fits the depiction of British society by television during the period Goodlad studied, but it does not fit American television's portrayal of American society. The contrast may result from the homogeneity of the British audience for popular drama. Social class differences did not seem to affect that audience's appreciation of popular drama. Goodlad (1971:141) also argues that those who controlled the supply of dramatic material in Britain in that period operated "within the same social nexus as those who consumed it." That is not the case for a very heterogeneous society, such as the United States, where mass media content cannot reflect the concerns of all segments of the society. To attract a wide audience, themes must be escapist rather than serious, because it is impossible to deal with serious themes so as to please all members of the audience. It even may be difficult to identify themes that are of interest to particular segments of the audience.[6] Unlike the creators of British television and popular dramas in the 1950s and 1960s, creators of American television dramas do not share the typical values and lifestyles of their audience. Cantor (1979) stresses that the creative people working in television

> do not necessarily express their own values but rather the values of those in control of their bureaucratic structures. . . . They must satisfy the producer, the production companies, the networks and, of course, finally some segment of the audience . . . most see themselves as different from the audience and agree that they subordinate their own personal values and tastes in order to work.

An alternative interpretation of the impact of the mass media is that of Gerbner and Gross (1976), who see television's primary function as that of reinforcing the legitimacy of established power and authority. In other words, Gerbner and Gross argue that the preoccupation with violence on American television reinforces the power of those who control society. It does so, supposedly, by inducing "a heightened sense of risk and insecurity," which increases acquiescence to and dependence upon established authority and legitimizes the use of force. They depict television as the chief instrument of enculturation and social control, in particular "the established religion of the industrial order, relating to governance as the church did to the state in earlier times" (Gerbner and Gross 1976:198).

Like the functionalist interpretation, the Gerbner-Gross argument seems plausible when applied to a single case. However, a recent reanalysis of their data (Hirsch 1980) finds little support for that argument. Moreover, the content of other mass media (e.g., radio, magazines) does not reveal a similar ideology. In order to compete with television, magazines and radio have become specialized, aiming their wares at specific segments of the audience (Hirsch 1979). As a case in point, the popular music industry is oriented primarily toward adolescents. This music expresses various themes, some of which appear to reflect very critical attitudes toward American society, and those attitudes are seemingly incongruous with the large corporations that dominate the industry. This suggests that the content of mass media is related to the organization of "cultural" industries. The cultural content of highly oligopolistic industries has been shown to be more homogenous than the cultural content of competitive industries (DiMaggio 1977; Lewis 1981). For example, at one time popular songs were produced and disseminated largely by a few large corporations. During that period (approximately 1930 to 1950), popular songs expressed the values of the white middle and upper class. The songs dealt primarily with romantic love in a very idealized and sentimental fashion. Social problems and world events were virtually ignored in this musical "picture" of an idealized fantasy world.[7]

Rather than describe the content of contemporary American television as an ideology that supports the status quo, it can be seen as an attempt to provide a message that is thrilling and scary enough to attract a very heterogeneous audience. However, once the organization of the television industry changes, its content will change. Given the steady increase in cultural differentiation in American society over several decades, the variety of "messages" in the content of television is likely to increase (DeLuca 1980).

The Implications of Cultural Differentiation for Cultural Integration

It appears that as the number of communication channels increases, the diversity of cultural products increases. Before 1950, when the number of communication channels were significantly smaller, the mass media and religious institutions disseminated a relatively consistent but narrow set of values. Those values appeared to be the dominant culture but they did not reflect the needs, interests, and values of all segments of the population.

In the 1950s and 1960s, this dominant culture was gradually replaced by an increasingly differentiated cultural scene. Major corporations lost their virtual control over channels for the production and dissemination of culture as "culture classes" acquired new channels for the dissemination of their views, along with increasing specialization of channels other than television for the production and dissemination of cultural products.

Therefore, the search for a dominant culture that encompasses widely shared values and integrates society seems less and less feasible. Escarpit (1977) has suggested that modern society consists of an intricate network of communication channels that correspond to the needs and identities of diverse social groups. If that interpretation is accurate, a new conception of the nature of cultural integration is needed. While symbolic interactionists emphasize the role of subcultures in contemporary society, they have not developed a new interpretation of the nature of cultural integration at a high level of cultural differentiation.

To understand cultural integration at that level, the social system of basic science is an appropriate model. Contemporary science comprises hundreds of distinct specialities, but each speciality has connections, both intellectual and social, with other specialities. Campbell (1969) has suggested that the entire system resembles the overlapping scales of a fish. However, Small and Griffith (1974) have shown that some clusters of specialties are more closely related than others.

From this point of view, cultural integration does not require that all cultural communities share the same intellectual values, beliefs, and norms. For example, while it has been argued that all scientists share certain very general norms concerning scientific work (Merton 1973), it appears that these norms are interpreted somewhat differently by each community of scientists. In a highly differentiated cultural system, cultural integration occurs because of overlapping memberships among cultural communities that lead to the dissemination of ideas and values. Individuals participate in a variety of cultural communities and, through their peregrinations, carry ideas from one community to another.

Consequently, one finds clusters of communities that share similar preoccupations. Examples are the so-called occult milieu (Campbell 1972) encompassing various small cults concerned with spiritualism and unidentified flying objects (UFOs), some of the communities concerned with science fiction, and the communities that are trying to apply scientific approaches to UFOs and parapsychology. Another milieu is concerned with bodily control and psychological adaptation. The aim is to give individuals greater control over their environment and hence more power in social relations. Secular movements include encounter groups, est, and transcendental meditation. Religious movements encompass Christian Science, Scientology, and Satanism. Still another cluster consists of the avant-garde arts, such as painting, music, and dance, where the social circles and culture classes clearly intersect and ideas move back and forth across highly permeable boundaries.

To what extent do various types of cultural communities serve essentially the same "societal functions," such as providing individuals with a sense of social identity or social control? A negative answer is suggested by the considerable variation in this respect. On the one hand, Wright (1976) says that the western film reveals to members of American society "what their society is like and how they as individuals should act in it." Much contemporary popular music is concerned with rejecting the social identities of the previous generation and creating new social identities for youth. On the other hand, in some cultural communities, there is scarcely any interest in problems of social identity, except possibly in an ironical or derisive manner. That is especially true of avant-garde arts during the past few decades, although with the growing acceptance of realist painting, there is some indication of increasing concern with social identity (Goodyear 1981). Moreover, some cults are preoccupied less with personal identity than with understanding man's place in the universe, which they interpret in terms of occult forces. Still other cults are concerned with ideologies more constrictive and authoritarian than anything ever perpetrated by the mass media.[8]

While the relationships among participants in a scientific speciality resemble a social circle,[9] the social bases for other cultural communities vary from the heterogeneous mass audiences for many prime-time television dramas; the taste cultures and culture classes that provide the audiences for many magazines, radio stations, and styles of popular music; and the culture classes and social circles that characterize the audiences for avant-garde arts and many religions. For example, collectors of particular styles of painting share at least a world view and sometimes, if very active, participate in a social circle that includes painters, critics, dealers, and museum curators. A religious cult draws its members from individuals who either share a world view or belong to a social circle that includes some who are already members of the group (Stark and Bainbridge 1980).

There are reciprocal relationships between the social bases of these communities and the kinds of messages that will be produced and disseminated for them. Paradigms are most suitable for transmission via social circles because in social circles, the audience can transmit information back to the producers and generate new ideas. By contrast, the standardization of a formula makes it suitable for transmission via the largely one-way channels between corporate producers and mass audiences or taste cultures. In most of the large popular culture industries, the producers of cultural materials receive little or no "feedback" from their audiences; and the producers may not be familiar with the concerns of the audience. In social circles, by contrast, ideas are defined and redefined in thousands of interactions among producers and between producers and their audience. Social relations between producers and audiences and the concomitant possiblity of exchanges of ideas affect the nature of the cultural product and the extent to which the product reflects the interests of its audience. The tendency of the mass media to present styles of life that are already dated is a function of the ways they are linked to their audiences.

Implications for the Future

The trend toward cultural differentiation—an increasing number of channels along which an ever-widening variety of cultural materials are conveyed—will continue and even accelerate. Moreover, the nature of the cultural differentiation will change. The trend is away from cultural differentiation based on economic and occupational distinctions (taste cultures) toward cultural differentiation based on culture classes and social circles.

If present trends continue, the nature of cultural integration will also change from a dominant culture transmitted along one-way channels toward a great variety of interlocking cultures transmitted along both one-way and two-way channels. With increasing possibilities for two-way channels through innovations in electronic communications, there is likely to be a gradual decline in the transmission of materials based on formulas and an increase in the transmission of materials based on paradigms.

Gerbner and Gross's image (1976) of the television viewer trembling with fear and apprehension will become unrealistic as a wider variety of other cultural channels becomes available. Undoubtedly, many viewers scarcely look to alternatives, but that group is likely to diminish as cultural differentiation increases.

At the same time, a conception of social control that postulates a dominant culture—a single set of norms and values that are widely shared—will become less and less applicable. The alternative is a complex model of interlocking cultural communities. Participation by individuals in a variety of "cultures" will lead to an appreciation and acceptance of normative dissensus, and it will become increasingly difficult for an elite to impose a one-dimensional interpretation of social reality on the public. Such forecasts make the specter of *1984* unrealistic.

NOTES

1. In this chapter, I will refer to (1) *cultural forms,* a particular type of recorded culture (e.g., the novel, painting, drama, poetry, basic science, religious faiths); (2) *cultural products,* specific instances of a cultural form (e.g., a particular novel, painting, play, poem); (3) *a set of related cultural products* within a particular cultural form that are associated with one another because they make use of the same style, version of a formula, theoretical model, world view, and the like; (4) *cultural communities,* the social group including producers, "middlemen" (e.g., executives, entrepreneurs, dealers, critics), and consumers that forms around the production and dissemination of a particular set of related cultural products; and (5) *cultural channels* through which cultural products are disseminated (e.g., television, film, radio, magazines, journals, public meetings).

2. Examples of five basic formulas in popular literature are provided by Cawelti (1976:39): adventure, romance, mystery, melodrama, and alien beings or states. The notion of a formula can also be applied to other cultural forms (e.g., the popular song, sidewalk painting). Most rapidly growing fields in the natural and social sciences contain paradigms that provide models or "exemplars" for research. Again, the concept has broader applications in the realm of avant-garde arts, whose practitioners

view themselves as using a particular approach to solve problems inherent in the use of their materials.

3. The following religious organizations had over five million members in 1975: the Roman Catholic Church, Southern Baptist Convention, United Methodist Church, and the National Baptist Convention of the U.S.A. The following organizations had between two-and-a-half and five million members: United Lutheran Church in America, the Episcopal Church, Lutheran Church-Missouri Synod, National Baptist Convention of America, and the United Presbyterian Church in the U.S.A. (United States Bureau of the Census 1977; Rosten 1975).

4. The percentage of respondents who voiced the opinion that religion is losing its influence in American society was 14 percent in 1957, 75 percent in 1970, and 61 percent in 1977 (Hyer 1977).

5. Philadelphia buses carry advertisements sponsored by Bell of Pennsylvania offering a telephone astrology service with different numbers for each sign of the zodiac. The knowledge gap between "Ma Bell" and her clients is nicely epitomized by these ads.

6. Frank and Greeberg (1980) show that the television audience consists of fourteen distinct segments, representing different interests, needs, demographic, and socioeconomic characteristics.

7. Similar observations could be made about American movies during this period (Wood 1975).

8. Cultural producers are often subject to social controls over their creative work. These controls are most stringent in esoteric fields, such as the sciences and the avant-garde arts, where recognition and rewards are given to cultural producers who conform to standards set by peers. By contrast, in popular culture industries producers must meet requirements set by management. In marginal fields, producers are constrained by the necessity of attracting and holding followers.

9. The entire group corresponds to a social circle, while a subgroup (known as an invisible college) provides a focal point for the group's activities.

REFERENCES

Albrecht, M. C. 1968. "Art as an Institution." *American Sociological Review* 33:383-97.

Allen, I. 1977. "Social Integration as an Integrating Principle." Pp. 235-50 in *Mass Media Policies in Changing Cultures,* edited by George Gerbner. New York: John Wiley.

Bell, Daniel. 1976. *The Cultural Contradictions of Capitalism.* New York: Basic Books.

Bellah, Robert. 1967. "Civil Religion in America." *Daedalus* 96:1-21.

Bellah, Robert. 1975. *The Broken Covenant.* New York: Seabury.

Berman, Ronald. 1981. *Advertising and Social Change.* Beverly Hills, CA: Sage.

Campbell, C. 1972. "The Cult, the Cultic Milieu, and Secularization." Pp. 119-36 in *A Sociological Yearbook of Religion in Great Britain,* Vol. 5, edited by Michael Hill. London: SCM Press.

Campbell, Donald. 1969. "Ethnocentrism of Disciplines and the Fish-Scale Model of Omniscience." Pp. 328-48 in *Interdisciplinary Relationships in the Social Sciences,* edited by Muzafer Sherif and Carolyn W. Sherif. Chicago: Aldine.

Cantor, Muriel G. 1979. "The Social Organization of Artistic Production: Art Through the Media." Unpublished paper presented at the Sociology of Art Conference, William Patterson College, Wayne, New Jersey, 1979.

Cawelti, J. G. 1976. *Adventure, Mystery and Romance: Formula Stories as Art and Popular Culture.* Chicago: University of Chicago Press.

Collins, R. 1975. *Conflict Sociology.* New York: Academic.

Crane, Diana. 1976. "Reward Systems in Art, Science and Religion." Pp. 57-72 in *The Production of Culture,* edited by Richard A. Peterson. Beverly Hills, CA: Sage.

DeLuca, Stuart M. 1980. *Television's Transformation: The Next 25 Years.* San Diego: A.S. Barnes.

DiMaggio, Paul. 1977. "Market Structure, the Creative Process, and Popular Culture." *Journal of Popular Culture* 11:436-52.

DiMaggio, Paul and Michael Useem. 1978. "Social Class and Arts Consumption." *Theory and Society* 5:141-61.

Downing, M. H. 1980. "American Television Drama—Men, Women, Sex, and Love." Pp. 299-341 in *Progress in Communication Sciences,* edited by B. Dervin and M. J. Voigt. Norwood, NJ: Ablex.

Escarpit, R. 1977. "The Concept of 'Mass'." *Journal of Communication* 27:44-47.

Fenn, R. K. 1972. "Toward a New Sociology of Religion." *Journal for the Scientific Study of Religion* 11:16-32.

Fine, G. A. and S. Kleinman. 1979. "Rethinking Subculture: An Interactionist Analysis." *American Journal of Sociology* 85:1-20.

Frank, R. E. and M. G. Greenberg. 1980. *The Public's Use of Television: Who Watches and Why.* Beverly Hills, CA: Sage.

Gans, Herbert. 1974. *Popular Culture and High Culture.* New York: Basic Books.

Gerbner, George and Larry Gross. 1976. "Living With Television: The Violence Profile." *Journal of Communication* 26:173-99.

Goodlad, J.S.R. 1971. *The Sociology of Popular Drama.* London: Heineman.

Goodyear, Frank H., Jr. 1981. *Contemporary American Realism Since 1960.* Philadelphia: Pennsylvania Academy of the Fine Arts.

Hartman, Warren J. 1976. *Membership Trends: A Study of Decline and Growth in the United Methodist Church, 1949-75.* Nashville: Discipleship Resources.

Heirich, M. 1974. "The Sacred as a Market Economy." Unpublished paper presented at the Annual Meeting of the American Sociological Association, Montreal.

Herberg, Will. 1955. *Protestant-Catholic-Jew.* Garden City, NY: Doubleday.

Hirsch, Paul M. 1978. "Television as a National Medium: Its Cultural and Political Role in American Society." Pp. 389-427 in *Handbook of Urban Life,* edited by David Street. San Francisco: Jossey-Bass.

Hirsch, Paul M. 1980. "The 'Scary World' of the Nonviewer and Other Anomalies: A Reanalysis of Gerbner et al's Findings on Cultivation Analysis, Part I." *Communication Research* 7:403-56.

Holzner, B. and J. Marx. 1979. *Knowledge Application: The Knowledge System in Society.* Boston: Allyn & Bacon.

Hyer, M. 1977. "Gallup Sees Big Religious Revival in U.S." *International Herald Tribune* (June 18-19).

Kadushin, Charles. 1968. "Power, Influence and Social Circles: A New Methodology for Studying Opinion Makers." *American Sociological Review* 33:685-99.

Kadushin, Charles. 1976. "Networks and Circles in the Production of Culture." Pp. 107-122 in *The Production of Culture,* edited by Richard A. Peterson. Beverly Hills, CA: Sage.

Kimche, Lee. 1978. "Science Centers: A Potential for Learning." *Science* 199 (20 January):270-73.

Lewis, George H. 1981. "Taste Cultures and Their Composition: Towards a New Theoretical Perspective." Pp. 210-17 in *Mass Media and Social Change,* edited by Elihu Katz and Tamás Szecskö. Beverly Hills, CA: Sage.

Luckmann, Thomas. 1967. *The Invisible Religion.* New York: Macmillan.

Masterman, M. 1970. "The Nature of a Paradigm." Pp. 59-89 in *Criticism and the Growth of Knowledge,* edited by I. K. Lakatos and A. Musgrave. Cambridge, England: University Press.

Melton, J. G. 1977. *A Directory of Religious Bodies in the United States.* New York: Garland.

Merton, Robert K. 1973. "The Normative Structure of Science." Pp. 267-78 in *The Sociology of Science.* Chicago: University of Chicago Press.

Meyer, J. 1977. "Education as an Institution." *American Journal of Sociology* 83:55-57.

Nelson, J. 1976. *Your God is Alive and Well and Appearing in Popular Culture.* Philadelphia: Westminister Press.

Newport, F. 1979. "The Religious Switcher." *American Sociological Review* 44:528-552.

Peterson, Richard A. 1979. "Revitalizing the Culture Concept." *Annual Review of Sociology* 5:137-66.

Peterson, Richard A. and Paul DiMaggio. 1975. "Cycles in Symbol Production: The Case of Popular Music. *American Sociological Review* 40:158-73.

Roof, Wade C. 1976. "Traditional Religion in Contemporary Society: A Theory of Local-Cosmopolitan Plausibility." *American Sociological Review* 41:195-208.

Rosten, Leo, ed. 1975. *Religions of America: Ferment and Faith in an Age of Crisis.* New York: Simon & Schuster.

Small, Henry and B. C. Griffith. 1974. "The Structure of Scientific Literatures: I. Identifying and Graphing Specialities." *Science Studies* 4:17-40.

Stark, Rodney and William S. Bainbridge. 1980. "Networks of Faith." *American Journal of Sociology* 85:1376-95.

Steinberg, C. S. 1980. TV Facts. New York: Facts on File.

Stone, D. 1976. "The Human Potential Movement." Pp. 93-115 in *The New Religious Consciousness.* Berkeley: University of California Press.

United States Bureau of the Census. 1977. *Statistical Abstract of the United States.* Washington, DC: U.S. Government Printing Office.

Wood, M. 1975. *America at the Movies.* New York: Basic Books.

Wright, W. 1976. *Six-Guns and Society.* Berkeley: University of California Press.

PART V

Perennial Issues and Prospects

Preoccupation with human liberty reached its apogee in the West during the eighteenth and nineteenth centuries, especially among writers now commonly identified as "bourgeois." Yet social control and human liberty are inseparable subjects, and one would be hard pressed to identify any civilization or historical period in which social critics were indifferent to this question: Who ought to control whom, how, and to what end? All of the central political issues in human history come down to that question, and it transcends politics. With the advent of democracy, both the idea of being controlled and controlling came to be distasteful, so much so that social or behavioral scientists are seemingly reluctant to recognize that benign behavior (e.g., inviting a friend out for lunch) can be control. But the common practice of implicitly equating control with evil is hardly mysterious. Far from distorting, Lord Acton's maxim is more meaningful if paraphrased as follows: Control corrupts and absolute control corrupts absolutely.

Whether benign or evil, control is the basis of power, and that relation points the way out of the quagmire into which the conceptual treatment of power has sunk. Briefly, unless power is defined as the *perceived capacity to control others,* the term serves no constructive purpose.

While the conceptualization of power in terms of control admits the possibility of individuals pursuing power as an end in itself, the conflict theory of social life suggests that control is not just a means and power an end. If social relations entail a conflict of interests, power is not a direct manifestation of that conflict; rather, the perceived capacity to control stems from attempts to resolve or conceal conflict to the advantage of one party over the other, and those attempts are necessarily attempts at control. Since control itself gives rise to a conflict of interests and power is best defined as the perceived capacity to control, control is the central notion rather than power.

All social control is suspect from the perspective of conflict theory, the assumption being that the interests of the controllers prevail over those who are controlled. The point is not made to suggest that the conflict theory is valid or invalid; rather, advocates of conflict theory simply view social control in a way quite different from advocates of functional theory. The latter are inclined to view social control as impersonal and benign, as something necessary to maintain society. Contemplate this argument: Penitentiaries are necessary to correct errors in socialization and deal with rare transgressors of widely shared norms. Whatever its merits, the argument does not stress the possibility that penitentiaries serve the interests of some social classes or factions more than others. Moreover, penitentiaries are surely conscious and deliberate control, but functionalists are prone to deny that social control is necessarily conscious and deliberate. If the conscious and deliberate character of social control is emphasized, it becomes difficult to avoid this question. Whose interests are served by social control?

Despite the foregoing, some arguments about social control do not support conflict theory. It may well be that some kinds of control solve some kinds of societal problems without benefiting particular classes or factions more than others, let alone without an exclusive benefit. For that matter, it could be that human societies are too complex for social order to be maintained through control in the conscious and deliberate sense. That possibility takes on added significance in contemplating the claim implied by Marxist theory that in slave, feudal, and capitalist societies control is monopolized by a propertied class.

So the argument is really this: The notion of control is pivotal in a perennial issue that haunts sociology and perhaps all of the social sciences. However, that consideration has not promoted the study of control, and the most damning commentary that can be made on the "counteraction-of-deviance" conception of social control is that after more than thirty years it has not generated impressive theories or lines of research. The reason is that the conception does not make control the pivotal notion in the perennial issue that divides advocates of conflict theory and advocates of functional theory. That claim is debatable, of course; but it does serve to underscore the importance of this question: What is necessary to further the prospects for impressive theories and lines of research in the study of social control?

As previously suggested, social scientists and sociologists in particular are seemingly reluctant to identify the manipulation of human behavior as social control if they perceive that manipulation as benign. The reluctance implies that social control is somehow inherently evil or dangerous. While such a conceptualization is hardly defensible, it is understandable in light of the relation between social control and social conflict, which is treated in this volume by Austin Turk (Chapter 11).

As Turk rightly suggests, the common nexus of social conflict is an unequally beneficial relation, and the party (be it an individual or collectivity) that benefits the most engages in control to maintain that relation. But control may be exercised with a view to establishing or maintaining social inequality, and in that sense social conflict may stem from control. In any case, an unequally beneficial relation is stable only insofar as the controlling party in the relation comes to be recognized as having authority over the other party. The viability of that authority depends on various conditions and the strategies pursued by those in authority. Those conditions and strategies are central subjects in Turk's chapter.

In Chapter 12, Robert Meier recognizes that progress in the study of social control has been stymied by the problem of conceptualization. He also suggests that the problem is not just one of contending and seemingly irreconcilable definitions of social control. Additionally, each contender is objectionable for one or more of various reasons.

Meier goes beyond the conceptual problem to an identification of the pivotal issue in formulating theories about social control or in conducting research on the subject. Social control is a dangerous phenomenon; and people have passionate feelings about it, even people who are not subject to extreme degrees of control. Meier points out that novelists are much more sensitive to those passionate feelings than are social and behavioral scientists. Many of the latter are reluctant to confront this question: Who should exercise control over whom, how, and to what end? The reluctance may be understandable, but Meier argues that any study of social control is incomplete (indeed, "lifeless") if it ignores the question.

11

Social Control and
Social Conflict

AUSTIN T. TURK

Social science, as all science, rests upon the twin assumptions that reality is not chaos but pattern, and that regularities of stability and change can in principle be detected and predicted. How best to approach the task of detection and prediction has long been at issue. Some philosophers and theorists have tended to view stability as the basic pattern and change as deviation from pattern, even a threat to "natural" order. Others have been inclined to the reverse conception, viewing change as reality and stability as largely illusion. One legacy of this bifurcation of perspective is the tendency of most social scientists and other people to see social control and social conflict as mutually exclusive. Control is presumed to be necessary because of conflict, and to be successful insofar as conflict is eliminated from social life. Or conversely, control is defined as alien repression of human life, while conflict is welcomed as the harbinger or means of liberation. Both positions have turned out to be more ideologically than analytically useful, as it has become increasingly clear that the relationship between control and conflict is not exclusionary but dialectical.

There will be no attempt here to review theoretical proposals and controversies regarding the nature and sources of either social control or social conflict (for recent useful analytical reviews, see Gibbs 1981, on social control; and on social conflict see Collins 1975, and Himes 1980). Each concept has proved to be indefinitely expansible; the intellectual history of each is one of conceptual imperialism—the agglomeration of concerns and observations whose relevance to one another is unclear. The inclusion of unintentional and even unconscious actions, unrecognized relationships, and unanticipated effects as "control" or "conflict" seems to have been especially pernicious in confusing and impeding research. As Gibbs (1981: *passim*) has emphasized, conceptions of social control without intentionality dissipate in a foggy imagery of social behavior as somehow automatically or incidentally patterned. Similarly, unless intentionality is specified, every way in which people impinge upon one another becomes "social conflict." The contexts in which conflict does or may occur become indistinguishable from the structural sources, means, paths, and effects of conflict.

In particular, the inequalities of life chances found in any complexly organized society may be facilely treated as evidence in themselves of current conflicts, ignoring the possibility that present inequalities may simply be the residue of past conflicts. Disproportions can then be illogically assumed to show discrimination (racist, sexist, or other); failures to observe antagonistic or intentionally discriminatory behavior can be discounted by invoking—without specification—such conceptions as "structural" or "latent" conflicts of interest, "objective group interests" versus "false consciousness," or "institutional" as distinct from interpersonal racism.

Conceptual and methodological problems are compounded when one tries to examine the *relationship* between social control and social conflict regardless of intentionality. In particular settings literally everything may be defined as "evidence." If A and B are, or seem to be, somehow functionally linked (e.g., through regional or international economic exchanges), they may be assumed to be in conflict. At the same time, the persistence of linkage may be taken as evidence that the conflict is being controlled—by physical coercion if clashes are observed, by ideological repression if they are not. Socialization, education, religiosity, electoral politics, consumer protection laws, policing, and all other patterning features of social life may thus be interpreted as "control," while anything short of perfectly equal or universally approved outcomes can be viewed as indicating "conflict."

The point is certainly not to deny the reality either of structural sources of conflict or of subtle controls. It is, rather, that these crucial realities are hopelessly obscured by notions of control and conflict that do not distinguish intended from unintended behavior, the objectives from the consequences of behavior, and interactive from functional (i.e., systemic) relationships. The question is, of course, not whether but how to make these distinctions, analytically and empirically. From what has been said, it follows that the logical possibilities of unintentional control and unintentional conflict must be excluded. This leaves the problem of developing a model of the control-conflict relationship that incorporates both (1) intentionality in defining each concept and (2) the facticity of unintended behavior, consequences other than those sought or expected, and functional as well as interactive relationships.

A Model of Social Life

Attempting to make sociological (predictively useful) sense of the available ideas and information about political criminality, I have been working from and toward a model of social life as constantly exhibiting the process and consequences of political organization (Turk 1982). The elemental postulate is that people try to secure and enhance the life chances of themselves and/or their own kind, as defined in social experience. As military stability and territorial identity are established, the process of politically organizing social life moves from the blatant manipulations of warfare to the relatively less crude and increasingly subtle manipulations of political *control* and *resistance*—the behavioral components of the process. The consequence of political organization is a hierarchical structure of relationships characterized by the channeling of greater resources to the more successful (superiors, authorities) and fewer resources to the less successful (inferiors, subjects). Anything, material or nonmaterial, that is valued by authorities and/or subjects is a resource, whose significance for their relative life chances is a composite function of the options it represents and the social bonds it affects (Dahrendorf 1979: 30-34, *passim*).

Control is, then, behavior intended to establish and maintain an unequally beneficial relationship. In a complex society (a polity), at the highest (policy) level of control decision making, the behavior of those who control may be called *statecraft*. As the strategies of statecraft are tactically adjusted to the pursuit of internal security (as distinguished from the concerns with interpolity relations and with material production and consumption), control behavior is more precisely focused as *political policing*.

Resistance may be behavior intended to terminate (and perhaps reverse) such a relationship, or it may be behavior expressing resentment without articulate political aims. In either case, resistance is not a prerequisite for control—which is always anticipatory as well as reactive.

Authorities engaging in control may or may not encounter or trigger resistance. If they do, there is *conflict* between them and those subjects who intentionally resist. Intentional resisters may be forced or persuaded to stop, provoked into self-defeating moves, or ignored, depending upon control tactics with regard to the scale, violence, and other aspects of the challenge. Persons whose resistant behavior is more expressive (merely resentful) than instrumental may be driven into greater political awareness and determination (radicalized), stopped, or ignored—again depending upon tactics. Whether directed against instrumental or expressive resistance, control tactics have unanticipated as well as anticipated effects. Most notably, conflict between controlling authorities and resisting subjects generates *interactive* relationships that help to create and sustain, but also undermine, the *functional* relationships linking the disparate life chances of everyone involved, knowingly or unwittingly.

If "success" is defined as the achievement of victory over an adversary, successful control results in an interactive relationship marked by subjects' deferential behavior complementing the dominant behavior of their social superiors. Initially, at least, deference may mean little more than the absence of intentional resistance, while dominance may be only slightly restrained aggression. In time, the interaction becomes more normatively constrained, and is extended by the casuistries of political socialization to legitimate the functional linkage of particular authorities and subjects who may never have any interaction with one another. The ultimate consequence is also the goal of enlightened authorities: an *authority* structure—a structure of inequality sustained mainly by ideological power, secondarily by political and economic power, and only minimally and occasionally by the threat and use of violence.

Unsuccessful control contributes to successful resistance—if defined as termination of the hierarchical relationship. However, if the relationship at issue is interactive—especially if limited to a particular locale or subset of authorities and subjects—it may be ended with little impact upon the polity. If not, the total structure of functional as well as interactive relationships between authorities and subjects may eventually collapse. The less definitive but more usual consequence of unsuccessful control is that control and resistance are routinized in a more or less conflictful interactive relationship. Insofar as functional relationships of inequality therefore lack normative support, the human and material costs of maintaining them will be relatively high for both authorities and subjects. A polity so constituted is less an *authority* structure than merely a *power* structure. To the extent that a polity is more a structure of power than of authority, it is expected to be more vulnerable to challenge and dissolution—though not necessarily more exposed to challenges as measured by the incidence of resistance acts (for an empirical illustration of the point, see Turk 1981).

The model of social life as collective struggle does not preclude the extension of group boundaries to include once-alien outsiders. It does imply that the process of inclusion is problematic and painful, that boundaries are never finally or irreversibly set, and that inequities in intragroup relationships always emerge and generate new conflicts. From this perspective, control and conflict are bound together in a dynamic interaction process that both produces and changes social structures while being at the same time channeled by them. In trying to anticipate the future directions and structural outcomes of the control-conflict process, we are led to consider (1) how authority structures are created and perpetuated; (2) the sources of deterioration of such structures; (3) possible indicators of their viability; and (4) the directions and forms of change expected under variable conditions. (The following sketches draw upon and supplement ideas developed more fully in Turk 1982.)

Constructing Authority

Authority grows out of power. Persistent inequalities in the distribution of resources tend to become a hardening reality as time passes. Most people find it easier to live with that reality than to struggle against it. Coping tends to displace questioning. Such is the social-psychological ground upon which unequal interactive realtionships are established, and upon which inequitable social structures ultimately depend.

Control strategies and tactics are intended minimally to perpetuate power structures, optimally to transform them into authority structures. The ideal is a *legitimate* as well as—at least from authorities' perspective—unchallengeable social structure. Strategically, the options of statecraft are to manipulate individuals and groups by controlling access to positions and resources, rewarding political conformity while punishing resistance, and fostering either apathy or enlightenment (see Gamson 1968:116-143). Within the broad framework set by whatever mix of options is adopted, the political policing of resistance is (at least in principle) designed to insure strategic success by a blend of intelligence gathering, information control (censorship and propaganda), neutralization of resistance by violence and/or other means, and intimidation tactics aimed at general deterrence. The organizational ideal—never fully attained—is an integrated control effort in which every governmental agency and social institution operates consistently to inhibit political deviance and encourage political conformity.

The particular form and direction of control depends upon not only the purposes and knowledge of authorities, anticipating or reacting to varying forms of resistance, but also the social environment in which the control effort is undertaken. The parameters of action, for resisters as well as authorities, are defined by all that affects how people are linked to one another within a particular setting: the demographic, cultural, organizational, territorial, economic-technological, and historical facts of their collective past and present relationships. For whoever would control or resist, the social environment delimits what is or may be possible. It is, however, improbable that either authorities or subjects will develop an objective understanding of the factual bases and possibilities of their relationship.

As resistance is experienced, statecraft incorporates such experiences as key elements in a theory of how resistance arises and can be controlled.

Such theories are of course partisan, and likely to be more implicit than explicit in the formulation of control policies. As interpretations of experience, partisan control theories are characterized to a greater or lesser degree by ideological distortions. Among the sources of distortion, and therefore of invalidity, are (1) the presumption that knowledge derived from participatory, partisan experience is more trustworthy than if derived from detached, nonpartisan observation (scientific research); (2) the strong tendency to exaggerate confirmatory evidence and belittle contrary evidence; (3) the related bias of equating self-fulfilling expectations with predictions; (4) emphasis upon proximate and more readily manipulated factors rather than on more complex and problematic factors; and (5) exclusion of propositions questioning the viability of the current social structure—especially any arguments for radical changes in the structure of power and privilege. One expects, then, that the control theories developed or favored by authorities will sometimes or often mislead them into ineffective or counterproductive moves.

Interpreting the same experiences, resisters will also develop partisan theories—of how to resist the control efforts of authorities. In their fullest expression such theories of resistance are theories of revolutionary praxis: how to destroy structures of power and authority. Resistance theories are subject to the same kinds of distortions (with appropriate modifications) as are control theories, with similar consequences.

Given that neither authorities nor resisters are likely to develop (or accept) objective understandings of their situations, their interaction can be expected to produce outcomes that often reduce instead of increase the chances for a more viable social order. The more their conflict is defined in zero-sum terms ("them" or "us"), the more vulnerable the social structure will be to deterioration.

The Mortality of Authority Structures

Contrary to the ancient notion that a given social order is mandated by nature's laws, sooner or later people appear who recognize that social structures are of human construction, and therefore subject to renovation—or even reconstruction. Inequalities of life chances cannot be forever cloaked or excused by legitimating ideologies and theories. Some people will question whatever legitimations are offered, some will be moved to resentment, and some will resist. Without entangling ourselves in a discussion of whether there is something "indomitable" about "the human spirit," there still are reasons to believe that no structure of power or authority is immortal.

First, political policing helps to cause that which the control effort is intended to eliminate: awareness, resentment, and resistance in regard to social inequalities. Because everyone is a potential threat to social order, political policing tends to become an ever-expanding program of surveillance and manipulation, while the criteria for distinguishing tolerable from intolerable opposition tend to be shifted (or ignored) so as to facilitate the prevention and neutralization of resistance. The definition of political deviance tends in practice, then, to include an ever-wider range of ideas and activities. Since authority exists to the extent that power is accepted without being questioned, political policing erodes authority structures insofar as it makes people see and feel power where they might otherwise see and feel only authority. Unless the tendencies of political policing can somehow be curbed, the result is insecurity for growing numbers of people—which tends to precipitate increasing resentment and resistance.

Second, if authority-subject conflicts are to be resolved, both parties must prefer compromise to victory or withdrawal; and each must be able to reward the other for concessions. Neither condition is likely to be satisfied when the structural foundations of unequal life chances are at stake. Authorities cannot be expected to concede enough resources to affect significantly the bases of inequality, nor can serious resisters (revolutionaries) guarantee that the kinds of people currently favored will not suffer diminished life chances—absolute as well as relative—if radical structural changes are accomplished.

Third, no authority structure can be insulated from the effects of variations in its natural and social environments. Declining resources, for instance, eventually make it impossible for everyone's needs to be met. One repercussion is that fewer resources can be conceded even as the less favored become increasingly desperate, so that authorities are under growing pressure to use repressive instead of cooptive controls. Even then, the more favored may begin to doubt the success of the control effort, and further weaken the structure by seeking alternatives to it—in ways ranging from withdrawing funds or emigrating to creating private armies or inviting foreign intervention (which itself tends to undermine local authority). Apart from specific exigencies, the distinction between authority structures and their environments becomes more and more difficult to maintain—empirically and analytically—in a world where economic self-sufficiency is mythological and political boundaries are increasingly permeable and tenuous.

Fourth, conflicts arise over the unequal distribution of symbolic as well as material goods. Relative differences in the social standing of groups or individuals imply differences in their relative worth—at least in empirical terms and often also in cosmological terms, in that human beings are prone to search for ultimate meanings in the varying circumstances of their existence. Whatever significance is attributed to status differences, the historical record indicates that the socially inferior do not forever grant the justice of their condition, and that some proportion of them will individually or collectively try to attain a more estimable and reassuring position—within the existing structure as far as possible, or by changing it if mobility is blocked.

And fifth, the combination of a genetic inclination to struggle for life and a socially learned disposition to value "our" above "their" life chances produces ethnocentrism in one form or another (familism, tribalism, parochialism, and the like). The differentiation of populations, especially when associated with differential life chances, is accompanied by divisions of allegiance and concern. Thus, efforts to assert and preserve the authority-subject distinction are finally self-defeating. Their respective ethnocentrisms make it impossible for authorities and subjects to trust one another much beyond the minimum level of a wary cooperation imposed by the functional linking of their respective life chances.

Assuming that the mortality of authority structures has been established, it is nonetheless evident that their lifespans may vary from the merest glimmer to an indefinitely long period measured in generations or millenia. We need not only to know that authority structures are mortal, but also—and more importantly—to understand why some are so much more viable than others.

Estimating the Viability of Authority Structures

Social scientists and political analysts have worked hard to learn the causes of rebellion, riots, strife, turmoil, and civil unrest of all kinds. An enormous literature has resulted, mostly addressing the questions of how to control such disorders and/or how to induce subjects to trust authorities. Myriad propositions about the relative efficacy and legitimacy of political systems have been advanced, sometimes based upon research findings, but more often derived from ideological commitments. The pressing task now is to develop objective indicators of the viability of political structures, for blindly partisan conflicts are increasingly costly and likely to have repercussions far beyond their initial loci.

To assess the viability of an authority structure means to estimate its capacity to persist without radical changes in the functional relationships by which life chance inequalities are perpetuated. Since no authority structure is universal, viability is always to be estimated in reference to a specified range of foreseeable contingencies. There are several possible approaches to the problem of estimation.

Probably the most common approach is to assume that viability is a simple function of inequality: The more inequality, the less viable the structure. Despite its popularity, the longevity and recalcitrance of many grossly inegalitarian structures leaves this approach empirically dubious, while the lack of specification (regarding dynamics, contingencies, time frames, and so forth) makes it analytically useless.

The classic inductive approach is to identify common features of cases in which authority structures have disintegrated or declined, then try to derive implications for the prospects of existing structures (Eisenstadt 1969, 1978; Moore 1966, 1978; Skocpol 1979). The great strength of this approach is that it leads to detailed specification of times and situations; its weakness is that it encourages historicist explanations assuming without demonstrating the applicability of findings regarding past failures to current situations in which failure is still problematic. Tilly's (1978) work is a notable exception; in it, historical materials are transformed into data amenable to quantitative analyses testing theoretical expectations and generating new explanatory propositions. Although such inquiries are a rich source of ideas, it remains unclear how they might eventually produce the methods and information needed to estimate the viability of existing authority structures.

A more direct inductive approach is to characterize existing authority structures with respect to such dimensions as "directiveness" (authoritarianism versus permissiveness), "participation" (subjects' role in influencing policy decisions), and "responsiveness" of authorities to subjects' preferences and needs (Eckstein and Gurr 1975: see especially 233-348). The major strengths of the Eckstein-Gurr approach are that it promotes detailed empirical description and facilitates comparisons. Its weaknesses reflect the basic difficulty with induction: Descriptions of existing structures do not explain how such structures originate and change. Scoring existing structures on the posited dimensions of authority does not provide indicators of viability unless the significance of particular scores has been established. Notably lacking is specification of the environmental conditions under which particular scores and variations are to be expected. However, one extremely important proposal is that the significance of scores does vary *within* authority structures according to the "bases of legitimacy"—i.e., "values which govern perceptions that authority patterns are rightly constituted and therefore worthy of support" (Eckstein and Gurr 1975:198). This suggests that viability indicators must be "weighted" according to the cultural (normative) meaning of particular features of authority-subject interactive and functional relatedness. One implication is that a given mode or level of authority-subject conflict may be more destructive to one kind of structure than to another, or may be progressive in some cases. Another and larger implication is that viability indicators are meaningful only in regard to a specified context.

Granted the importance of the "internal" context, it may well be that the significance of viability indicators also varies with variations in the "external" context—i.e., environmental factors in addition to cultural ones. If so, estimates of viability presuppose knowledge of how the significance of particular indicators is affected by the *interaction* of internal (subjective, interactive) and external (objective, functional) contextual variables. Previous discussions of the nature, creation, and deterioration of authority structures indicate several variables for possible inclusion in a model for estimating viability. Instead of displaying and discussing all possible combinations of variables so far mentioned or implied (an exercise precluded anyway by space limitations), some examples (hypotheses) will be offered of how selected variables interact to affect the control-conflict process so as to increase or decrease the viability of authority structures. (A "first model" for assessing the relative viability of the South African and American authority structures has been specified for the interaction of environmental factors with legal system characteristics; see Turk 1977.)

Example 1: The Breakdown of Traditional Authority Structures

Proposition: The less people expect equality of life chances, the less significance inequality will have as a viability indicator.

Although no culture can fully justify life chance differentials, the association of authority with greater life chances is less onerous under such conditions as the following:

(1) Sacred (ideological, religious) conceptions and evaluations of reality are unchallenged by secular (analytical, scientific) views; the wickedness as well as the futility of resisting authority is stressed. *Effect:* Justifications for resistance are not readily available, so a considerable intellectual effort is needed to create them in the absence of ideas as well as information.

(2) The welfare of collectivities is given priority over that of individuals. More specifically, the welfare of subcollectivities (e.g., families, ethnic associations, residential communities) is emphasized. In contrast to the functional relationships characteristic of political structures of the highest degree (polities), interactive relationships are the primary constituent elements of subcollectivities. *Effect:* Obligations of social participation restrain inclinations to risk even relatively low subcollectivity life chances in the hope of improvement.

(3) At every level of social organization—from the most proximate subcollectivity interaction to the highest echelons of power—ascribed status is ordinarily valued more than achievement. *Effect:* Incentives and opportunities for political as well as other innovations are minimal.

(4) The level of technology promotes labor-intensive rather than capital-intensive economic activities. Because the division of labor is minimal and complex skills are rarely needed, virtually everyone—especially including young people—can and does engage in productive activity. *Effect:* Norms of responsibility for contributing to subcollectivity economies (subeconomies) are applicable in practice.

(5) Productivity is high enough to sustain the ritual and other components of the interactive relationships constituting the subcollectivities. *Effect:* Subcollectivities are not threatened by extinction or declining life chances in comparison to those of other subcollectivities; therefore, resistance is not encouraged by subcollectivity commitments.

.(6) Productivity is not high enough to stimulate or sustain subcollectivity efforts to increase life chances at the expense of other subcollectivities or of the polity itself; nor will many individuals be encouraged or able to overcome the status limits imposed by their subcollectivity involvements. *Effect:* Ethnocentrism is checked by the lack of resources, both as goals and as means.

(7) The rate of population growth is low, and the relative size of subcollectivities remains fairly constant. The age-sex composition of residential and ethnic communities is in virtually every case approximately normal. Dependency ratios are low. The mortality and morbidity rates of subcollectivities are consistent with the expectations of their members. *Effect:* Normative expectations regarding the life-cycle can usually be met; most people see "their kind" getting their "due" out of life.

The features of "traditional" and "primitive" societies are, of course, familiar both as descriptions and as elements in ideologies (of either resistance or control) or "integration-consensus" theories of social order. Partly as consequence and partly as cause, there is a common tendency to construe the meaning of authority in essentially traditional terms—even in otherwise penetrating analyses of differences between traditional and modern societies (e.g., Bendix 1964, 1978: note especially 16-18, 265-272). However, the record—mainly anthropological, partly historical—shows only that empirical approximations to the model of traditional authority *have* existed, and that the closest approximations have been found where social life was extremely small-scale and isolated.

No part of the world can now be so insulated (few parts ever were), and the process of political organization becomes increasingly global. Every one of the conditions noted above changes drastically under the impact of great-power economic, cultural, political, and military expansion and rivalries. To the extent that the great powers are not limited by technological capacity, internal control problems, or mutual deterrence, the breakdown of relatively traditional authority structures will continue despite reactionary efforts (e.g., Iran) to stop and reverse "modernization" and "Westernization." What direction, then, is the control-conflict process likely to take in the future?

Example 2: The Costs of Social Transformation

Proposition: Attempts to create alternatives to traditional authority structures (e.g., the American and French postrevolutionary "experiments") have demonstrated the impossibility of reconciling traditional "bases of legitimacy" with the rationalism and materialism of both bourgeois and socialist ideologies of progress. The breakdown of "pockets" and "vestiges" of traditional authority indicates not the lesser or declining viability of truly modern authority structures, but rather the nonviability of traditional authority structures in modern contexts.

Indicators of the nonviability of traditional authority structures may also be viewed as the (variable, not fixed) costs of transforming them into modern authority structures. Any effort to create a nontraditional alternative confronts a situation in which:

(1) isolation and small-scale social life are precluded;

(2) secular ideas and modes of thought either predominate or increasingly challenge sacred ones;

(3) individualism either has priority or strongly challenges collectivism;

(4) achievement is increasingly valued more than ascribed status;

(5) technological innovation promotes capital-intensive instead of labor-intensive economic activities;

(6) goods and services accrue to some subcollectivities at enormous cost to others, possibly including their extinction;

(7) high and increasing productivity stimulates ethnocentric conflict among unequally matched subcollectivities, and among groups and individuals within them; and

(8) population growth rates and dependency ratios are high; some communities have skewed age-sex distributions; and variations among subcollectivities in their mortality and morbidity rates are increasingly intolerable to the less favored.

The implied material and psychosocial costs (see Naroll 1962, for a pioneering effort to develop "culture stress" indicators) will be less insofar as the control-conflict process involves more progressive than destructive moves by *both* authorities and resisters—e.g., authorities evidence more concern with increasing than limiting subjects' life chances; resisters promote specific alternatives instead of merely trying to weaken the existing structure; both parties eschew terror (random violence) and try to minimize violence in general. Despite everyone's best efforts, there will still be costs. Against most assumptions regarding indicators of viability, the point must be stressed that lower costs do not necessarily indicate greater viability, while higher costs may be necessary to create a more viable authority structure. In any case, how the costs are distributed affects viability more than whether they are relatively high or low for the population as a whole. The crucial issue is whether viability is maximized by allocating the costs equally or according to some discriminatory criterion. Given the hierarchical and conflictful nature of political organization, the possibility of equally distributing the costs of social transformation is as remote as that of insuring equality of life chances. Clearly there will and must be discrimination, with some criteria and forms likely to be more progressive than others in terms of increasing viability.

Attempts to restore or recreate traditional authority structures reduce the viability of modern authority structures (insofar as some empirical approximations are to be found). Progressive strategies of control and resistance seek to impose the costs of social transformation upon traditional subcollectivities and individuals. The extent to which traditionalists can be made to bear the costs of their own destruction varies with whether authority-subject conflict is coterminous with traditionalist-modernist conflict: the more coterminous, the less viability.

In addition to their degree of traditionalism, the relative power of subcollectivities and individuals will and must be a criterion for the allocation of costs. Realism in political struggle means taking into account the capacity of others to help or hinder. Those with minimum capacity are politically inconsequential, until and unless they somehow acquire greater resources—economic, organizational, ideological, or military. The control-conflict process is more likely to increase viability when the conflicting parties are more realistic than idealistic in dealing with one another and with other present and potential supporters and enemies. Because of their greater defensive and offensive capacity, it is unrealistic to expect those with greater life chances to accept readily the costs of changes that may reduce them. The costs of social transformation have to be borne disproportionately by those who already bear disproportionately the costs of social continuity. This is not to say that exploitation is the route to a more viable authority structure. Whether political realism contributes to viability depends upon the degree to which authorities and resisters give priority to replacing traditionalism rather than imposing the costs upon the powerless or each other. Discrimination against the already disadvantaged contributes to viability only to the extent that powerlessness is associated with traditionalism.

Two major propositions have been offered: that traditional authority structures are unviable under modern conditions, and that the costs of social transformation will and must be disproportionately borne by the more traditional and less powerful. Such propositions imply that openness, secularism, individualism, achievement values, and technological innovation characterize modern authority structures—but also that great and intolerable inequalities, heightened ethnocentric conflict, and increasing demographic pressures accompany efforts to create them. Modernization thus increases options at the price of destroying existing social bonds and impeding the formation of new ones. Whether the net result is an increase or decrease in human life chances is still at issue (Dahrendorf 1979); and it is clear that the costs of social transformation might be dramatically less than they have so far been (Bauer 1981). It is, then, not surprising that estimates of the viability of existing authority structures—or attempts to create them—are invariably contested and frequently wrong (as all intelligence analysts quickly learn). Yet, the world moves on to better or worse. Estimates must be ventured if the authority structures of the future are to be worth the human costs of their creation.

Toward A New World

Insofar as they have from choice or necessity sought an alternative authority structure, modern authorities have reversed the traditional strategy of control. Traditional authorities rely heavily upon the interactive relationships of established social bonds, and limit the resources (options) available to their subjects. Unable to depend upon crumbling or never-existent interactive bonds, modern authorities displace and replace them with the functional relationships imposed by centralized bureaucracies, and try to "buy off" subjects by increasing (or promising to increase) the material resources available for their discretionary use. There is some evidence (Cereseto 1979) that the socialist version of the strategy (more centralized bureaucracy, more equal distribution of a lesser product) may so far have been more successful than the capitalist version (less centralized bureaucracy, more unequal distribution of a greater product). However, socialist or capitalist, the centralist-materialist strategy has deferred rather than produced a solution to the problem of creating a really modern authority structure.

The problem has at least two major facets:

(1) Especially under growing demographic pressure, secular individualism combines with ethnocentrism to generate expectations that eventually surpass both (1) the productivity limits set by available technology, and (2) authorities' ability (regardless of their willingness) to concede additional resources without changing the structure of power and privilege to the point of endangering their own position—and therefore their own

life chances. Further, there is a growing discrepancy between what is necessary to keep local populations in line and what is required to deal with foreign relations problems—particularly those arising from the association between the increasing functional interdependency among erstwhile sovereign nations and the internationalization of the control-conflict process.

(2) Paraphrasing Dahrendorf (1979:31), though social bonds without resources are likely to be oppressive and unviable, resources without social bonds eventually become dangerously unsatisfying. To the extent that resources are only markers in an open-ended competition for personal status, they promote increasingly unstable and/or vicious interactive relationships. Without supportive bonds, people do not find life meaningful enough to refrain from acts destructive to their own and everyone else's life chances (e.g., crime, suicide, addictions, waste, absenteeism, apathy, irresponsibility, short-run hedonism).

No authority structure can exist under such conditions. How to change them is not nearly as clear as dogmatists and romantics, of right and left, tend to believe. A checklist of policy goals is, of course, implied by the nature of the problem: reduce population pressure; temper secular individualism with social responsibility and philosophical enlightenment; extend and rationalize the collective bounds of ethnocentrism, perhaps (though improbably) to include all humanity; increase productivity without destroying its bases; balance the destruction of traditional social bonds with the creation of new forms of interactive support; minimize violence, deceit, and exploitation in authority-subject relationships; eliminate archaic political boundaries, moving toward a viable worldwide authority structure.

Aside from inevitable controversies over the desirability of the goals, debates over the means of attaining them still reflect ideological more than technical concerns; and whatever technical counsel is sought reflects the current lack of relevant knowledge. The problem of authority will not be solved without research; it may be solved indefinitely if sufficient knowledge is acquired and applied before the chance for a solution is lost in a new barbarism. Excluding that possibility, Wright (1979) has considered several possible transitional futures defined by varying forms of "interpenetration" between capitalism and socialism (see also his analysis of how existing bureaucratic structures might be used to promote socialist rather than other alternatives; Wright 1978:181-252). If it is achieved, a viable modern authority structure will be the product of a control-conflict process transcending the contemporary distinctions between capitalism and socialism—or between evolution and revolution.

REFERENCES

Bauer, P. T. 1981. *Equality, The Third World, and Economic Delusion.* Cambridge, MA: Harvard University Press.

Bendix, R. 1964. *Nation-Building and Citizenship.* New York: John Wiley.

Bendix, R. 1978. *Kings or People: Power and the Mandate to Rule.* Berkeley: University of California Press.

Cereseto, S. 1979. "Critical Dimensions in Development Theory: A Test of Four Inequality Models." Boulder, CO: Red Feather Institute.

Collins, R. 1975. *Conflict Sociology: Toward An Explanatory Science.* New York: Academic.

Dahrendorf, R. 1979. *Life Chances: Approaches to Social and Political Theory.* Chicago: University of Chicago Press.

Eckstein, H. and T. R. Gurr. 1975. *Patterns of Authority: A Structural Basis for Political Inquiry.* New York: John Wiley.

Eisenstadt, S. N. 1969. *The Political Systems of Empires: The Rise and Fall of the Historical Bureaucratic Societies.* New York: Free Press.

Eisenstadt, S. N. 1978. *Revolution and the Transformation of Societies: A Comparative Study of Civilization.* New York: Free Press.

Gamson, W. A. 1968. *Power and Discontent.* Homewood, IL: Dorsey.

Gibbs, J. P. 1981. *Norms, Deviance, and Social Control: Conceptual Matters.* New York: Elsevier-North Holland.

Himes, J. S. 1980. *Conflict and Conflict Management.* Athens: University of Georgia Press.

Moore, B., Jr. 1966. *Social Origins of Dictatorship and Democracy.* Boston: Beacon.

Moore, B., Jr. 1978. *Injustice: The Social Bases of Obedience and Revolt.* White Plains, NY: M. E. Sharpe.

Naroll, R. 1962. *Data Quality Control—A New Research Technique: Prolegomena to a Cross-Cultural Study of Culture Stress.* New York: Free Press.

Skocpol, T. 1979. *States and Social Revolutions: A Comparative Analysis of France, Russia and China.* New York: Cambridge University Press.

Tilly, C. 1978. *From Mobilization to Revolution.* Reading, MA: Addison-Wesley.

Turk, A. T. 1977. "The Problem of Legal Order in the United States and South Africa: Substantive and Analytical Considerations." *Sociological Focus* 10:31-41.

Turk, A. T. 1981. "The Meaning of Criminality in South Africa." *International Journal of the Sociology of Law* 9:123-55.

Turk, A. T. 1982. *Political Criminality.* Beverly Hills, CA: Sage.

Wright, E. O. 1978. *Class, Crisis, and the State.* New York: Schocken (NLB edition).

Wright, E. O. 1979. "Capitalism's Futures: A Provisional Reconceptualization of Alternatives to Capitalist Society." Working Paper No. 7. Toronto: Structural Analysis Programme, Department of Sociology, University of Toronto.

12

Prospects for Control Theories and Research

ROBERT F. MEIER

Prospects for fruitful social science theories about control are not promising. The primary reasons are the reluctance of social scientists to emphasize the intentional or purposive quality of human conduct and conceptualizations that do not distinguish control and other concepts (e.g., influence). Both problems are conspicuous in the history of the notion of social control in sociology.

Sociology and Social Control

Sociological interest in control stems largely from E. A. Ross. He began his influential *Social Control* (1901) with a distinction between peace and order. The distinction is an important one because Ross claimed that effective social control is necessary for order but not for peace. Ross (1901:1-2) argued that if "the weaker of two hunters that have brought down the same stag avoids a fight by yielding up the game, there is peace, but no order. But if the dispute is settled according to the rule that 'first struck' decides the ownership of the game, the solution is an orderly one." The argument suggests that order stems from agreement on rules to govern behavior rather than from the simple use of power and the correlative fear of sanctions. That suggestion in turn implies that Ross thought of social control in terms of norms and normative consensus rather than power.

Actually, Ross's arguments about peace and order did little to clarify the meaning of social control, and subsequent sociologists failed to go beyond Ross's vague conceptualization. Instead, they have used the term as though it needs no clarification. And use it they have; social control is clearly a popular term. The reason for the popularity is not difficult to discern: The term gives the appearance of linking individual conduct and social structure. But while most sociologists agree that social control has something to do with rules, influence, and social order, both the conceptual (logical) and empirical character of the relation remain obscure.

Major Contending Conceptions

There are two contending conceptions of social control in sociology. The first, stemming from Ross and dominant until about 1950, equates social control with virtually anything that presumably contributes to social order. As such, social control is implicitly defined by reference to a notion—social order—that is even more abstract.

The second conception has developed since 1950—initially in the works of Parsons and LaPiere. This conception equates social control with conformity to norms or the counteraction of deviance. Such an approach has the advantage of identifying potentially researchable control mechanisms (e.g., the law, public opinion); but it is based on an untenable assumption—that social scientists agree in defining deviance and in identifying instances of it.

Particular Conceptual Problems

Social control has not received much conceptual attention since Ross's initial effort. As a result, several serious problems haunt contemporary usage.

Conceptual Redundancy

The most obvious problem in defining social control is to distinguish it from other key concepts in the social sciences. Hannah Arendt (1972:142) lamented that it is "a rather sad reflection on the present state of political science that our terminology does not distinguish among such key words as 'power,' 'strength,' 'force,' 'authority,' and, finally, 'violence'—all of which refer to distinct, different phenomena and would hardly exist unless they did." Arendt's argument can be extended readily to the term "control." Given the way that sociologists commonly use the term "social control," it is difficult to see any obvious difference between the meaning of the term and socialization or even social interaction. Moreover, if social control is not distinguished from "influence," then it becomes virtually synonymous with all of sociology's subject matter. The problem of conceptual redundancy is especially conspicuous in the case of control, power, and authority.

The *Oxford English Dictionary* informs us that "control" can be used either as a noun or a verb but not as an adjective. The words "power" and "authority," on the other hand, may be used either as nouns or adjectives but not as verbs. True, we sometimes construct sentences in which power and authority appear to be verbs; but such sentences merely highlight the subtle differences between these words by casting them as metaphors. Consider the following sentences:

(1) X is an authority.
(2) Y has power.
(3) Z is controlling.

By conventional usage, the first sentence means that X *is not doing* anything overt; the second sentence means Y *need not be doing* anything overt; and the third sentence means Z *is doing* something. The implication is that, unlike power and authority, control is not an adjective because it adheres neither in particular persons nor positions.

Specific Issues

None of the distinctions pertaining to authority, power, and control answers this question: What is "social" about social control? That question gives rise to several issues.

The Issue of Coercion

Although he does not define the term explicitly, Morris Janowitz (1978) speaks of social control as excluding coercion. For Janowitz, social control is persuasive influence. Janowitz appears to draw on Ross's original conception of social control, but Ross made frequent references to coercive means of control. Why, then, must coercion be excluded?

One possible reason is to narrow the meaning of the term "social control." Any attempt to narrow the meaning would seem welcome, but all of them are likely to be disputable. Some theorists (e.g., Goode 1972) have suggested that conceptions of social control without coercion are suspect on that ground alone.

The Issue of Effectiveness

Another way to narrow the meaning of social control is to recognize only successful attempts to influence conduct. Specifically, if an attempt is successful, it is social control; otherwise, it is something else. Thus, if the threat of prison does not deter potential offenders, it would not be considered social control.

The immediate objection to treating success as a defining feature of social control is that it precludes theories about the effectiveness of social control. If only successful attempts to influence conduct are social control, then *by definition* social control is effective in all conditions. Now consider the implications for theories pertaining to the causes of historical and international variation in the punitiveness of legal reactions to crime (see Sutherland and Cressey 1978:347-358). Since the effectiveness of legal punishment as a means of preventing crime is most disputable, the theories in question are not theories of social control if only successful attempts to influence conduct constitute social control.

The literature on the deterrence doctrine (see Tittle 1980 for a review) makes it abundantly clear that legal punishments cannot be readily identified as either successful or unsuccessful attempts to influence conduct. Some types of legal punishments may deter some types of individuals from some types of crimes in some types of situations, but investigators have yet to identify those types. The inconclusive nature of the findings illustrates the difficulty of assessing the success of attempts to influence conduct, especially at the aggregate level. Moreover, it is puzzling to regard deterrence research as bearing on social control if and only if the findings demonstrate that legal punishments prevent crimes through deterrence. That is all the more the case because there is a quite different rationale for identifying legal punishments as social control. If legal punishments are intended to prevent crimes, whether through deterrence or incapacitation, they are social control. However, that argument gives rise to another issue.

The Issue of Intentionality

The notion of "the ends of social control" implies that social control is a conscious, directed endeavor. Ross (1901:viii) made this explicit when he described social control as being "concerned with . . . domination which is intended and which fulfills a function in society." However, Ross's terminology raises two questions. First, how are social scientists to judge the intention of human behavior, especially in the context of institutional arrangements, such as legal punishments? And, second, what do we make of unintended mechanisms that promote social order or conformity to norms?

The import of the questions can be illustrated by examining contrasts in penal policies. It is commonly assumed that retribution and deterrence are contending penal policies, but the two cannot be distinguished by reference to the severity of legal punishments. So it appears that the only distinction lies in the intention of those who prescribe the kind and magnitudes of punishments for particular types of crimes. However, if statutory penalties are prescribed by a collectivity, such as a legislative body, there is no accepted procedure for inferring the intentions of that collectivity. But suppose that by one procedure or another the criminal laws of a particular jurisdiction have been rightly described as reflecting a retributive penal policy. Such a policy does not aim for crime prevention through rehabilitation of offenders, deterrence, or incapacitation; rather, offenders are punished solely because they deserve it. Yet retributive punishment could prevent crime through deterrence or incapacitation.

There are at least two arguments for defining social control as intentional behavior. First, it is the only way to preserve the distinction between successful and unsuccessful control. And, second, such a definition narrows the meaning of social control and avoids conceptual redundancy. The second argument ignores the point that conceptual redundancy can be avoided by other strategies. Thus, Wrong (1980:3-5) prefers a definition that makes power intentional; but he does so to realize a distinction between power and social control, meaning that social control, in Wrong's view, is unintentional influence.

Eliminating conceptual redundancy is commendable but only if arbitrary distinctions are avoided. Defining social control as intentional influence would not be arbitrary if it could be assumed that conformity to norms is solely or even primarily promoted by intentional efforts to that end, but no sociologist is likely to accept that assumption. Internalization of norms, for example, supposedly promotes conformity independently of control in the intentional sense; yet that is the case only if internalization is somehow "automatic," a view that has been seriously challenged (Scott 1971).

Of all the arguments considered, the most important one is this: It is difficult to infer the intentions of a collectivity. That difficulty possibly led to the two major contending conceptions of social control, and it is relevant in identifying the adherents of each conception. Sociologists who are not fearful of reductionism lean toward a definition of social control as intentional behavior, while staunch antireductionists are inclined to define social control as any mechanism (intended *or* unintended) that contributes to social order. The exception is the case of Marxist sociology. Marxists are opposed to reductionism, but their conception of social control appears to emphasize the intentional (indeed, self-interested) character of social control. Paradoxically, however, the principal agent of social control in Marxist theory is a collectivity—a particular social class.

Naturalism and Control

Normative concepts—those that make reference to what "ought" to be—and the notion of intention are rarely defended by social scientists. The reason is a commitment to naturalism in the social sciences, a view of human action as more determined than chosen.

Social thought around the turn of the century was heavily influenced by Darwin. Sumner and Ward were vocal social Darwinists in sociology; Justice Holmes argued that common law developed through natural selection; Veblen examined the growth of economic institutions from the same viewpoint; William James, John Dewey, and Edward Thorndike treated the "mind" as an adaptive physiological function of the body rather than as a separate metaphysical entity; and James, Dewey, and Charles Sanders Pierce began their critique of philosophy (called pragmatism) by arguing that truth is a matter of practical consequences (i.e., there are no *a priori* truths, only hypotheses).

Prior to Darwinism, nature was thought of as a part of a comprehensive divine order, and truth was believed to be a matter of moral absolutes that can be revealed by reason alone. With the triumph of Darwinism, nature ceased to be thought of as divine creation, and truth came to be regarded as a relative matter, revealed only through empiricism. Reason was no longer sufficient; observation, measurement, and analysis were required. And these newer ideas were not simply a reaction against an older theistic philosophy; they constituted a reaction against both Hegel and Aquinas.

The shift from a reflective, introspective scholarship to scientific empiricism produced disquieting results. In political science, scholars examined and rejected three cardinal principles of democratic government: the possibility of a government of laws rather than men, rational electoral behavior, and the practical possibility of a popular government itself (Purcell 1973). The new empiricism also reoriented jurisprudence, in that judicial decisions were no longer seen to result from impartial logic or natural law but from the personal values of judges themselves. In psychology between 1913 and 1919, John Watson laid the foundation for the new empiricism by emphasizing complete objectivity. Watson's aim was to make psychology a completely observational, physical, and empirical science. He advocated that psychologists abandon the method of introspection, study only observable behavior, and abjure the concept of consciousness. By the 1930s, Tolman, Hull, and Skinner emerged as leading spokesmen for behaviorism.

The pattern was similar in economics, sociology, and anthropology. Scholars like Berle, Commons, and Mitchell in economics studied not hypothetical principles of money flow but actual cash transactions and business cycles. In sociology, Park and Burgess were committed entirely to an observational methodology; indeed, the Chicago school of sociology was almost defined by its emphasis on observation, sending students into cities as laboratories for empirical studies of social processes. In anthropology, Franz Boas led the empirical school, and under his tutelage the field prospered. Along with his students—Kroeber, Sapir, and Montagu—Boas moved anthropology out of the museums and into the universities as full partners in the empirical exercise.

What each discipline shared was an antimetaphysical commitment. As Purcell (1973:21) has characterized it:

> Keenly aware of the moral assumptions and personal value judgments of their predecessors, many scholars insisted that scientific knowledge must be wholly objective and based on concrete, universally verified data. Sharply skeptical of all nonempirical concepts and theories, they accepted a highly particularistic, nominalistic epistemology.

The new orientation actually came to be etched in stone. The inscription over the new social science building completed in 1929 at the University of Chicago told the entire story: "When you cannot measure," it proclaimed, "your knowledge is meager and unsatisfactory."

The inevitable concomitant of naturalism is relativism. Since nothing is absolute, there can be no superior values; and anthropologists began to proclaim that different cultures are no better or worse, only different. Cultural relativism in anthropology and the rise of legal realism in jurisprudence were signs that social scientists had rejected absolutism and with it the burden of pronouncing moral judgments. Even morals themselves were conceived to be empirical:

> The morality of a group at a time is the sum of the taboos and prescriptions in the folkways by which right conduct is defined. Therefore morals can never be intuitive. They are historical, institutional, and empirical [Sumner 1940:41].

To be sure, there were critics of the ethical implications of naturalism. Frank H. Knight in economics and Charles A. Ellwood in sociology were particularly outspoken, decrying ethical neutrality. Ellwood would be joined in sociology later by MacIver and Sorokin, and later still by Alfred McClung Lee, who presently echoes Ellwood's theme of two generations ago. But against those voices were the collective weight of entire disciplines, each with strident spokespersons, like George Lundberg in sociology, who expressed total indifference to any social phenomenon that was unquantifiable (hence, not naturalistic).

A commitment to naturalism required a commitment to ethical neutrality, to objective description, to an avoidance of normative judgments (see Catton 1966). To speak of what "ought" to be was to speak as a private citizen (as Lundberg saw it) or, worse, as a popularizer of social science findings or, worse yet, as a one committed more to an alternative social system than to naturalistic principles.

Naturalism could not provide a vocabulary to express the feelings of people when they are objects of control. Naturalists discussed how anxiety could best be measured, how fear could be operationalized, and the quantification of the process whereby anger translates into rebellion. But people appeared to have been displaced by methodological procedures, and relativism prohibited judgments of control as good or evil. So it is no wonder that control was treated more compassionately by novelists, who deal primarily with human passions. There is no place for passion in naturalism; hence, the passionate features of control came to be ignored in the social and behavioral sciences.

The Future of Control and Its Study

The most unfortunate consequence of "ethical neutrality" in the study of control is the indifference to the dangerous quality of control. That quality deserves all the more recognition in speculating about the future of control.

The Context of Control

"America's first democratically distributed privilege," according to historian Robert Wiebe (1975:3), "was the right to dream." But with that privilege came the possibility of nightmares. The nightmares revolved not around personal failure but diminished liberty. Autonomy, life chances, and freedom of association mattered more for American immigrants than personal success. The promise of America for them was never the guarantee, merely the chance for personal advancement. Freedom from religious and political oppression, opportunity for economic well-being, and a place where the future was earned not inherited; these were the promises that early Americans took seriously.

The ideology of democracy and the reality of control are antithetical, and the relation cannot be fully appreciated without reading More (Utopia), Andreae (Christianapolis), and Bellamy (Looking Backward), Huxley (Brave New World), Zamyatin (We), and Orwell (1984). Those writers suggest that true freedom and control are mutually exclusive. But the total loss of human spirit and abject acceptance of control under, say, Orwell's Big Brother is inconsistent with the rebellious predispositions of individuals who are actually objects of attempts at total control. There are no "freedom fighters" in Orwell's novel.

The fear of control exists simultaneously with the desire for order that control supposedly provides. We are ambivalent about control. This is similar to observations by Richard Sennett (1980) on authority, William Goode (1978) on prestige, and Dennis Wrong (1980) on power. We may control, but dread others' control over us; we may covet authority, but we experience anxiety and may be hostile toward others in authority over us; we enjoy prestige, but we resent the more prestigeful; and we may view our power over others as altruistic or at least benign but loathe others' power over us because its exercise appears to be motivated by self-interest.

Social scientists have yet to really examine the implications of human ambivalence about control or what is a great paradox. Total control is the very negation of freedom, but total freedom supposedly results in anomie. Indeed, the Marxian notion of alienation makes sense only under conditions of complete freedom, for total estrangement is the absence not of domination but of control. Yet fiction writers suggest that the only alternative to total freedom is paternalism or, worse, totalitarianism. Orwell is a case in point. His fear of communism, more common among intellectuals in the 1940s and 1950s than is generally recognized (see Podhoretz 1979), led him to sketch a portrait of total control. The portrait is overdrawn and ignores considerations (e.g., the rebellious character of human reactions to total control) that are emphasized in Bettleheim's and Arendt's observations on totalitarianism.

The paradox of control has received little attention from social scientists. Consider James Coleman's (1975:91-92) observation that John Rawls in *A Theory of Justice* makes only three incidental references to contemporary sociologists (Homans garners two, Runciman one) and only two to classical social theorists (one each to Weber and Durkheim). Rawls evidently saw no need to review sociological ideas about justice and inequality. Coleman concludes:

> The irony . . . lies in the fact that sociologists carry out more empirical research on inequality than do members of any other discipline, and sociologists' values lead them on the whole to be more concerned about inequalities in society than are most scholars. . . . Yet, in their theoretical work, there is little or no normative content concerning inequality.

The question that Coleman does not address is the extent to which naturalism requires ethical neutrality in the study of control. The future of the study of control is largely contingent on the answer to that question.

There are two alternative directions for work on control. If the naturalistic direction is taken, social scientists will be concerned with identifying means of control, assessing the relative effectiveness of those means, and explaining differences among social units as to the relative predominance of particular means of social control. If the normative direction is taken, work will center around arguments about the justness of means and goals of social control. Those arguments will be akin to debates over the "best" political system or economic system. However, those debates are a tradition, and a similar tradition in the study of control will not be established until those engaged in that study abandon the "value-free" approach.

The problem with naturalistic direction is that it will have little bearing on the central concern of most persons about control: how it should be used and to what ends. That concern is conducive to a normative direction in studies of control, but there is a problem in taking that direction. No normative theory of control can be disconfirmed by conventional scientific procedures.

Recent Developments in the Naturalistic Direction

As suggested earlier, the conceptual problem in the study of social control has been crippling. So it is not surprising that the most recent development in the naturalistic direction has been a reconceptualization of social control (Gibbs 1981). Another recent line of work (Black 1976) is relevant in considering a different problem in the naturalistic tradition, one best stated as a question: What is the central question in the study of social control?

Gibbs's (1981:109) recent definition of social control is innovative: "Social control is an attempt by one party to manipulate the behavior of another party through still another party by any means other than a chain of command." Gibbs's definition represents a rejection of the traditional "prophylatic conception" of social control, which equates it with the counteraction of deviance; and the definition reflects Gibbs's concern with the conceptual problems treated earlier. In particular, his conception stresses the intentional quality of social control, but it does not make successful manipulation of behavior a criterion of social control. It admits the possibility of coercion (or threatened coercion) as a means of social control, but it does not postulate any necessary connection between social control and social order.

Whatever its merits, Gibbs's conceptualization departs from the traditional concern in the study of social control with the counteraction of deviance and social order. For that reason alone, the conceptualization may never be widely accepted.

Black's (1976) conception of social control is, to use Gibbs's word, "prophylatic" in that it equates social control with responses to deviance. However, unlike most advocates of the prophylatic conception, Black is not concerned with the consequences of those responses (i.e., whether they counteract deviance). Rather, he views social control as simply another facet of social life, one that varies according to circumstances and conditions (e.g., modes of social organization). Black's purpose is not to identify effective means of social control but to explain variations in the character of social control itself. As Black (1980:41) puts it: "A theory of social control seeks to understand patterns of normative life and their relation to other aspects of social organization."

Black's approach implies this argument: The effectiveness of means of social control should not be the central question. While a truly impressive theory about variation in the character of social control would lend support to the argument, it would not preclude an equally impressive theory about the effectiveness of means of social control. For that matter, it remains to be seen whether variation in the character of social control can be explained without any consideration of the effectiveness question. The more general point, however, is that neither of the two contenders for the central question in the study of social control is obviously superior to the other.

Normative Directions

For reasons previously indicated, the normative treatment of control is dominated not by social scientists but by fiction writers, George Orwell in particular. His *1984* is the most dramatic prophecy in this century about the future of control. However, the crucial question is not whether Orwell's predictions have proven accurate (Goodman [1978] claims that over 100 of the 137 predictions culled from *1984* have proven accurate; but Beckwith [1979] finds Goodman's evidence on these points "unconvincing"). Rather, the question is whether Orwell portrayed the passionate dimensions of control in realistic terms.

If events in American history since World War II are taken as the criterion for assessing the "realism" of Orwell, the conclusion depends on the decade considered. Contemplate the willingness of Americans in the 1950s to accept if not endorse attempts to control in the name of anticommunism or crime prevention. That willingness appears consistent with one of Orwell's themes—the rarity of passionate resistance to control. But the 1960s witnessed the erosion of consensus as to appropriate targets of control, and control became tied inextricably with political concerns. Also during that decade, sociologists came to question the conventional definition of deviance and the idea that social control served "societal" interests. Events in the 1970s, such as the Vietnam war, oil dependence, and runaway inflation, demonstrated the vulnerability of institutional controls in the United States. Thus, whereas Orwell depicted social control as invincible, many Americans in the 1960s and 1970s came to perceive social control as corrupt and ineffective.

In light of the foregoing, the immediate challenge in coping with control is not to avoid Orwell's *1984;* rather, it is that of identifying effective institutional bases for the exercise of control in times of scarce resources. The cult of individualism has gone beyond a concern with legal rights to the very rejection of authority on which control is based, and the quest for total freedom has promoted anarchy rather than happiness. Perhaps we should fear precisely the opposite of *1984,* for in choosing total freedom over total control one abandons what may be the only hope for humanity, the balance point between total freedom and total control.

REFERENCES

Arendt, H. [1970] 1972. "On Violence." In *Crises of the Republic.* New York: Harcourt, Brace, Jovanovich.

Beckwith, B. 1979.. "*1984* is Not Our Future." *The Futurist* (April):111-15.

Black, D. 1976. *The Behavior of Law.* New York: Academic.

Black, D. 1980. *The Manners and Customs of the Police.* New York: Academic.

Catton, W. R. 1966. *From Animistic to Naturalistic Sociology.* New York: McGraw-Hill.

Coleman, J. 1975. "Legitimate and Illegimate Power." Pp. 221-236 in *The Idea of Social Structure,* edited by Lewis A. Coser. New York: Harcourt, Brace, Jovanovich.

Gibbs, J. 1981. *Norms, Deviance, and Social Control.* New York: Elsevier-North Holland.

Goode, W. 1972. "The Place of Force in Human Society." *American Sociological Review* 37:507-19.

Goode, W. 1978. *The Celebration of Heroes.* Berkeley: University of California Press.

Goodman, D. 1978. "Countdown to *1984:* Big Brother May Be Right on Schedule." *The Futurist* (December):345-55.

Janowitz, M. 1978. *The Last Half Century.* Chicago: University of Chicago Press.

Podhoretz, N. 1979. *Breaking Ranks.* New York: Harper & Row.

Purcell, E. A. 1973. *The Crisis of Democratic Theory.* Lexington: The University Press of Kentucky.

Ross, E. A. 1901. *Social Control.* New York: Macmillan.

Scott, J. F. 1971. *Internalization of Norms.* Englewood Cliffs, NJ: Prentice-Hall.

Sennett, R. 1980. *Authority.* New York: Knopf.

Sumner, W. G. [1960] 1940. *Folkways.* Boston: Ginn.

Sutherland, E. H. and D. R. Cressey. 1978. *Criminology,* 10th ed. Philadelphia: Lippincott.

Tittle, C. R. 1980. *Sanctions and Social Deviance.* New York: Praeger.

Wiebe, R. H. 1975. *The Segmented Society.* New York: Oxford University Press.

Wrong, D. 1980. *Power: Its Forms, Bases, and Uses.* New York: Harper & Row.

About the Authors

RICHARD N. ADAMS is Professor of Anthropology at the University of Texas at Austin, Austin, TX 78712. His major interests include evolutionary processes, complex societies, energy in society, social power, and theory construction. His most recent publication is: *Paradoxical Harvest: Energy and Explanation in British History* (New York: Cambridge University Press, 1982).

IVAR BERG is Professor of Sociology and Chair of the Department of Sociology at the University of Pennsylvania, Philadelphia, PA 19104. His major interests include industrial sociology, organization, and economy and society. His most recent major publication is: *Sociological Perspectives on Labor Markets,* editor (New York: Academic Press, 1981).

EUGENE BURNSTEIN is Professor of Psychology at the Institute for Social Research, University of Michigan, Ann Arbor, MI 48106. His major interests include social influence and persuasion, and group processes. Most recent major publication, co-authored with K. Sentis, is: "Attitude Polarization in Groups," in R. E. Petty, T. M. Ostrom, and T. C. Brock (eds.), *Cognitive Responses in Persuasion* (Hillsdale, NJ: Lawrence Erlbaum Associates, 1981).

GEORGE A. COMSTOCK is S. I. Newhouse Professor of Public Communication at the S. I. Newhouse School of Public Communications, Syracuse University, Syracuse, NY 13210. His major interests include mass communication and public behavior, psychology of media events, and theory construction. His most recent major publication is: *Television and Human Behavior* (New York: Columbia University Press, 1978).

LEWIS A. COSER is Distinguished Professor of Sociology at the State University of New York at Stony Brook, Stony Brook, NY. 11794. His major interests include: sociological theory, sociology of knowledge, political sociology, and history of sociology. His most recent major publication is: *Books: The Commerce and Culture of Publishing,* with Charles Kadushin and Walter Powell (New York: Basic Books, 1981).

ROSE LAUB COSER is Professor of Community and Preventive Medicine and Sociology at the State University of New York at Stony Brook, Stony Brook, New York 11794. Her major interests include: social structure, mainly of hospitals and of the family. Her most recent publication, co-authored with Cynthia Fuchs Epstein, is: *Access to Power* (London: Allen & Unwin, 1981).

DIANA CRANE is Professor of Sociology in the Department of Sociology, University of Pennsylvania, Philadelphia, PA 19104. Her major interests include: sociology of science, sociology of art, and sociological theory. Her most recent major publication is: "Science Policy Studies," in Paul T. Durbin (ed.), *A Guide to the Culture of Science, Technology and Medicine* (New York: Free Press, 1980).

JACK P. GIBBS is Professor of Sociology and Chair of the Department of Sociology and Anthropology, Vanderbilt University, Nashville, TN 37235. His major interests include: deviant behavior, social control, sociology of law, human ecology, and methodology of theory construction. His most recent major publication is: *Norms, Deviance, and Social Control: Conceptual Matters* (New York: Elsevier, 1981).

LEONARD KRASNER is Professor of Psychology in the Department of Psychology, State University of New York, Stony Brook, NY 11794. His major interests include: behavior modification, abnormal psychology, environmental design, and values and science. His most recent major publication is: *Environmental Design and Human Behavior: A Psychology of the Individual in Society* (Elmsford, NY: Pergamon, 1980).

SAMUEL KRISLOV is Professor of Political Science at the University of Minnesota, Minneapolis, MN 55455. His major interests include: judicial process, constitutional law, organizational theory, and comparative legal systems. His most recent major publication is: *Prepresentative Bureaucracy and the American Political System,* with David H. Rosenbloom (New York: Praeger, 1981).

ROBERT F. MEIER is Associate Professor of Sociology in the Department of Sociology, Washington State University, Pullman, WA 99164. His major interests include: deviant behavior, criminology, social control, and sociology of law. His most recent major publication is: "Perspectives on the Concept of Social Control," *Annual Review of Sociology* (1982).

AUSTIN T. TURK is Professor of Sociology and Criminology at the University of Toronto, Toronto, Canada M5S 1A1. His major interests are sociology of law, criminality, deviance, social control, social conflict, and theoretical sociology. His most recent major publication is *Political Criminality: The Defiance and Defense of Authority* (Beverly Hills, CA: Sage, 1982).

Name Index

Subject Index